Joomla!®
Templates

Joomla!® Templates

Angie Radtke

♦♦ Addison-Wesley

Upper Saddle River, NJ • Boston • Indianapolis • San Francisco
New York • Toronto • Montreal • London • Munich • Paris • Madrid
Capetown • Sydney • Tokyo • Singapore • Mexico City

A Message from Open Source Matters

Since Joomla! launched in September 2005, it has grown to become one of the most popular content management systems in the world. As this book goes to press in July 2012, Joomla! has been downloaded over 32,000,000 times and provides support for 64 different languages. Joomla! has received multiple awards, and estimates indicate that approximately 2.8% of all Internet Web sites are using Joomla!.

The key to Joomla!'s success has always been the help and contributions freely given by a large and diverse group of volunteers from all over the world. The Joomla! project isn't backed by venture capital firms, and it isn't led by a single individual or corporation. It is volunteers who write the code and then test it, translate it, document it, support it, extend it, promote it, and share it.

Volunteers are also continually planning and organizing events all over the world where people come together to learn, connect, and share about Joomla!. These events include hundreds of local user groups, as well as national and international conferences. The first Joomla! World Conference will take place in November 2012 in San Jose, California (go to *http://conference.joomla.org* for more information).

Work is underway on many improvements and new ideas aimed at keeping Joomla! on a path of continued growth and innovation. Our community is open to all. If the idea of working alongside a diverse group of bright and passionate volunteers from all over the world who are helping to make Joomla! better sounds fun and rewarding to you, then I invite you to join us. To learn more, please go to *http://www.joomla.org*.

Best regards,

Paul Orwig
President, Open Source Matters

Open Source Matters is the nonprofit organization that provides legal, financial, and organizational support for the Joomla! project.

The publisher offers excellent discounts on this book when ordered in quantity for bulk purchases or special sales, which may include electronic versions and/or custom covers and content particular to your business, training goals, marketing focus, and branding interests. For more information, please contact:

U.S. Corporate and Government Sales
(800) 382-3419
corpsales@pearsontechgroup.com

For sales outside the United States, please contact:

International Sales
international@pearson.com

Visit us on the Web: informit.com/aw

Library of Congress Cataloging-in-Publication Data

Radtke, Angie.
    Joomla! templates / Angie Radtke.
        p.   cm.
    Includes bibliographical references and index.
    ISBN 978-0-321-82731-9 (pbk. : alk. paper)
1. Joomla! (Computer file) 2. Web sites—Authoring programs. 3. Web site development. I. Title.
    TK5105.8883.R32 2013
    006.7'8—dc23   2012017878

Text printed in the United States on recycled paper at RR Donnelley in Crawfordsville, Indiana.
First printing, July 2012

Editor-in-Chief
Mark L. Taub

Executive Editor
Debra Williams Cauley

Development Editor
Songlin Qiu

Managing Editor
John Fuller

Project Editor
Elizabeth Ryan

Packager
Kim Arney

Copy Editor
Carol Lallier

Indexer
Richard Evans

Proofreader
Diane Freed

Technical Reviewer
Andrea Tarr

Editorial Assistant
Kim Boedigheimer

Compositor
Kim Arney

Contents

Introduction

Joomla! is one of the best known Open Source content management systems with many hundreds of thousands of applications in the most varied areas of use. It offers the best possible conditions for implementing a comprehensive and accessible Web presence. Thousands of extensions for almost any purpose are freely available. The developer and user community is huge. On the Internet you can find many different platforms for exchanging information with other users and developers. That's an advantage you should not underestimate! But a Web site without individual design is inconceivable. After all, it's not just the content that makes a Web site truly unique; above all, it's the individual design. This design is the job of the Joomla! templates. In addition to the design aspect, they are also responsible for structuring the content. They create the framework and are basically a template for the content. So they control not only what something looks like but also where the content is located within the document. Joomla! template designers are responsible not only for the design but also for the architecture of the information. When designing a Web site, you need to take into account all requirements of the client as well as the expectations of the visitors.

A small, but important part of these requirements is accessibility. With Joomla!, it's really easy to create accessible Web pages.

To develop Joomla! templates, you need some knowledge of different areas of Web technology, much of which has little to do with Joomla! itself. In our time of increasingly manifold technical possibilities, it is difficult to be an expert in all available Web technologies, so we tend to specialize in certain areas. For instance, you have the front-end developer who knows all there is to know about HTML and Cascading Style Sheets (CSS), the designer who can use Photoshop with all its functions, the PHP specialist, and the JavaScript expert. To develop Joomla! templates, you need some of all this specialized knowledge.

Why This Book Is Unique

This book does not replace a specialized reference work on usability, CSS design, information architecture, PHP, JavaScript, accessibility, or HTML5, but it discusses certain aspects of these topics and others. The aim of this book is to give you the required basic knowledge you need to develop Joomla! templates.

I offer you a readily comprehensible guide that makes it easier for Web designers and programmers to develop their own Joomla! template by working through practical examples. All topics mentioned in this book are condensed to their essence, which was particularly hard to achieve because I could easily have written whole books on each topic. I hope I succeeded and that you find my book helpful.

How This Book Is Organized

My first aim is to show you how Joomla! templates are constructed and how you can create an accessible, standards-compliant template by using the technical possibilities offered by Joomla! in combination with the most modern forms of technology.

In the opening chapters of the book, you will find general basic information on the individual Web technologies, comments on design, and a list of helpful tools. In principle, the things I describe in this part are the basic requirements you need to build a template in the first place. They are meant to help you get started with these topics. If you are a Web designer, you will probably already be familiar with most of the information contained in this part. In that case, you can move straight on to the second part.

The subsequent chapters discuss the technical background of constructing templates. Using concrete examples, I show you the technical options and internal interrelations.

The final chapters are more practical and presented in the form of a workshop. I demonstrate how to turn a template created in Photoshop to a Joomla! template, step by step.

As happens with any vigorous, ongoing project, Joomla! is always evolving. This book contains the most recent information available at the time of publication but see *informIT.com/title/0321827317* for bonus chapters on future releases.

What You Need to Know Before Using This Book

This book is not a "click instruction" but aims to explain contexts and encourage working independently. It is not a CSS book either, although CSS is an important component in building your Joomla! template and is discussed frequently. Photoshop, JavaScript, and PHP are also important tools for your Web design. This book doesn't provide tutorials on these tools, so you may find it helpful to consult textbooks on these topics.

When you start reading this book, keep these hints in mind.

- As an Open Source project, Joomla! is subject to constant changes. In some chapters I refer to code by specific line numbers. It may well be that these lines move about a bit during the development, because code sections are inserted or removed. I added the references anyway to help you get close to the right place. So if you look something up and it's not on the specified line number, please just look a bit above or below it.

  The potential changes that affect the line references usually result from new features being integrated or old ones removed in different Joomla! versions. Most of what I describe here should apply to older versions as well, and major changes are not expected in the newer versions. But please do not be surprised if there are some slight differences.

- To get the most out of the book, you should install Joomla! (with the sample data that comes with it) onto a Web server. You need to have full access to the file system. The best option is to install a local Web server on your computer, such as XAMPP (*www.apachefriends.org/en/xampp.html*). This is especially important by the time you get to Chapter 8, "Now for the Details: A First Look at Templates."

- You will also find it very helpful if you can work with Firefox and install the extension Firebug, which will make your work much easier. You can find out what Firebug is and where to get it when you get to Chapter 7, "Tools."

Joomla! templates is a wide topic. I have tried very hard to cover all the important points in sufficient detail, but I may have missed something. If you do notice anything, I would be grateful if you could get in touch. Just e-mail me at a.radtke@derauftritt.de.

I hope you have fun reading and working your way through this book!

Acknowledgments

In 2010, Joomla! was at the center of my creative activities. I spent much time using—and greatly enjoying—Joomla!. Working with the templates and the default output has helped me both professionally and personally. I have learned so much and am happy with the outcome of my work. This book was created as a result of it.

Those people with whom I spent a large amount of my time chatting on Skype were also involved. We worked out concepts, made plans, and contrived specific solutions. This includes the always prepared Jean-Marie Simonet, whose commitment I can only admire. Then there is Andrea Tarr, who turned out to be a fellow campaigner for accessibility. There is also Elin Waring, who never seems to sleep. My gratitude goes to Mark Dexter, who always remains calm, and Bill Richardson, the good spirit of bug tracking, who sometimes had to test my patches twice. And I should not forget to mention my "rubber ducky," Sam Moffat, who was able to solve my problems just by listening to me (maybe he has magic powers?). I also owe thanks to Mahmood and Ofer, who took care of the RTL-CSS of the templates, and to Henk van Cann for listening, to Ian MacLennan, Andrew Eddy, Louis Landry, Jennifer Marriott, and many others.

Special thanks to my colleague and friend Michael Charlier, who supported me with many helpful tips and important advice. I would also particularly like to thank my friend Biggi Mestmäcker for having the *patience of a saint, for providing the linguistic fine polish, and for the fact that she still answers the phone when I call.* Also I would like to thank the editor of the German edition, Boris Karnikowski, for his encouraging words and his trust in me.

I am very happy that my book has also been translated into English and would like to thank the U.S. team at Pearson for their wonderful work. Special thanks are due to Almut Dworak, the translator, whose valuable feedback has certainly helped improve this edition significantly.

But my biggest thanks go to my family. I am very grateful to my husband, Markus Kummer, for having strong nerves and quietly suffering my temper. I would like to apologize to my daughters, Malou and Joelle, for not listening to them and sometimes not being quite sure what I just agreed to. And last but not least, I want to thank my parents-in-law, who always made sure that I also got a bit of the Sunday roast.

About the Author

Angie Radtke, along with her colleagues at her communications agency, Der Auftritt (*www.der-auftritt.de*), has been conceiving, designing, and implementing targeted communications solutions since 1999, primarily in the areas of Internet and print. She specializes in marketing-oriented, accessible Web presences and tends to use the open source content management system Joomla!, depending on the customer's wishes.

Appealing design, accessibility, and use of a content management system are not mutually exclusive, and therein lies the basis of Radtke's work. She invests a lot of time and energy in further developing Joomla!. Radtke was actively involved in promoting accessibility in the previous version, Mambo, and her dedication continues today. She developed the two default templates, Beez 2.0 and Beez 5, and she sees herself as an interface between Joomla!'s program logic and its actual output of contents.

Radtke is increasingly involved in passing on her knowledge to others—for example, in training sessions, presentations, and workshops on Joomla! and through accessible Web design. In 2006, she and coauthor Michael Charlier published *Barrierefreies Webdesign: Zugängliche Websites attraktiv gestalten* (München: Addison-Wesley), a book on designing attractive, accessible Web sites.

Angie Radtke is married, has two children, and lives in Bonn, Germany.

The Basis: Designing the Content and Visual Concept

Creating a Web site is a constant challenge. You need to combine content, design, and interaction and use the technology you have available to create a unified whole. At the same time, you need to incorporate the existing corporate design used by the business or institution. Good Web sites are always geared toward specific target groups and ensure that as many people as possible can access the content. They support the user in absorbing the information provided but do not limit the user to just a single way of using it. Successful businesses want to set themselves apart from the competition and project a specific image—good products and services alone are no longer enough.

A good corporate design reflects the company's philosophy and the underlying corporate culture. The effect of the design is determined by the interaction of its basic elements. Are the colors harmonious? Is the logo expressive? Does the design contain typical features that people will recognize? And so on.

Design is a very powerful form of communication. It creates emotions, transmits a message, and triggers different reactions in the viewer. An overall design that differs too much from common expectations will cause visitors to leave your site.

The first impression is crucial. When users visit a Web site, they decide in the first few seconds whether or not to stay. We all know what it's like when you meet someone for the first time. Your first impression decides how you behave. Your impression and response have a lot to do with your own experiences and your own personal perception. People react on the basis of their personal backgrounds and social context. For example, things that have a positive connotation in the United States may trigger negative reactions in Europe or Asia.

It All Starts with the Structure

A good Web site and its design are always based on the content. The content should be in place before you even start thinking about the visual design. But in practice, it's often a different situation.

The client hires a designer to create a pretty shell that corresponds to the corporate identity of the company. If the designer does a good job, the client is happy and gets someone to integrate the whole thing into a template. And that's where the first problems arise. A template can look however you want it to look, but certain conventions still must be observed.

With Joomla!, almost anything is possible: it just depends how much effort you are willing to invest.

Once the design is implemented correctly, the next step is inserting the content. But what if the designer failed to allow room for longer words in the navigation, or what if the headers are too long and suddenly spill over onto two lines? It does not take much to ruin the whole design.

A good content-related structure makes a Web site much more usable. The prettiest design and the best technology are of little use if the content is insufficiently structured.

Before you start designing, you should have finished developing your underlying concept with regard to the content. The design is only there to enhance the content and help the viewer absorb the information.

This of course does not mean that all content has to be available in its entirety right from the start. After all, we are working with a content management system that can be expanded. But you should at least know what type of information must be displayed and how it will be presented.

Tip

It pays to get a good copywriter!

Recognizing User Expectations

Web applications have to be based on the motivation, the aim, and the expected behavior of the user because human beings are creatures of comfort and want to have as little as possible to do with operating your Web site. Usually, users are looking for information. The aim should be to lead them to this information as quickly and with as few complications as possible. You need to take into account that users follow their habits and experiences when searching for information. The Web has become an accepted part of life in recent years. Web sites with technical, visual, and structural defects are not readily accepted because, with the huge deluge of information out there, anything the users cannot find directly on your Web site they will try to find elsewhere.

One of the most important aspects in the Web design process is finding out the goal of the users. What is their motivation to visit the Web sites you have designed, and how can you support them in terms of visual design and technology?

Information architecture plays a central role. Depending on the amount of content you are dealing with, a good content-related structure can pose a huge challenge. Try to put yourself in the user's place and arrange the contents logically from that point of view.

This process is not always easy, as your view of the content may be significantly different from that of the user. Do not forget: you know your information and how it's organized, but your user does not.

Page Layout—Visually Structuring Content

The layout design of the individual site areas is a central element for presenting content. The term *column layout* became common in the times of table layouts. A table layout is nothing more than a structural grid that enables you to arrange your content consistently. Originally, it was a term from newspaper layouts, and site designers later brought this type of presentation to the Web. Tables were the first choice for presenting content online.

You may have heard the term *the golden ratio*. Artists and architects have long used this ratio, which appears frequently in nature. Wikipedia offers the following definition:

> In mathematics and the arts, two quantities are in the **golden ratio** if the ratio of the sum of the quantities to the larger quantity is equal to the ratio of the larger quantity to the smaller one.[1]

This sounds very technical and hard to understand. Simply put, you could describe it as a ratio of one-third to two-thirds. Elements that are arranged on the screen in this ratio often appear very harmonious and well balanced. Figure 1.1 shows what a golden ratio looks like.

Designing with Grids

In addition to the golden ratio rule, using the grids can make your design process simpler. In every graphics program you will find a grid view. If you use the grids, you will find it considerably easier to position individual elements on the screen.

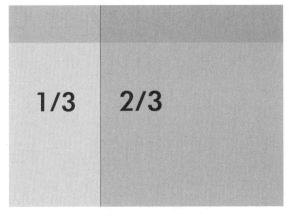

Figure 1.1   The golden ratio

---

1. *http://en.wikipedia.org/wiki/Golden_ratio*

In principle, grids are a combination of vertical columns, horizontal areas, and empty spaces. Grids help designers find structure and patterns within their design. The result is usually a more harmonious, well-proportioned overall picture. An example of a typical grid is shown in Figure 1.2.

Grids, positioned as background images in the graphics program, serve as guidelines for the chosen design. This makes it easier to position columns and boxes.

To create suitable grids, you need to use a little bit of math because you have to combine the width of the individual columns with a corresponding amount of blank space so that the whole layout stretches over the total selected width. Fortunately, others have already taken care of the math for you.

On the Web site *www.960.gs* you will find a collection of grid patterns for various graphics programs, each with a total width of 960 pixels.

If you want to create grids for individual page widths, Grid Designer by Rasmus Schultz *(http://grid.mindplay.dk)* can help. This program gives you the option of entering individual data on the total width, number of columns, and desired distances. Grid Designer then automatically creates the desired template for you. See Figure 1.3 for an example of using Grid Designer.

Among other reasons, designing with grids will become more important in the future because of CSS3. CSS (Cascading Style Sheets) was developed by the World Wide Web Consortium (W3C) and first released in 1996. The requirements for modern Web design have changed since then. The CSS Working Group of the W3C has been thinking about a more flexible positioning model. One of the group's ideas is the grid-positioning module of CSS3. This concept is based on the idea of grids, but although it is eagerly awaited by users, its development is not yet finished. The grid-positioning module offers, for example, the two properties `grid-columns` for columns and `grid-rows` for rows. Unfortunately, you cannot test it yet because browsers do not currently support it.

Figure 1.2   12-column grid with 960-pixel width

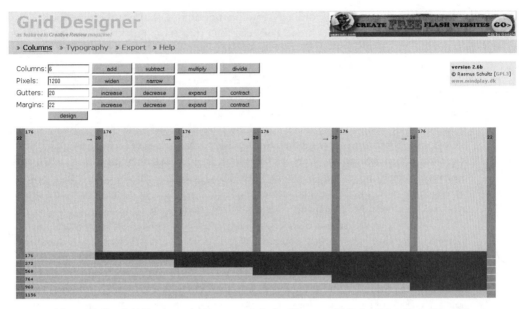

Figure 1.3   Grid Designer by Rasmus Schultz (Rasmus Schultz, *http://mindplay.dk*)

For further information, have a look at *Transcending CSS: The Fine Art of Web Design* by Andy Clarke and Molly Holzschlag (Berkeley, CA: New Riders, 2007) or visit *www. alistapart.com/articles/outsidethegrid*.

Implementation

Once your structure is established, you can visually arrange the various basic elements—information on the company, the navigation, and content of the columns—on the screen. Doing so allows users to understand the site as a whole and find their way around it easily.

Over the years, a few clear conventions for layout designs have developed on the Web. The header usually contains information about the company, the purpose of the site, central navigation elements such as company and contact information, and possible navigation aids such as links to a sitemap or a search function. As a header, this type of information is in the viewer's direct field of vision and can be easily found if there are any problems.

In our Western direction of reading, the eye moves from left to right and top to bottom over the pages, so the logo is usually placed at the top left in the primary visual area.

The average user expects to find the navigation on the left side. However, this design is often debated because some say it is boring and lacks innovation. But people follow familiar patterns, even when moving around the Internet. They have their own experiences and will react accordingly. Familiar positioning shortens the time users require to grasp the overall content. They can then turn more quickly to specific content on the site. The first few seconds are crucial because users who do not directly find what they are looking for can soon lose interest.

The main content is generally placed on the center of the page. Larger Web sites and portal sites frequently feature additional information on the right, offering a brief summary and then linking to more detailed information.

Usability experts generally use eye-tracking systems to test a site. These systems track the eye movements and viewing direction of users when they are looking at a Web site. It records which areas of the Web site users look at, how long they look at it, which area they look at first, and so on. Tests done with this system have shown that familiar positioning leads users to take in the content more quickly. For a short demonstration of an eye-tracking system on a Web site, check out *www.youtube.com/watch?v=lo_a2cfBUGc*.

This setup is of course not obligatory, but because of its success, it is recommended. Consider municipality or utility company Web sites. In general, they are not visited frequently, and when they are visited, it is usually in situations of stress: for example, the trash was not collected or there was a mistake on a bill. In such cases, users are glad to find their way around without having to search an unfamiliar layout. So adhering to the (relatively few) design conventions of the Web is generally an indispensable requirement for achieving a high level of accessibility.

Many designers prove that the three-column design does not have to be boring. A List Apart, shown in Figure 1.4, is a striking site that uses a three-column design.

Figure 1.4   Three-column design, *alistapart.com* (Reprinted with the permission of *A List Apart* magazine, *www.alistapart.com*)

A relatively new approach to this traditional concept relates to the arrangement of the contents on the start page.

Push to Front Principle

On large portal sites in particular, the tendency is often to link directly from the start page to deeper contents to show the complexity of the site. This approach is called the "push to front" principle. The term was coined by my colleague and friend Dr. Michael Charlier. He clearly pinpoints the problems of very large portal sites: the larger the offerings of a Web site, the more difficult it becomes to effectively structure the contents in terms of usability.

Whereas the classic navigation design merely attempts to offer visitors paths toward the desired content, the push to front method aims to visually present as many teasers as possible to visitors on the top levels of a site, and then direct them to the content on the lower levels. This approach helps users discover content that, due to unfamiliarity, they might not have been looking for but that is relevant to the topic and provides clear information. Increasingly, context-sensitive methods are used as well.

The development of the push to front principle was triggered by the information explosion of recent years, particularly on large portals. Web sites with tens of thousands of individual documents are no longer an exception—such an amount of material cannot be clearly and logically categorized in practice, nor can it be made manageable with the classic navigation design.

Instead of presenting many links to different content, which would be confusing, the new architectural model works with teasers and information boxes that have enough content to give users a first impression of what each topic is about. Because such teasers require a relatively large amount of space, they are constantly being replaced and in some cases even automatically rotated. The aim is to present as much content as possible, as early as possible, and as close to the front as possible. At the same time, the indispensable navigation links are radically reduced—four to seven basic categories give visitors (and also the site maintainer) a clear initial overview of what goes where.

At the end of the page, the main menu with the always-visible items of the second navigation level is usually repeated. This solution, which is becoming increasingly popular, removes, in one fell swoop, all accessibility and usability problems of the normal slide-out navigation. Furthermore, as a mini sitemap, it can offer an excellent guide, especially to visitors who are unfamiliar with the site. Even if you do not need this navigation, it will not get in your way.

The Graphical Layout—Visual Appearance Matters

The spatial arrangement of the content in a design grid is always the first step. Next is the specific design. Visual elements assist visitors in taking in the information offered on the Web site. They show users possible options for interacting and expressing the corporate identity of the site owner. They lead viewers in a logical sequence through the most important content of a site and help them grasp the overall concept.

The start page forms the center of the concept. It guides user behavior on the site and ultimately determines whether the site will be successful. Its design should correspond to the expectations and the usual reading behavior of the visitors and should keep offering them new visual anchor points that they can hold on to.

Colors—A Central Element

Colors have a great influence on human emotions and moods. Their effects are complex because they vary according to cultural background and gender. Even the shade of a color can produce different moods. Dark blue appears more serious than a light, glowing blue, for example. Colors can often be adapted to target groups: women prefer shades of red, whereas men find blue more appealing, and colors such as black and silver-gray appear elegant. In many cases the choice of colors is determined in advance by the corporate design of the client.

The effects of colors and the visual materials used should not be underestimated. In Figures 1.5 and 1.6 you can see two identical designs that differ only in their choice of colors and the images used. The difference in their effect is astonishing.

Finding Colors

Often you need to find a color complementary to the company color you are already using to emphasize certain content. The Adobe Kuler *(http://kuler.adobe.com)* is a very special tool. A Flash application helps you find the most suitable color combinations. You simply enter hexadecimal color values and the program finds the matching color combination. See Figure 1.7.

If you are interested in colors, you may also find this Web site fun to investigate: *www.colorlovers.com.*

Until a few years ago, for technical reasons, you were fairly limited when it came to selecting colors. You were only able to choose the so-called Web-safe colors to ensure a fairly uniform presentation. Computer technology has greatly improved since then. Millions of different colors now are at users' disposal.

Many designers encountered clients who stood next to the monitor with a pantone color guide to check whether the company color was correctly implemented. They then had to explain that you can never assume that colors are represented in the same way on different systems. The representation can differ greatly due to different, uncalibrated monitors and different graphics cards. Old cathode ray tube monitors usually have colors darker than thin-film transistor screens as well as clear differences among their operating systems. Also, not many users have properly calibrated their monitors.

Colors in the Context of Accessibility

Certain color combinations can cause problems when designing an accessible Web site, so color selection is especially important.

Total colorblindness is rare, and as the name indicates, people with total colorblindness have no color perception at all. If you convert a layout to grayscale, you get a rough impression of how people with colorblindness see. But the perception is very individual and can differ greatly depending on the degree of vision impairment. Many colorblind

Figure 1.5   Design dark

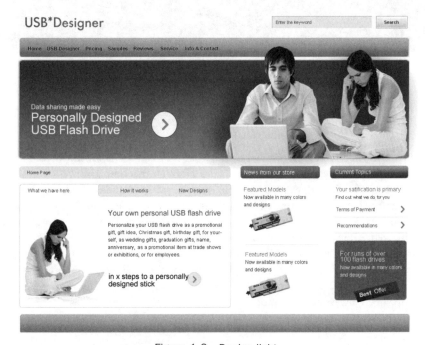

Figure 1.6   Design light

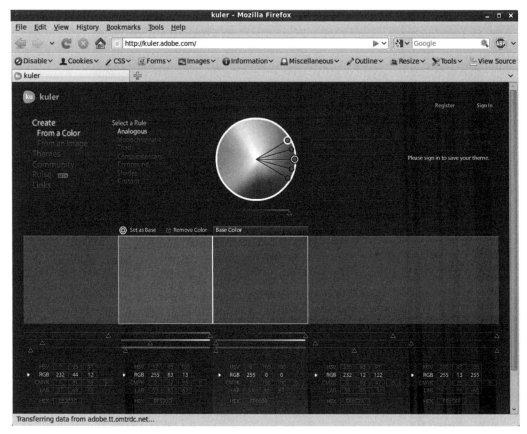

Figure 1.7   Adobe's Kuler (© 2012 with express permission from Adobe
Systems Incorporated, *http://kuler.adobe.com*)

people have learned which colors lay behind what they can see. They know, for example, that grass is green and can identify other shades of green by comparison.

Much more common than total colorblindness is red-green colorblindness. People with this impairment have a genetic anomaly that prevents them from being able to distinguish between the colors red and green. Mixed colors that contain red and green appear blurred. About 9 percent of men suffer from red-green blindness. Usually the people concerned do not perceive this colorblindness as a great restriction. It only becomes a problem if recognizing the color difference is essential for taking in important information. The traffic light is a good example of compensating for colorblindness: red is always at the top, green always at the bottom.

Online tools such as *www.vischeck.com* or *http://colorfilter.wickline.org* can help us get an approximate impression of what colorblind people actually see.

Contrasts

If the contrast in a Web site is too low, the design can appear washed out and boring. Too high a contrast, on the other hand, can make the design look too busy and chaotic.

Contrast not only is important for the overall appearance of a Web site, but it is also a critical aspect of making a Web site easy to read. If you are thinking about creating an accessible site, you should choose your foreground and background colors so that the difference remains visible even for visitors with impaired color vision or visitors who may be viewing the page on a grayscale monitor.

The foreground and background colors should clearly contrast with your text elements. But it is not possible to select color and contrast settings that suit everyone. Black text on white background has the greatest color contrast. To avoid annoying glare effects, it may be appropriate to slightly tint the background. Some people with vision impairment require very strong contrasts to be able to separate the individual elements of a page. For these people, color combinations such as white text on a light orange background do not have enough contrast. For others, strong contrasts can result in a type of distortion called "blooming," and the content becomes harder to read. Figure 1.8 demonstrates the need for contrast as well as hue so that differences can be seen by more people.

Color values also influence accessibility. Colors with hues that are very similar in value are no longer distinguishable when converted to grayscale. In certain designs—whenever information is not just represented through color differences—you can make a compromise with this area. But you should still be aware that people with color vision impairments may not be able to distinguish the design very well.

Figure 1.8   The colors red and gray are easy to distinguish for people with normal vision. When converted to grayscale, the color differences are no longer visible and the red square looks black.

At *http://juicystudio.com/services/colourcontrast.php* you will find the color contrast analyzer. You enter two color values, and the system tells you whether the colors have enough contrast in the context of accessibility.

Designing the Navigation—The Core of the Design

The navigation should be clearly set apart from the content of the page. It forms the design anchor point that guides users even when they advance further into the lower levels of multilayered Web page offerings.

Each page should indicate as clearly as possible

- Where the visitor is currently located in relation to the Web presence as a whole
- Which other main areas are present
- How these can be reached

You can achieve this by

- Emphasizing the navigation items and their parent elements
- Adding margins, making the text bold, or using small graphics
- Indicating information not just by using different text color, as, for example, to accomodate people with impaired vision
- Indicating visited and not-visited links
- Creating a uniform design for your links
- Clearly highlighting links located within the text flow and creating a uniform design presentation for links within the text and navigation
- Arranging the links in a logical, consistent order so they can be reached via the tab key on a keyboard
- Offering breadcrumb navigation

Content Design—To Make It Fun to Read

Graphical elements such as small icons or photos give the eye something to focus on. They guide viewers from one section to another so they can absorb the information one step at a time.

We have all come across veritable text deserts on Web sites that make reading the text on the screen unbearable. Lines get blurry because there are no striking points for the eyes to focus on. The design of the page should make it clear what the main content is. Headers serve to emphasize text sections and reflect semantically relevant structures. They should stand out from the main content in color and size. Dark headers appear more striking than light ones. The more succinct the wording of the header, the clearer you should make it stand out. The sections are easier to read if the lines are not too long, because in a long line of text, the eye finds it hard to go back to the beginning of the next line. This can be difficult to implement, particularly with scalable layouts, depending on the screen resolution. Lines that are too short can also be hard to read, as the relevant content is harder to grasp if there are too many line breaks. Long sections of continuous text should be broken up with headers, or the eye gets tired too quickly. If the distance between the lines is too large or too small, it can also make it hard for the reader to understand the content of your text.

With CSS you have the option of formatting the line spacing very simply via the property `line-height`. This property can be specified as an absolute value in pixels or as a relative value in the form of percentage or em.

```
p { line-height:1.4em}
```

The text formatting itself has great importance. Text formatting is the specification of font type, font size, font weight, character and word spacing, and font color. CSS offers a number of such text formatting options.

Font Design—We Do Not Have Many Options

When selecting the font type, we as designers are restricted. This statement would have been universal until fairly recently were it not for Web fonts. But first we need to explain a few fundamental points.

Fonts can be classified generally into two categories, those without serifs (sans serif) and those with serifs. Serif fonts, such as Times and Georgia, have little lines or flares at the ends of strokes in each letter; sans serif fonts, such as Arial and Helvetica, look smoother because they are composed of only the letter strokes without the decorative touches. Sans serif fonts are easier to read on the screen, and serif fonts are better suited for use in printing. Smaller fonts used in continuous text are harder to read: on the screen where everything is represented in pixels, serifs tend to clump together or even disappear. On paper, even fine serifs are clearly visible and help us grasp the word from its shape.

The design effect of fonts can be very different. Sans serif fonts appear clearer and more modern; serif fonts can appear old-fashioned.

Recently, there is a growing tendency to combine both types of fonts on a page by using sans serif fonts, such as Arial or Helvetica, on the Web in the continuous text and serif fonts, such as Times or Georgia, in the generously sized headers. Have a look at the Web site *www.alistapart.com* as an example of the effect this kind of combination can produce.

When constructing your Web site, make sure your CSS contains the generic font family as well as the font itself. This ensures that at least the desired font type is displayed even if the font you selected is not available on the system of the user.

```
p { font-family: verdana,sans-serif;)
```

Web Fonts

With CSS2 there was an attempt to make implementing fonts within a Web site possible by offering the option of embedding external fonts within the page via `@font-face`. This would have worked beautifully if the font manufacturers had not dug in their heels and objected. Like texts, photos, and graphics, fonts are subject to copyright protection. As soon as a font is directly integrated into a page, it resides on the Web server and is thereby publicly accessible and open to abuse. This is not in the best interest of commercial font providers.

Until recently, the safest option to make sure that the font was displayed as intended was to use system fonts. But there is hope: the Web fonts are coming and will offer more design freedom in the future.

The W3C has formed a working group focused on Web fonts. The result is a new file format for Web fonts: WOFF (Web Open Font Format). The format was developed by Erik van Blokland and Tal Leming together with Mozilla developer Jonathan Kew.

WOFF fonts are compressed, so they have a much shorter loading time. You can also save meta information, such as information on the copyright. Ultimately, the data of OpenType or TrueType fonts is only repackaged in WOFF, so basically no new functions are required. Via @font-face, WOFF fonts can be embedded in Web pages together with TrueType and OpenType fonts.

The Beez template by Joomla! makes use of this technique and integrates the selected font Titillium Maps via CSS.

```
@font-face {
 font-family: 'Titillium Maps';
 src: url("../fonts/TitilliumMaps29L002.eot")

 }
@font-face {
 font-family: 'Titillium Maps';
 src:
 url("../fonts/TitilliumMaps29L002.otf") format("opentype"),
 url("../fonts/TitilliumMaps29L002.woff") format("woff")
 }
```

Here you can see that this font is embedded several times with different file extensions. The reason is that not all browsers currently support the .woff format. In addition to Firefox, the following browsers do offer support for the .woff format:

- Safari, v.5.1
- Opera, v.11.10
- Microsoft Internet Explorer, v.9
- Camino, v.2.1a
- Mobile Safari under iOS v.5
- Chrome, v.6

Other browsers can only integrate fully fledged OpenType fonts, and Internet Explorer requires the Embedded OpenType (EOT) format. A big disadvantage in this method is the long loading time for the different file formats. If you are building a very large Web site, it makes sense to load the files after first checking the browser.

Once you have integrated the font into the page, you can use it very easily without further complications.

```
h1
{ font-family: 'Titillium Maps', Arial;
}
```

You should choose your font carefully because there are still browsers that do not support any of the specified file formats or cannot interpret the statement @font-face at all. In the preceding example, you can see that an alternative font—in this case, Arial—is specified for this case.

Different fonts have a different default tracking and height. Web fonts are often smaller than system fonts. If you adapt them to the right size with CSS font-size, the font size may differ from the size of the alternative font. You can test font sizes in Firefox 2 and other browsers.

Free fonts under the SIL Open Font License can be converted to WOFF files. You can find a converter at *www.fontsquirrel.com/fontface/generator.*

Font manufacturers had to rethink their licensing models, and many providers have now added Web fonts to their offerings.

The ever-innovative Google has considered the topic of Web fonts and now offers the Google Font API. Currently, there is a limited pool of available fonts that can be easily integrated into your page via a CSS link. You can see some of the fonts available from Google in Figure 1.9.

To include these fonts in your site, link to the Google Font API with the following code in your head section:

```
<link rel="stylesheet" type="text/css"
 href="http://fonts.googleapis.com/css?family=Font+Name">
```

Droid Sans Mono by Steve Matteson

Droid Sans Mono

Droid Serif by Steve Matteson (4 variants)

Droid Serif

IM Fell by Igino Marini (10 families)

IM Fell

Inconsolata by Raph Levien

Inconsolata

Josefin Sans Std Light by Santiago Orozco

Josefin Sans Std Light

Lobster by Pablo Impallari

Lobster

Molengo by Denis Jacquerye

Molengo

Figure 1.9   Selection of Google fonts

The offered fonts are on the Google server and from there are directly integrated into the page. The API takes care of browser compatibility and makes using the fonts very simple.

There is a downside: normally, every designer creates a draft in a graphics program, and for that you need the fonts in readable format. The Google API does not offer the fonts in their original format, so you have to go searching on the Web. I quickly found doing so was tedious and unproductive. Only with Lobster was I able to relatively quickly find what I was looking for.

There are other methods for integrating your own fonts into your design. For example, you can use image replacement techniques, using Flash or Cufon *(http://cufon.shoqolate.com/generate/)*, a JavaScript solution.

But none of these solutions are completely without disadvantages. The image replacement methods limit the usability regarding the accessibility, especially for blind people, while the other two methods require Flash or JavaScript to work.

Font Size—Scalability of Text

It is often tempting to use very small fonts to get more information to fit onto the screen. Also, larger fonts appear less elegant. But small fonts are hard or impossible to read, not just for people with vision impairment and the elderly. Fortunately, the common browsers still offer the option of zooming in on fonts or even the whole page, but you should still offer an easy-to-read standard font size.

Fixed and Fluid Layouts

In Web design, a distinction is made between fixed and fluid layouts. Fluid layouts adapt to the screen size and offer space to scalable text. The Web makes it possible for viewers to actually influence what they are seeing. Windows can be adapted in size, fonts can be tailored to individual needs, and even color settings can be edited by users. Fluid layouts place special demands on design implementation because they need to work independently of the width of the relevant browser window or the monitor resolution.

The column width of the design is specified in percentage (%) or ems, which offers the option of using the whole view area of the screen if the user finds it optimal. If the browser window changes, the content display changes automatically.

Tip
The golden ratio for a two-column layout is 62 percent to 38 percent.

This flexibility is a good thing, but it can lead to massive problems in our design. If pages have only a small amount of text, they can appear homogeneous and well balanced when viewed with a resolution of 800×600 pixels. But if you look at the same page with a resolution of 1280×1024 pixels, all the content may be crammed up at the top edge of the screen. Besides being unattractive, it makes the text hard to read. The eye begins to waver and can no longer connect the end of a line with its beginning. In such cases, it makes sense to specify a maximum width for the view area. Standard conforming browsers offer the CSS property max-width for this purpose.

Internet Explorer 6 does not support max-width. Whether you still want to support this browser is a decision you need to make for yourself. Keep in mind that some large companies, governments, and people, particularly in developing countries, still use this browser (or, rather, have to). If you decide to support Internet Explorer 6, you have to use a little trick to get the same result as in other browsers.

```
*html #content
 { width: expression((body.offsetWidth >1000)?'1000px':'auto'); }
```

expression is a proprietary property of Internet Explorer and is only understood by this browser. This solution is not compliant to standards and therefore is not valid, but it can be useful in certain cases. If the browser window is wider than 1000 pixels, our container #content is assigned the fixed width of 1000 pixels. If it is smaller than 1000 pixels, it behaves according to our relative specifications.

Fixed design layouts offer the designer the option of controlling the representation more precisely. Individual page areas remain consistent in their arrangement: no elements will start sliding around. It is much easier to integrate graphics because you will know how large they need to be to fill certain page areas. Also, the length of the text lines is easier to manage.

When using scalable fonts in a fixed layout, the design has to give enough space to the fonts that they can expand. If there is not enough room, page areas can suddenly overlap or parts of the content become inaccessible. To ensure that scalability is practicable, you may have to mix relative and absolute specifications. With any combination of relative measurements and other specifications, you should ensure that the overlapping effects do not occur by carrying out appropriate tests. A second method for ensuring scalability is working with floating areas that arrange themselves below one another within the relevant viewport when the font is enlarged. The problem of scalability should be considered when developing and selecting graphical layouts. Not everything that is visually pleasing and appears conceptually sensible will be possible to scale and implement pixel by pixel.

2

Accessibility—What Is It?

For most people, using the Internet has become so commonplace that they take it for granted. Information from all over the world is ready for you to retrieve. Perhaps more important is the local information available to you with just a few keystrokes: you can look up the special offers of local retailers, the operating hours of most businesses, and even phone numbers from your home computer. You no longer need to bother with inconvenient trips to the library or numerous phone calls: you just look online to get the information you need.

But not everyone benefits from the convenience of today's technology. In particular, people with physical or mental disability face barriers that make accessing information or using services difficult or even impossible for them. Many of these barriers can be overcome if a Web site's content is designed to be accessible to everyone.

Building in accessibility—that is, designing the Web experience so that all people have access to the information and functionality on a site—is fundamental to Web design. You need to be aware of the issues that hinder accessibility and the techniques that enhance it when you build your template. The accessibility of your Web site can be crucial to its success because online businesses want to reach the greatest number of people possible, and those with disability constitute a considerable target group. Accordingly, accessible Web design aims to make content and interactions on the Web as accessible and barrier-free as possible for all user groups.

A significant percentage of the U.S. population have a physical impairment that makes it difficult for them to access information on the Internet. The types of impairments are manifold, and the resulting requirements for design and technical implementation are therefore also varied. People who are blind, for example, have different requirements than people with other types of visual impairments. Some people have difficulty with the usual input methods: for example, not everyone can use a mouse or operate a standard keyboard. About 35 million Americans are hearing impaired. Some of them are children, and their hearing loss is so severe that they have trouble learning sign language. This makes it all the more important that texts are presented clearly.

Another type of limitation is "contextual disabilities," such as slow connection speeds in hotels, unpredictable lighting conditions while on a train, and mandatory absence of sound in the workplace. These and other environmental factors should be kept in mind as you design for accessibility.

Building accessibility into your Web design is not always about meeting recommendations and legal requirements (which government authorities are obliged to do). Even small steps toward accessibility can significantly improve the usability of Web sites for all visitors.

Joomla!, with its widespread use, can have a big impact on Web accessibility. With the standard templates Beez 2.0 and Beez 5.0, it has now become relatively simple to create accessible sites that many people can use.

In this chapter, after we examine the legal reasons for being concerned with accessibility, I describe the problems that various user groups are faced with when trying to access online information. Guidelines and derived checklists offer points of reference for reducing barriers, but the barriers themselves can only be effectively reduced if you have a precise idea of where the problems lie and which solutions are available.

The Legal Basis

Efforts to make computers accessible for people with disabilities are in fact older than the Internet. In December 1982, the United Nations General Assembly adopted the World Programme of Action (WPA) concerning Disabled Persons, in which the accessibility of modern technologies for people with disabilities plays a significant role. In the following years, large IT companies such as IBM, Microsoft, and Sun Microsystems made the first important contributions to improve this accessibility. In December 1993—HTTP was hardly 2 years old—the UN General Assembly adopted a resolution demanding equal access to information and communication for people with physical disabilities. Soon, the first countries began to draw up regulations, and laws were implemented.

With the creation of the World Wide Web Consortium (W3C) in 1994, an expert advisory board took on the task of creating guidelines for a more accessible Web in addition to many other standardization measures. These efforts were largely complete in 1998 and formed the basis for Section 508 of the Rehabilitation Act Amendment, passed by the United States in December 1998, making it a legal obligation for the U.S. government and its agencies to adhere to certain accessibility requirements. The W3C Web Accessibility Initiative adopted these guidelines in May 1999 as Web Content Accessibility Guidelines 1.0 (WCAG1.0). Other countries soon followed suit and introduced similar laws and guidelines.

The WCAG 2 was published in December 2008. It differs significantly from the previous version in a few respects.

According to the WCAG 2, Web sites should be

- *Perceivable* for every person and every technical device, for example, by providing text alternatives for images, subtitles for audio, and adaptable presentation and color contrast

- *Operable* by every person and every technical device, for example, by ensuring simple keyboard operation, reasonable time limits for input, and ease of navigation and avoiding visual stimuli that could induce seizures in users with photosensitive epilepsy

- *Understandable*, for example, by being readable and predictable and offering help with input

- *Robust*, for example, by being compatible with assistive technologies

In practice, you should be aware of the following improvements:

- Improved requirements for color contrasts.

- More precise requirements for forms.

- Scripting: Web sites can now manage without fallback solutions, but the JavaScript itself should be accessibly structured.

- More precise requirements for multimedia (subtitles, synchronization, operation, etc.).

- More precise requirements for operation via keyboard.

- More precise requirements for dynamic updating of contents.

So far, the guidelines are just recommendations, and the law for private sector companies is still somewhat vague. Section 255 of the Telecommunications Act, which does apply to private sector companies, requires telecommunication products and services to be accessible whenever accessibility is "readily achievable" (see U.S. Legal Activities on Web Accessibility, *www.uiaccess.com/us-legal.html*). It is a good idea to be aware of these guidelines; you can read the W3C recommendations at *www.w3.org/TR/WCAG/*.

Visual Impairment

When most people think about Web accessibility, they think first about people who are blind. There is more to visual impairment than just blindness, just as there is more to accessibility than accommodating those with visual impairments.

Initial Situation and Findings

The monitor is basically the classic symbol of a computer, and for people who have difficulty seeing or cannot see at all it is a problem. I am not talking about a small minority: about a quarter of the working population has problems with vision to different degrees of severity, and with growing age that number rapidly increases. Some vision problems can be easily corrected with eyeglasses or contacts, and others are only partially corrected. Some eye problems, such as cataracts or glaucoma, are operable or can at least be alleviated. Others, such as retinitis pigmentosa or diabetic retinopathy, cause a progressive decrease in vision and often lead to total blindness. People who suffer from tunnel vision lose their peripheral vision and have an extremely restricted field of vision, sometimes just the size of a coin held at arm's length.

About 9 percent of the male population suffers from mild forms of colorblindness, which generally entails being unable to distinguish certain shades of red and green. Blindness toward other colors, complete color blindness, and red-green blindness in women is very rare.

People are considered legally blind if their visual acuity—*with* corrective lenses—is 20/200 or less or if their visual field is 20 degrees or less. The number of people who are legally blind in the United States exceeds 2 million. Some of them can decipher text on the computer only by enlarging text on the screen and adjusting color settings; others must rely on acoustic output or must feel the text using a braille display. To do so, they require assistive technologies.

The requirements of different people affected by vision impairments are extraordinarily different. It is therefore not possible to achieve a general optimization of colors, contrast, or font size. Whereas a person with tunnel vision may prefer tiny yellow letters on a dark blue background, a person with presbyopia (age-related farsightedness) may be grateful for large black letters on a slightly tinted background. Accessibility for people with vision impairment is therefore primarily about avoiding any barriers that could prevent them from being able to adjust the page display to suit their needs. You have a rich assortment of tools available to choose from.

Technical Aids

Some technical aids are already included as standard features of every personal computer and can be used without limitations, but others have to be purchased and are costly.

Adjusting the Screen Resolution

The average Internet user today uses a screen resolution of 1024 × 768 pixels or 1280 × 768 pixels on a 17- to 19-inch monitor. This does not mean that you can optimize your Web site for these parameters without problems, although some Web sites do. Depending on the monitor, graphics card, and operating system, there are different settings available, and they are used in different ways. Older users often set a resolution of 800 pixels width or less even on large monitors. This causes all elements (not just the text, but also icons and frames) to appear considerably enlarged, which is considered more pleasant by these users even though pixels may be clearly visible or pictures may look blurry. Windows offers another method of globally adapting size, which primarily affects fonts. Web sites that are intended to be accessed by the greatest possible number of visitors should be generally set up so that they are still usable at a resolution of 800 pixels, with medium-sized fonts, and if possible, without scrollbars.

Adapting Font Size

Until a few years ago, a user could enlarge only the font size of a Web site's text. Now, most browsers enable users to scale the entire page by using Ctrl (or Command for Mac) plus to increase the size, Ctrl (or Command) minus to decrease the size, and Ctrl (or Command) 0 to reset to the default size. Full scalability is very useful, but it can force the page outside of the viewport, resulting in parts of the page being cut off. For that reason, some people still prefer to zoom only the text.

The WCAG 2 states that it should be possible to resize the selected font by 200 percent of the original size in text zoom mode. This requirement is not always easy to fulfill.

If you have a demanding design with lots of words and long sentences, your design can start to fall apart at this zoom level.

If you want to optimize your site for Internet Explorer 6, you should also ensure that you choose relative size specifications, such as in percentage or ems, for the font. Theoretically, px is also valid for specifying a size and should be scalable by all browsers, but Internet Explorer does not change the display size for font changes only when px is used. Because of this limitation and because many designers are unaware of it, some Web sites with fashionable and space-saving small fonts are inaccessible for many visitors.

Standards-compliant browsers scale the font even with fixed pixel sizes specified. In Firefox, you will find the corresponding function in the menu View → Zoom → Zoom Text Only.

Opera can even scale graphics—although the quality suffers.

In Internet Explorer, version 7 and later, use Page → Text Size.

Defining Custom Stylesheets

The common browsers offer the option of creating custom stylesheets, but they are not always easy to find. On Web sites where the separation of content and presentation has been implemented consistently, and the entire layout is in the stylesheets, users can use this method to adapt the appearance of the Web site entirely to their own needs. This is a strong argument in favor of implementing the separation of content and presentation stated in the WCAG 2 guidelines. Following are instructions for setting up personal stylesheets for the two most common browsers, Firefox and Internet Explorer.

Firefox

Each system offers the option of loading user-specific data: programs can even be adapted individually. You probably are familiar with the following Windows folders:

Documents and Settings → User Name → Application Data

In this area, you will find user-specific settings for the various programs, including the browsers.

Firefox uses an external stylesheet for representing Web sites only if it does not find an alternative in the user settings.

Once you have created your individual stylesheet, it is important that you save it under the name userContent.css in the folder Chrome, because the browser uses naming conventions to detect whether a corresponding file is present or not. You can find this folder as follows:

Under Windows: Documents and Settings → User Name → Application Data → Mozilla → Firefox → Profiles → Xyz → Chrome

Under Mac OS X: User Name → Library → Application Support → Firefox → Profiles → Xyz → Chrome

Once you have saved your file there, it should be loaded automatically, and the selected Web site should then be displayed accordingly.

Internet Explorer

In Internet Explorer, the option for integrating your own stylesheets can be found in the menu Internet Options → Accessibility (see Figure 2.1).

The stylesheet does not follow any naming conventions. You can name it anything you like and integrate it.

Screen Magnifiers

Software magnifying glasses for screen output can make individual areas of the display considerably larger. Simple versions are available in most operating systems (see Figure 2.2), and others can be purchased as add-ons.

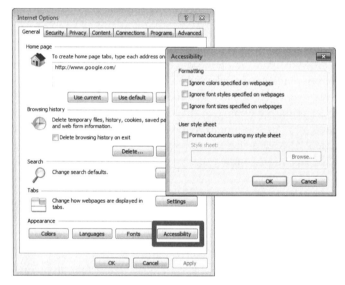

Figure 2.1   Accessibility options in Internet Explorer

Figure 2.2   Magnifier under Windows

In Windows 7, you can find the integrated screen magnifier by typing "magnifier" in the Start menu (see Figure 2.3).

In Windows XP, you can find the integrated screen magnifier under

Start → All Programs → Accessories → Accessibility → Magnifier

Onscreen Keyboards

Windows 7 also includes a simple onscreen keyboard as default (see Figure 2.4), which can be operated with just one key (normally the space bar). You can find it by typing "keyboard" in the Start menu.

In Windows XP, you can find this program under

Start → All Programs → Accessories → Accessibility → On-Screen Keyboard

The keyboard functions in a way that will feel very strange at first. You start the keyboard with the space bar. A blue bar cycles through all the rows in order from top to bottom. You can adjust how fast it cycles. Once it is in the row where the desired key is

Figure 2.3   Finding the magnifier in Windows 7

Figure 2.4   Onscreen keyboard in Windows

located, you stop it by pressing the space bar. Then the individual keys of that row are highlighted in sequence from left to right. Once the desired key is highlighted, press the space bar to use that key. This is faster than you might think, and practice makes perfect. Commercial versions offer considerably more comfort and higher speed.

There are also mouse keys that work under a similar principle: bars or lines run over the screen to form a coordinate system to enable the user to navigate to any point on the screen and trigger a function there.

With Mac OS X Snow Leopard, you can activate an onscreen keyboard under

> System Preferences → Language & Text → Input Preferences → Keyboard & Character Viewer

This puts a tiny American flag (with just one star) on your menu bar. Click on it, and then click on the Show Keyboard Viewer for the onscreen keyboard to appear.

Inverting the Screen Color

You can enable and configure the settings for screen color inversion in Windows under

> Start → Settings → Control Panel → Accessibility → Display → Settings for High Contrast

You can enable and configure the settings for screen color inversion on Mac OS X under

> System Preferences → Universal Access → Seeing → Display

Note

The operating systems Mac and Windows also offer an option for inverting the screen to increase the contrast. In Windows, the user can decide between different color combinations for foreground and background color and can choose a custom font size.

Screen Readers and Braille Displays

For people who need to use screen readers and braille displays, the commonly available computers have little to offer. You need to buy the screen reader software with output options via voice synthesizers separately, and the same goes for the extremely expensive and fragile braille display for reading braille.

The braille display is a tactile device you can connect to the computer. Every letter of the alphabet is represented by eight pins that can move up or down. Users feel the pattern by touching it with their fingertips and can thereby read text letter by letter. There are also braille devices with 24 × 36 individually navigable image points to make simple graphics accessible by touch in the corresponding resolution. If you are not dependent on this technique, you will probably find it hard to imagine how it works—again, with a little practice, a lot is possible.

Software for outputting screen content on nonvisual devices is offered by several suppliers. We distinguish between screen readers that read out the entire content of the screen—independent of the program currently used—and Web readers or voice browsers that are specifically designed for reading Web content. Acrobat Reader now offers its own voice output.

JAWS (Job Access with Speech) by Freedom Scientific is a screen reader available only for the Windows operating system. The active content of the screen is output acoustically via the computer soundcard. You can also enable output via the braille display. As a real screen reader, JAWS can make not only Web content but also a number of computer applications accessible. The program has an extraordinarily large range of functions and can work very effectively once you get used to it. JAWS is deeply rooted in the operating system once you install it, so if you want to test it, you should do so on a separate computer that you do not need to use every day. If you use several screen readers in combination, it can cause problems.

Other screen readers are Virgo by BAUM Retec AG and Blindows by Audiodata. They have a range of features similar to JAWS, and both use the WebFormator for representing Internet content.

Note

The WebFormator is a plug-in by Audiodata for Microsoft Internet Explorer. Not only can it be used as an add-on for screen readers but it can, in some cases, access a braille display on its own.

Once again, many features are available to support the user in accessing information. An integrated search function helps you find what you need. You can skip selected text blocks, navigate through forms, skip link lists if you wish, and see which links have already been visited. The WebFormator does not yet have its own voice output, but there are plans to include one. The WebFormator is available free of charge. Further information on the WebFormator can be found at *www.webformator.com*.

Mac OS X has several accessibility aids, including VoiceOver. For more information, see *www.apple.com/accessibility*.

Practical Example

Learning to use a screen reader can be a laborious task because it relies on the user's acoustic perception. People who are blind tend to have well-developed acoustic as well as tactile senses, and using the screen reader becomes easier with practice. Also, a screen reader can represent only one word or line at a time, regardless of whether it uses a speaker or braille display for output.

With the help of Eva Papst, who uses screen readers daily and knows far more about them than I do, I will try to describe what the intake of information via a screen reader is like.

Try to imagine you are looking at a Web site through a narrow window that is one text line high and about 80 characters wide. In this tiny "observation slit" you cannot see any formatting, such as different font colors or distances to neighboring elements; there is no context. This little slit is all that people with visual impairment can see when they first look at a Web site.

> **Note**
>
> That sounds worse than it is, because screen readers offer a vast number of commands with which you can move this narrow "slit" very precisely. (Eva Papst)

Of course, you can also move the reading window automatically from top to bottom, which makes sense for continuous texts. But before you can read, you first need to navigate to the right place and do so as accurately as possible. Screen readers offer a multitude of functions for moving around on a page. Here is just a small selection of available commands.

- To the next/previous header
- To the next/previous list
- To the next/previous paragraph
- To the next/previous form (element)
- To the next/previous table

Most screen readers also offer the option to list, for example,

- All links
- All headers
- All form fields

so you can temporarily hide the continuous text and reduce the information to a minimum. With function keys, you can request the page title or start a search function to make navigating easier.

What Can We Do?

For these features to work, you always need a semantically correct markup and a well-thought-out linearization of the contents. If the developers cannot fulfill the necessary requirements, the users cannot optimally use their tools and aids.

The first and most important rule for developers is therefore the complete separation of content and layout. This means, specifically,

- Clean HTML code for the content
- No superfluous layout tables
- Formatting exclusively via CSS

Only then can assistive technology process the content as desired while discounting the visual presentation. Saving the presentation in separate stylesheets can also give users the option of defining custom stylesheets in their browser to adapt the Web pages exactly to their needs. When specifying colors, you should always specify foreground and background colors. Using red and green as signal colors alone should be avoided because not everyone can see the difference.

Another very important rule: design the font sizes to be variable so the user has the option of changing them. Accommodating different font sizes will affect the design of your page because the frame layout has to accord sufficient room for the font to expand without breaking the layout. Depending on your other design specifications, it can become a big challenge. In Web sites where accessibility is the highest priority, using variable font sizes may mean that not all design ideas can be implemented or that—and this is what customers prefer to hear—you offer an alternative "accessibility style" in addition to the fancy design with all its graphical tricks and shiny sidebars. By providing an alternative design, you can fulfill all conceivable requirements for adaptability.

Frequently, Web designers use text in images with transparent backgrounds as headers. Transparent backgrounds are permissible only if all precautions are taken to prevent the text from disappearing if the user's choice of background color is the same as the designer's choice of text color. If possible, you should try to avoid transparent backgrounds in your design.

Following are the main requirements for designing to accommodate visual impairment:

- Separation of content and layout
- Semantically logical structure
- Well-reasoned choice of colors
- Sufficient level of contrast
- Variable font sizes
- Scalable layouts
- No textual graphics (don't replace real text with images)
- No transparent backgrounds for graphics

Motor Disabilities

Visual impairments are not the only type of disability that can affect a person's ability to use the Web. Certain types of motor disabilities can also negatively impact the ease with which a person can navigate the Web.

Initial Situation and Findings

The wheelchair has become the universal symbol of disability. But at the computer workplace and on the Internet, wheelchair users who can move their arms fully are as fit and able as any other user. The people who require special consideration are those who cannot use the keyboard or mouse as the default input device, for example, because of paralysis, loss of limbs, or inability to move or control their hands. Provided a person is able to trigger a binary signal—the famous 0 or 1—he or she can learn how to use a computer and all of its functions with the help of suitable software.

Technical Aids

A wide variety of adaptive keyboards (too many to discuss individually) have been developed to accommodate the many different types and degrees of disability that prevent users from operating standard devices. Other adaptive tools include head-motion devices, foot pedals and switches, eye-tracking devices, mouth controllers (also called sip-and-puff devices), and more. These tools enable users to operate a Web browser and other software—often with surprising speed. Ingenious software takes care of relating the signals produced by the user to the desired functions or actions (see Figure 2.5).

What Can We Do?

For accessibility software, and therefore the user, to work as efficiently as possible, Web sites should be clearly and logically structured. The clearer the structure, the easier the user can click, using only a few commands, to the place he or she wants to reach. For the optical design, one point is particularly important—both for severely disabled people who control their computers via eye movements (eye-tracking devices) and for older people who may have difficulty in getting the mouse to go exactly where they want it to go: the control elements should not be too small, and the distances between them should not be too narrow.

Following are the main requirements for designing to accommodate motor disabilities:

- Clear and logical structure
- Sufficiently large navigation elements
- No mouse-controlled events

Figure 2.5   Mouth controller (Used with permission by LIFEtool/Austria)

Deafness

It's not as obvious a factor as blindness, but deafness, contextual as well as actual, can also negatively impact a person's experience with a Web site.

Initial Situation and Findings

In the United States, approximately 10 million people are deaf or hard of hearing. Some of them are so severely affected that they cannot learn verbal language. American Sign Language (ASL), based on a system of gestures and facial expressions, provides a means for them to communicate. Many Web sites therefore include ASL videos for important information.

People with limited hearing are not the only ones who surf the Internet with the sound turned off. Libraries and some offices, for example, require a quiet atmosphere. All users find navigation and computer interaction easier when visual cues, not just acoustic cues, are provided.

Technical Assistance

Videos in sign language can be integrated into Web sites without technical problems. This makes it possible for providers of governmental or other important information to offer content in an additional "translated" sign language version.

What Can We Do?

The Web site sponsor and/or the Web editors should decide what information is made available in sign language on a Web site. The task of the person designing the Web site is to ensure that the videos are integrated cleanly in technical terms and to incorporate them into the general navigation so they are easy to find.

It makes sense to use an appropriate icon to indicate that videos in sign language are available. The videos should be offered in different qualities where possible to accommodate different bandwidths. They should also be available in different formats. The Quicktime, Windows Media Player, and Real formats are the most widely used plug-ins for multimedia content and should be covered. It makes sense to specify the file size so the user can decide whether the offered information is important enough to put up with the potentially long loading time.

Learning Disabilities

Learning disabilities can affect how a person is able to use a Web site. How the Web site is set up, how complex it is, the type of language used, and sometimes even the colors chosen can determine whether people with various learning disabilities can successfully interact with your Web site.

Initial Situation and Findings

As the Internet becomes increasingly vital for communication, accessibility specialists are focusing on people whose use of the Internet is limited by a cognitive, psychological, or other mental disability. People with these disabilities do not form a uniform group, and their very different needs have been only partially researched.

Where specific target groups are addressed—for example, on an information site that motivates adults with poor writing or reading skills to take part in literacy sessions—presentation forms can usually be developed in cooperation with specialists in communication and didactics that can then be applied to meet the needs of the identified group. It is difficult and impractical to build special assistive material into sites aimed at the general public because the needs of people with learning disabilities are widely diverse. For some people with learning difficulties, access to a site can be made easier by using lots of symbols. People with concentration problems, however, may find excessive use of symbols irritating and confusing. Colors that most people perceive as calming and favorable to concentration may be distracting or repulsive to others, making them less likely to look at the Web site content.

A wide variety of solutions exist to overcome many—but by no means all—communication and accessibility barriers encountered on Web sites. The idealistic claim expressed by some of the founders of the Internet—to make all information accessible to all people—is undoubtedly unrealistic and has created exaggerated expectations. Increasingly, the Internet is being used, and in some cases *required*, for interactions between citizens and business and government entities; for example, some companies accept only online job applications, and many people commonly use the Internet for such activities as paying bills, renewing licenses, and so on.

Note

There will always be people who are unable to master the targeted use of the Internet technology but who are otherwise able to cope well in everyday life, including managing red tape, as long as they get a little human support.

What Can We Do?

There is no single solution that can address the multitude of potential barriers encountered by people with cognitive, learning, or other mental disabilities. When designing a Web site intended to reach a very broad audience, such as a local government site, you must consider all the usual issues of usability and accessibility with the highest attention to detail:

- Simple and clearly structured navigation
- Clean and optically clear fonts
- Many headers with signal-giving keywords

- Short texts with brief sentences that avoid "difficult" words
- Content reduced to its essence or most basic form
- Large selection of aids (FAQs, glossaries, etc.)

In some cases, the following measures can be helpful:

- Using color coding
- Using ideograms and symbols
- Providing translation into several languages (including ASL)

Occasionally, a translation into "simple language" is also suggested. Inasmuch as this assumes such a thing as simple language that is comprehensible to the majority of people who have problems with the "standard language," you need to be a little bit skeptical here. But it makes sense to keep texts aimed at a broad general public as simple and easy to understand as possible. Try to avoid specialist terminology, administrative jargon, and in-house idioms without offering explanations.

Seniors

The last group we look at are people ages 50 and over, many of whom develop some or all of the limitations discussed earlier: impaired vision and hearing; limited motor skills; and deteriorating memory, concentration, and cognitive skills. Many people in this age group are not as famliar with today's technology. By following a few basic guidelines, you can provide this group with an opportunity for a positive experience on your Web site.

Initial Situation and Findings

The average age of our population continues to rise. Seniors are coveted as a target group for many products and services. Although new portals for seniror users arise on the Internet constantly, in most cases the technical aspects of a site fail to consider the needs of seniors, and many members of this target group are lost. You can greatly reduce the barriers many seniors face, such as inexperience with using the Internet and deteriorating vision, by making Internet sites accessible to this demographic. They require clear structure of content, even more so than younger people, so they can find their way around the site, and they benefit from scalable font sizes and sufficient contrast between the site colors.

A Personal Example

My father-in-law bought his first computer when he was 78 years old. My task was to explain to him how to use it. I quickly noticed that many things I found self-explanatory were a problem for him. Younger people grow up with computers. My daughter knows what e-mail is, but for my father-in-law, this was a new and unknown form of communicating. The first real problem was that I set his 17-inch monitor to a resolution of 1024 × 768 pixels. The result: he was unable to see the display. Text and objects all looked too small to him, despite his glasses. The solution was that my father-in-law now surfs the Web with a resolution of 800 × 600 pixels.

All too often Web designers are faced with the problem of wanting to adapt their design to a resolution. Scalable layouts are often the best solution in this case, but scalability does not always work because many graphic designers create designs that require fixed sizes. In this case, we stick to the solution for the lowest common denominator. Allowing for 800 × 600 pixels still makes sense, even if statistics show that most Internet users prefer a resolution of 1024 × 768 pixels.

Venturing into the Internet for the first time was a complete shock to my father-in-law. On most Web sites, he was completely lost. Too much information on one page, for example, was very confusing too him. He felt utterly overwhelmed. Seniors and less-practiced Internet users require comprehensible and clearly structured layouts so they can find their way around more easily.

What Can We Do?

People "acquire" disabilities and limitations over time and to very different degrees. From around the age of 40, vision and hearing start to decrease. Fine motor skills become more limited in people over 60, and they may have trouble with concentration, memory, and information processing. None of these factors mean that these seniors are seriously "disabled," but their needs still must be considered. In practice, accommodating the needs of seniors simply requires incorporating the measures discussed throughout this chapter in the context of other groups.

We have to get away from the notion that the Internet is only for people with sharp eyes, quick wits, precise mouse control, and who have long-standing computer competence. This is an illusion reflected by many Web sites and their youthful designers. In real life, it's a very different story.

3

CSS and HTML—Getting the Basic Structure into Shape

HTML and Cascading Style Sheets (CSS) are part of the basic knowledge of every Web designer. HTML is relatively easy to learn, but it takes quite a lot of practice before you can master the tips and tricks of CSS. It is not so much the theory that causes a problem but the practical application. Different browsers still implement CSS instructions differently, which is sometimes infuriating for Web designers.

The details of using CSS correctly are beyond the scope of this book, but I include a little introduction for context. My experiences in the forum have shown that even people with no previous experience in this area do create Web sites with Joomla!. I will do my best to base my description on classic Joomla! examples. If you are already an expert in CSS and HTML, you can safely skip this chapter.

A Few Words about the History

The Internet speaks HTML. HTML is a markup language and is as old as the Internet itself. Tim Berners Lee developed this language in 1990. His aim was not the design of information but simply the pure structuring of content. For that reason, you can use HTML only to represent semantic structures. You can assign heading hierarchies to documents and create lists or process tabular data in HTML, but in those early days, there were almost no design options.

The information you could find many years ago on the Web was much more accessible than many documents are today. The desire to be able to adapt content visually as well as textually has contributed to creating barriers to accessibility for many people. For example, tables originally intended for presenting data structures were misused for placing content on the screen. The semantic markup of headings was largely omitted, because rows in tables were easier to design in terms of visual appearance.

CSS is a kind of formatting language for HTML. When I first started designing Web pages in 1999, one of the first books I read on this topic was *Cascading Style Sheets* by Eric Meyer. I became acquainted with it but realized after a few weeks that the time for using CSS was not yet ripe because of a lack in browser support. So I learned how to do layouts with tables.

Fortunately, the situation is very different today. With CSS, nothing stands in the way of separating content and layout.

To develop standards-compliant sites that perform well using CSS is indispensable. You need to have sufficient knowledge in this area for designing Web sites with Joomla!, too.

This book briefly summarizes HTML and CSS. For more in-depth information, the following books are excellent:

- *Bulletproof Web Design* by Dan Cederholm (Berkeley, CA: New Riders, 2011)
- *Sams Teach Yourself Web Publishing with HTML and CSS in One Hour a Day: Includes New HTML5 Coverage*, 6th ed., by Laura Lemay and Rafe Colburn (Indianapolis, IN: Sams, 2011)
- *HTML5 & CSS3 Visual QuickStart Guide* by Elizabeth Castro (Berkeley, CA: Peachpit, 2011)

Which Version of HTML Should I Use?

A question that often arises when discussing HTML is which version of HTML to use. The choice is between HTML 4.01 and XHTML 1.0—and each has Transitional, Strict, and Frameset versions from which to choose. Recently, HTML5 is also an option.

HTML 4.01 and XHTML 1.0

The difference between HTML 4.01 and XHTML 1.0 is often overestimated—both are identical in terms of language scope and capacity and differ in only a few formalities. You can automatically convert anytime between HTML 4.01 Strict and XHTML 1.0 Strict.

The HTML output of Joomla! is based on XHTML, so the question about the version does not arise.

More relevant for both languages is the difference between the *Strict* and the *Transitional* versions. Transitional allows the use of attributes that are no longer recommended or have become deprecated. *Deprecated* means "superseded, no longer wanted." Deprecated attributes include, for example, `vspace` and `hspace` of the Image element and `align`.

In connection with Joomla!, I recommend using the Transitional version even if the standard edition of Joomla! allows Strict:

```
<!DOCTYPE html PUBLIC "-//W3C//DTD XHTML 1.0 Transitional//EN"
  "http://www.w3.org/TR/xhtml1/DTD/xhtml1-transitional.dtd">
```

You may find this surprising, because Strict would be the more elegant and standard choice. The reason is that the frequently used text editors that are shipped with Joomla! sadly still continue to use the deprecated attributes. The HTML validator, a tool that checks your Web site for correctness, would invariably flag these "incorrectly used" attributes as wrong.

But if you are managing without the editors, editing the code manually, or using the editor Xstandard, then it is certainly better to use the Strict version:

```
<!DOCTYPE html PUBLIC "-//W3C//DTD XHTML 1.0 Strict//EN"
  "http://www.w3.org/TR/xhtml1/DTD/xhtml1-strict.dtd">
```

HTML5

The Web is moving fast toward using HTML5. You can find numerous Internet sites that are already using HTML5. Have a look yourself. You can see a showcase of sites using HTML5 markup at *http://html5gallery.com/*. Even large companies such as Google are now using HTML5.

I am particularly thrilled by the declaration of the document type:

```
<!Doctype html>
```

Finally, something is really easy!

The semantically significant elements are also particularly interesting. For example, the elements nav for the navigation; header, footer, and aside for additional information; section for sections; and article for content have caught my eye. These elements alone are a huge plus.

While Opera, Firefox, Safari (always in the current version), and Internet Explorer 9 can handle these elements beautifully, Internet Explorer versions 6, 7, and 8 refuse to play along. The elements cannot be addressed and styled via CSS—these browsers do not recognize them. To solve this problem, you currently have two options. Either you surround these elements with the traditional div elements and style them accordingly, or you add the unknown elements via JavaScript to the document object model (DOM) of the browser.

```
<!--[if lt IE 9]>
<script type="text/javascript">
document.createElement('section');
document.createElement('nav');
document.createElement('article');
document.createElement('header');
document.createElement('footer');
document.createElement('aside');
document.createElement('figure');
document.createElement('legend');
</script>
<![endif]-->
```

The disadvantage of this method is that it does not work when JavaScript is disabled.

Within the beez5 template, you can choose between XHTML and HTML5 as the markup language to be used in the back end. This option was implemented via the template overrides, whose function I explain in more detail in Chapter 14, "Designing Default Output Individually."

The Basic HTML Structure

You determine the basic HTML structure of your site in the template. The HTML in your template controls the general page structure and determines where the individual page areas such as headers and footers are located within the flow of the document. The HTML for a Joomla! template looks very much like the HTML for an ordinary Web site. To add the dynamic content from Joomla!, you just add a couple of statements. This is explained in detail in Chapter 10, "The index.php: The Heart of the Matter." You will find out how to have even more control over the output in Chapter 14.

In earlier versions of Joomla!, the HTML used tables for layouts. Layout tables were necessary before CSS was widely supported by browsers. However, tables are cumbersome, inflexible, and inaccessible. Since version 1.6 was introduced, Joomla! has replaced layout tables with layouts using CSS for positioning, as is the current standard practice.

HTML is responsible for the structure of the content. The presentation, the look and feel, is handled by the CSS. The same basic structure in HTML can look totally different depending on which CSS you use.

A Brief Introduction to CSS

CSS in just one chapter? Sounds impossible. There are whole books, even book series, on this topic. I cannot explain the entire feature range of CSS in one chapter or one section, but I can give you a basic understanding of the design possibilities offered by CSS.

CSS is a markup language for structured documents. By using CSS, you have direct control over the design of the output HTML code. You can format headings, lists, and paragraphs or arrange content in a structured way on the screen. You can find the complete CSS specification at *www.w3.org/TR/CSS2/*.

Adding CSS Statements

CSS statements can be added to your page in different ways. Its weighting within all CSS declarations depends on where you add it in a document, and that's where the name "cascading style sheets" derives from. The three main ways are to put the CSS statements in an external file, to add them in the <head> section of the HTML, or to add them directly to HTML statements with the style attribute.

In an External File

One option is to place style specifications into an external file in the page head:

```
<link rel="stylesheet" href="/templates/beez/css/layout.css"
  type="text/css" media="screen,projection" title="" />
```

This choice is the most popular one, and it is also the most effective, because you can separate content and layout completely. If you are relaunching your Web site and changing the design, you can move all the style data into such a file without having to touch the code itself.

You can integrate any number of CSS files using this method. It makes sense if, for example, you want to separate the positioning of the content from the color scheme. You can also integrate special style files for Internet Explorer or create targeted files for print previews. If you look at the index.php file of Beez, you will find a large number of CSS files referenced there.

In the Document Head

Another method for adding CSS statements is to insert the style specifications directly in the page head. Many free Joomla! extensions also use this method to integrate their special stylesheets.

```
<style type="text/css">
<!--
div.mycomponentdiv
{
background:#000
}
-->
</style>
```

The style data of the external Joomla! extensions often does not match your own layout, and you may want to override it. The styles you define in the source code of your own CSS files and added via `link rel` have higher priority because they will appear after the extension CSS. This is the cascade. So you can simply place any styles you want to override in your own CSS files.

As Inline Styles

Another complication may arise when external components use inline styles. You cannot change them because inline styles have the highest priority and override everything else.

HTML elements have the `style` attribute, which you can use to individually format each element inline:

```
<p style="color:#cc0000"> This is a paragraph in red.</p>
```

There are many reasons to avoid using inline styles.

- When redesigning a Web site, you have to painstakingly remove the inline styles from the existing code.
- People who are vision impaired often create individual styles in their browsers and apply them to all Web sites. Because inline styles have top priority, alternative styles cannot be applied on a site already containing inline styles.
- Inline styles inflate the HTML code unnecessarily.

But despite these possible drawbacks, do not be discouraged by people who virtually hate inline styles. In certain situations, inline styles can be useful. For example, you may want to insert a background image within a module and perhaps replace the image from time to time. In that case, it does not make sense to adapt CSS files because that would require much more effort than using inline styles.

Tip

The styles are best located in an external file at the top of the page. Just use a pure text file that you can edit with a simple editor such as Notepad.

CSS Selectors

Selectors may sound confusing and complicated, but don't worry, they really aren't. The CSS needs to know where it should be applicable, and that's why it needs selectors. HTML elements such as p, h1–h6, div, and span are such selectors. You can also assign classes and IDs to the elements, which can then function as selectors as well.

Element Selectors

First let's look at the syntax using a very simple CSS statement. In the preceding example of inline styles, you added red font color to a paragraph. You can now apply this statement to all p elements within a document:

```
p {color:#cc0000;}
```

p acts as a selector here, followed by curly brackets that enclose the property, separated from its value by a colon. A semicolon concludes the statement. (In this case, you could omit the semicolon because it's the last—the only—statement in your declaration.)

A semicolon is required if you want to add several declarations to an element:

```
p
{
 color:#cc0000;
 background:#eee
 }
```

If you want to assign this statement to different elements, you can group them by separating the elements with a comma. Notice that the last selector is **not** followed by a comma.

```
p, h1, h2
{
 color:#cc0000;
 background:#eee
 }
```

Class Selectors

If you want to assign the font color red only to certain paragraphs within a document, the easiest way to do it is to assign a class. This technique is especially useful if you want to reuse the class several times. In your source code, it would look like this:

```
<p class="attention"> Paragraph in red color.</p>
```

Here is the corresponding CSS:

```
.attention   {color:#cc0000;}
```

As you can see, there is a period (.) before the word attention. This period specifies a class within the CSS code.

Classes can be applied to all kinds of HTML elements. For example, you could assign the font color red to the top-level heading with:

```
<h1 class="attention"> This is a heading </h1>
```

ID Selectors

The most important information first: IDs may appear only once in a file. This explains why they are frequently used for positioning individual page areas in the basic HTML framework. In HTML code, it looks like this:

```
<div id=" header">
<p> Anything at the top of the page</p>
</div>
```

In the CSS file, you can reference it as follows:

```
#header
{
background:#000;
color:#fff
}
```

The # is the CSS indicator for the IDs.

The positioning of individual page areas is an advanced level of CSS and not always easy to implement because of different browsers.

Context Selectors

The context selectors are a useful and code-saving method of formatting individual page areas via CSS. Suppose you have a list in your header area that you now want to format.

The HMTL code would look like this:

```
<div id="header">
      <ul>
            <li> List item 1 </li>
            <li> List item 2 </li>
      </ul>
</div>
```

You could reference it as follows:

```
#header ul li {color:#cc0000;}
```

This code ensures that all list items in the header get the font color red. Elegantly done, isn't it?

Child Selectors

The child selectors described in the next section are very useful. If you are still support-ing Internet Explorer 6, you should be aware that that browser does not recognize child selectors. The following formats all p that are a direct child of body.

```
body >p
```

Direct child in this case means that no other element exists between the parent element and the child. In the following example, the selector would not be applied because the paragraph <p> is not a direct child of the <body> element but is instead a direct child of the subordinate <div>.

```
...
<body>
<div>
<p> This is a paragraph within a div </p>
</div>
</body>
```

The following formats the first li item within a list:

```
ul li:firstchild
```

And this line formats the first div following a paragraph:

```
p + div
```

Universal Selectors

Surely you already know the wildcard * from the Windows search function. For exam-ple, if you want to find a file with the extension .png, you can simply enter *.png, and

Windows searches your computer for all files with that file extension regardless of the file name before the extension. Wildcards are placeholders for other characters.

In CSS, this method is also used. For example, the following:

```
* {margin:0; padding:0}
```

sets the margin and padding of all elements to 0.

Because different browsers automatically assign margins to different HTML elements, this is a sensible formatting instruction to get all browsers onto the same initial level. For example,

```
body * p {margin:0; padding}
```

sets the margins of a paragraph to 0 if there is another element between it and the body.

Pseudoclass Selectors

A special form of formatting is done via the pseudoclass. Pseudoclasses do not influence HTML elements themselves but overwrite browser-internal formatting.

The most important pseudoclass is the one used for formatting links. If you have ever clicked your way through your browser configuration, you may have noticed that you can specify, for example, the color of links (see Figure 3.1). In most cases you can select whatever color you want; it no longer affects the modern Web sites you surf, which usually use CSS to overwrite your settings.

These are the pseudoclass selectors for the <a> tag:

- a:link for a normal link
- a:visited for a visited link
- a:focus for a link that becomes active when tabbing through the page
- a:hover for the condition of the link when you hover the mouse pointer over it
- a:active for a currently active link/Internet Explorer 6 active when tabbing

The sequence of your formatting arrangement in CSS is important. You will encounter display errors if your code is out of sequence.

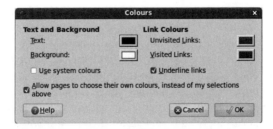

Figure 3.1   Selecting the colors of links in Firefox

Other pseudoclasses or pseudoelements include the following:

- `li:first-child` formats the first child element of the list item.
- `p:first-letter` formats the first letter of a paragraph.
- `p:first-line` formats the first line of a paragraph.

There are quite a few more pseudoclasses, though many of them are not supported by Internet Explorer 6.

Attribute Selectors

Attribute selectors are used to format attributes of HTML elements, such as the `title` attribute of a heading:

```
h1[title] { color: 0000ff; }
```

These selectors are rarely used now, mainly because there is no comprehensive browser support for them.

Tip

For further information on this topic, see this link:

www.w3.org/TR/CSS2/selector.html

Inheritance

Certain CSS properties are passed from parent elements to their children, so the children inherit the parent properties. The system of inheritance saves a lot of typing. For example, if the `body` element has the font color black, all paragraphs within it will also inherit this font color unless a different color is explicitly specified.

Not all properties are inherited—for example, inheritance does not apply to `margin` or `border`.

Using Multiple Classes Together

You can group multiple CSS classes together for more flexibility. I explain this process using the example of the Joomla! default output, which is far more relevant to practical application than any theoretical explanations. You may not yet know very much about the structure of Joomla! templates, but don't worry about becoming confused. Just read this section first, and don't go running to your computer to look at the template.

As you probably know, Joomla! lets you determine the number of columns to be represented via the parameters in the blog views. In the table variation of Joomla! 1.5, this is not a problem: the table simply adds an additional column if you increase values in the parameters by one. Nothing slips around—your page is simply stretched accordingly.

Now we use individual `div` elements for implementing this representation. `div`s are semantically meaningless elements that can be arranged on the screen to construct the visual grid of a page. They can contain any number of other elements and can be safely nested:

```
<div><p>Paragraph</p></div>
```

In a multicolumn view, the elements require a certain width to be arranged correctly. This means you need at least one class that you can assign a width to. If you then want to design the first column in a different color than the second one, you need another class (see Figure 3.2). Now you have the option of assigning two classes to an area.

The width can be assigned via the `width` property and expects an absolute value in pixels or a relative value in em or percentage. This topic is discussed further under "Positioning and Box Model" later in this chapter.

```
<div class="width color"> <p> Paragraph </p> </div>
<div class="width color2"> <p> Paragraph </p> </div>
```

The corresponding CSS looks like this:

```
.width {width:200px}
.color { background:#cccc99} // light green
.color2 {background:#999900} // green
```

In a single-column design, you have the following code:

```
<div class="item column-1" ></div>
```

In two-column design, the code looks like this:

```
<div class="item column-1" ></div>
<div class="item column-2" ></div>
```

And in three-column design, like this:

```
<div class="item column-1" ></div>
<div class="item column-2" ></div>
<div class="item column-3" ></div>
```

Figure 3.2   Assigning two classes to an area

You could now add general formatting to the class item that would apply to all columns. This could include the font type. With the classes column-1, column-2, and column-3, you could determine the width and positioning of the different columns. The result would be similar to that shown in Figure 3.3.

You can also design each row individually.

Let's assume you have six articles and three columns to be represented in two rows (see Figure 3.4). The Joomla! code would look like this:

```
<div class="items-row cols-3 row-0">
<div class="item column-1" ></div>
<div class="item column-2" ></div>
<div class="item column-3" ></div>
</div>
<div class="items-row cols-3 row-1">
<div class="item column-1" ></div>
<div class="item column-2" ></div>
<div class="item column-3" ></div>
</div>
```

[One Column]

Paragraph

[Two Columns]

Paragraph   Paragraph

[Three Columns]

Paragraph   Paragraph   Paragraph

Figure 3.3   Columns positioned and designed via CSS

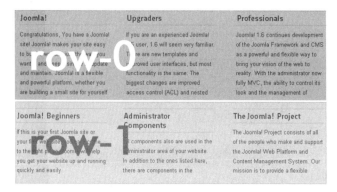

Figure 3.4   Columns and rows

Joomla! always surrounds each article in a row with a separate `div` element. This element also has its own classes: a universal class that remains the same for each row, `items-row`; another class that indicates the number of columns; and one that states which row is being output.

- `.items-row` indicates a universal class, the same for each row.
- `.cols-3` indicates the number of columns.
- `.row-0 –row-xx` indicates the number of rows.

The result is a great number of design options. Depending on which column design you choose, you can adapt your formatting individually. There are no limits to what you can do.

Another great advantage is that you are no longer limited to the number of representable columns. For example, you can select ten rows in the back end without any problems, but you then have to format them accordingly via CSS.

Positioning and Box Model

Positioning individual elements on the screen is the most difficult task you will carry out with CSS. You have to imagine that all elements appearing on a page take up rectangular boxes on the screen and then reserve enough space for their content. Each box can be assigned properties regarding its width, its margin and padding, and its border. You can also assign a height to it, but usually this is tricky because of dynamic content. Plus you can specify each box's visual position on the screen (see Figure 3.5).

Let's use an example to make this clearer.

```
<div id="content">
<h1> This is a heading</h1>
<p> Now we want to format this box. </p>
</div>
```

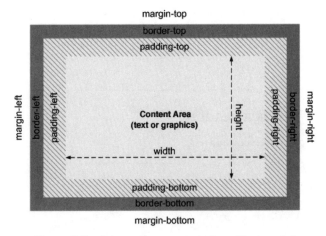

Figure 3.5　Schematic representation of box model

This snippet assigns the id="content" to the container and can now format it via the id selector.

First you assign a border to the box to make it easier to see what you are doing (see Figure 3.6).

```
#content { border:solid 1px #0000cc}
```

As you can see, the content is closely stuck to the border, which does not look nice. For that reason, you assign padding to the box (space on the inside), which you format with the property padding. You can define it individually for each side of the box:

- padding-top: padding at the top
- padding-right: padding at the right
- padding-bottom: padding at the bottom
- padding-left: padding on the left

You can group the properties, so you do not need to list every property individually. Let's start with padding-top and then specify the other padding settings in a clockwise direction. You can see the result in Figure 3.7.

```
#content
{
border:solid 1px #0000cc;
padding:10px 20px 10px 20px;
}
```

This is a heading

Now we want to format this box.

Figure 3.6   The box before it is formatted

This is a heading

Now we want to format this box.

Figure 3.7   Box with padding

You can also specify the margins of a box (the space around the outside), as shown in Figure 3.8.

- `margin-top`: margin at the top
- `margin-right`: margin on the right
- `margin-bottom`: margin at the bottom
- `margin-left`: margin on the left

```
#content
{
border:solid 1px #0000cc;
padding:10px 20px 10px 20px;
margin: 70px 0px 0px 240px
}
```

Now, with the browser bar, you can better see that your container is positioned 240 pixels from the left border and 70 pixels from the top. To integrate this container into a proper layout in the second step, you can assign a width to it.

Pages rarely have just one element. To implement different designs, you need a basic understanding of CSS positioning mechanisms.

In the following example, you implement a simple two-column layout using the CSS properties `float` and `margin`. This example gives you a feeling for the CSS positioning methods. The method shown is not always the method of choice for positioning elements next to each other on the screen. The properties of the container `id="content"` remain identical for now.

Figure 3.8   Box with margins

The source code of the example has the following structure:

```
<div id="navigation">
<ul>
<li><a href="#">Menulink</a></li>
<li><a href="#"> Menulink </a></li>
<li><a href="#"> Menulink </a></li>
<li><a href="#"> Menulink </a></li>
<ul>
</div>
<div id="content">
<h1> This is a heading</h1>
<p>paragraph text paragraph text paragraph text paragraph text paragraph
text paragraph text paragraph text paragraph text</p>
</div>
```

The container with the `id="navigation"` contains a list with navigation items and is to be positioned to the left of the actual content. To achieve this, you first assign it a width; you then use the property float to position it on the left-hand side. Floated elements are taken out of the normal document flow and allow other elements to flow around them.

As soon as one element is assigned this property, it automatically becomes a block element. In other words, you can assign a height and width to it. If floated elements do not have a width, you may get unexpected results in some circumstances.

```
#navigation
{
border:solid 1px;
width:220px;
float:left;
}
```

By assigning a `margin-left` of 240 pixels to the container via the `id="content"`, you make sure the content does not slip under the navigation box if this box is shorter than the actual content. In addition to `margin-left`, the container has the property `margin-top:70px`. This property is now no longer needed because the upper edge of both elements should be on the same level, so it is simply removed.

```
#content
{
border:solid 1px #0000cc;
padding:10px 20px 10px 20px;
margin: 0px 0px 0px 240px
}
```

If you want to arrange footers below the two areas later on, make sure to remove the floating behavior of the navigation container again. Otherwise the subsequent elements would also flow around the floated container.

```
<div id="navigation">
<ul>
<li><a href="#">Menulink</a></li>
<li><a href="#"> Menulink </a></li>
<li><a href="#"> Menulink </a></li>
<li><a href="#"> Menulink </a></li>
<ul>
</div>
<div id="content">
<h1> This is a heading</h1>
<p>paragraph text paragraph text paragraph text paragraph text paragraph
text paragraph text paragraph text paragraph text</p>
</div>
<div id="footer">Footer</div>
```

You can achieve this, *among other results*, with the CSS property `clear`. The `clear` property can be assigned the values `left`, `right`, or `both`. An element that has this property is always the first element that no longer flows around the floating element and causes a break. In our example, the code would look like this:

```
#footer {clear:left}
```

`clear` is not the only method to achieve this behavior. For example, if you place another container around the elements `navigation` and `content` and assign it the property `overflow:hidden`, the footer will also be placed below the two containers.

This was just a very simple example. On the Internet you can find a whole range of good examples based on CSS2, which can help you with more complex layouts. The relatively old but still rather clearly structured Web site *www.intensivstation.ch/en/templates/* offers a quick overview of possible positioning methods, as does *http://little-boxes.de/lb1/ IV-css-positionierung.html*.

CSS is constantly evolving. If you are interested in finding out more about the new CSS3 positioning concepts, have a look at the exciting information available at these links:

- *www.css3.info/introducing-the-flexible-box-layout-module/*
- *www.the-haystack.com/2010/01/23/css3-flexbox-part-1/*
- *http://hacks.mozilla.org/2010/04/the-css-3-flexible-box-model/*

CSS Hacks and Browser Problems

You will need CSS hacks whenever browsers do not interpret the code as they should, which results in the pages not being displayed as you intended.

There is certainly a bug here or there in any browser, but the main problem is definitely with Internet Explorer in any version up to version 7. With version 8, much has changed and hacks are hardly necessary anymore. And version 9 finally offers support for CSS3.

The following section provides a quick overview of the most important problems and solutions. At *www.positioniseverything.net* you will find further information on display errors and bugs of the common browsers.

Conditional Comments

To get Internet Explorer on the right track, it makes sense to assign it a separate CSS file. This is a huge advantage because you can later remove desired files simply and without complications once you no longer need them.

Microsoft is aware of errors and therefore offers something called *conditional comments.* These are special HTML comments that are integrated into the head of the page and execute the code contained within depending on the browser version.

Only Internet Explorer users use these statements because no other browsers support them. In the Beez template you will find exactly those statements to ensure a consistent display for Internet Explorer 6 and 7 as well.

```
<!--[if IE 7]>
<link href="<?php echo $this->baseurl ?>/templates/beez5/css/ie7only.css"
rel="stylesheet" type="text/css" />
<![endif]-->

<!--[if lte IE 6]>
<link href="<?php echo $this->baseurl ?>/templates/beez5/css/ieonly.css"
rel="stylesheet" type="text/css" />
<![endif]-->
```

The first statement identifies Internet Explorer 7 and assigns it the individual CSS file. The second statement identifies all versions of Internet Explorer that are smaller or equal to version 6. Table 3.1 shows you how to specify the different Internet Explorer versions.

Conditional comments have operators that you are familiar with from math. With these operators, you can check conditions. In this case, I used lte, for "less than or equal."

There are many more. Table 3.2 shows you the operator options.

The * Hack

Likely the best known CSS filter is the * hack (asterisk hack). This filter is interpreted only by Internet Explorer 6 and lower. HTML is normally the first element appearing on a page. Internet Explorer up to version 6 has another, nonvisible element that encloses the HTML element.

Table 3.1   **Selection of Internet Explorer Versions**

Internet Explorer Identifier	Condition Description	Conditional Comment
!IE	if no Internet Explorer	`<!--[if !IE]>`
IE	if Internet Explorer	`<!--[if IE]>`
IE 5.5	if Internet Explorer 5.5	`<!--[if IE 5.5]>`
IE 6	if Internet Explorer 6	`<!--[if IE 6]>`
IE 7	if Internet Explorer 7	`<!--[if IE 7]>`
IE 8	if Internet Explorer 8	`<!--[if IE 8]>`
IE 9	if Internet Explorer 9	`<!--[if IE 9]>`

Table 3.2 **Operators**

Operator	Condition Description	Conditional Comment
!	not equal	`<!--[if !(IE 6)]>`
lt	less than	`<!--[if lt IE 6]>`
lte	less than or equal	`<!--[if lte IE 6]>`
gt	greater than	`<!--[if gt IE 6]>`
gte	greater than or equal	`<!--[if gte IE 6]>`

Via the * selector, you can address an HTML element that is surrounded by another element. Because this only applies to Internet Explorer 6 and lower versions, this filter applies to precisely these versions. The statement itself remains hidden to standard-conforming browsers.

```
#all
{width:960px;}
* html #all
{width:900px; }
```

With the second statement, you overwrite the first statement (applicable to all browsers) only in Internet Explorer 6 and lower.

Internet Explorer Again: hasLayout

Internet Explorer has a property called hasLayout that often causes display problems. The underlying concept determines how elements display and limit their content, how they behave in relation to other elements, and how they react to user interaction.

Some elements have this property, others do not. This can lead to display problems.

The elements with `hasLayout` include

- `html, body`
- `table, tr, th, td`
- `img`
- `hr`
- `input, button, select, textarea, fieldset, legend`
- `iframe, embed, object, applet`

If you come across display problems in Internet Explorer during the design process, the reason may be that certain elements lack the property `hasLayout`. You can force `hasLayout` by adding the property `zoom` to the concerned element. Using this property generally helps if the cause of the problem is in the concept of the layout itself.

I also use this method in the Beez template; for example, nested lists in the right-hand column are not displayed properly unless I put:

```
#right ul.menu ul
{zoom:1;}
```

But you can also try this solution:

```
position:absolute
height: numeric value
width: numeric value
display: inline-block
[float: left | right
```

In Internet Explorer 7 you can also force `hasLayout` with the property `overflow: hidden|scroll|auto`.

CSS Tuning

Whenever you are using Joomla! to construct a large page that will have many visitors, it can become important to keep the page loading time as short as possible.

In the Beez template, I integrate several CSS files: one for positioning, one for the distances, one for the colors, and one for the different Internet Explorer versions. These files make it easier for designers to handle and understand. But for each file, you need to send a request to the servers, which affects the performance.

Sometimes it can make sense to combine the contents of the files (not the one for Internet Explorer) into a big file, which invariably leads to a large file that is not very clear.

Here are some other tips.

- Avoid redundancies in your CSS rules.
- Remove the semicolon after each final statement in a statement block.

- Combine value statements:

```
{
margin:0 10px;
instead of:
margin-top:0;
margin-right:10px;
margin-bottom:0px;
margin-left:10px
}
```

- Avoid too many indents and spaces.
- Remove comments if necessary.
- You can also use the free tool CSSTidy to automatically optimize your CSS file: *http://csstidy.sourceforge.net/*.

CSS3—A Brief Overview

Many browsers already support the new properties of CSS3 that make complex layouts easier to implement and provide a range of amazing visual effects. Visual effects range from the simple rounded corners to shadows and even complex CSS animations. In the scope of this book I provide a brief overview of the new options and introduce the three most exciting CSS3 features.

Browser behavior is an important basis for working with CSS3. If a browser stumbles across a CSS statement that is does not know, it simply ignores the statement. This behavior is a great advantage because it prevents display errors. Internet Explorer up to version 9 behaves in this way. So if you are using, for example, the statement `border-radius:5px`, it will simply be ignored and the corners will be displayed as normal.

Some tools, such as CSS3 Pie, are available that help display certain CSS3 properties even in Internet Explorer up to version 8.

Vendor Prefixes

While the browser manufacturers are working on implementing new CSS properties in their products, they are using vendor prefixes in front of the CSS statements. These prefixes remain in use until the new property is fully implemented. With this approach, until the implementation is working reliably, you can use the vendor prefixes to add separate specifications for individual browsers in order to avoid display errors.

```
-moz    -> Firefox
-webkit -> Safari
-o -> Opera
-ms -> Internet Explorer
```

Overview of the Three Most Useful CSS Statements

Depending on the browser version, the three CSS3 properties reviewed in this section are supported with or without a prefix. You can find an up-to-date list of the currently used prefixes at *http://peter.sh/experiments/vendor-prefixed-css-property-overview/*. Here is a brief summary of the three most useful CSS statements: `border-radius`, `box-shadow`, and `linear-gradient`.

border-radius

With `border-radius` you can specify the degree of the curvature of an element, such as the corners. The following example gives `#myelement` an even curvature of 5 pixels.

```
#myelement {
    -moz-border-radius:5px // for Firefox < version 4
    -webkit-border-radius: 5px // for Safari < 5 and chrome < 5
    border-radius:5px;  // official standard for all supported browser
    ➥versions
}
```

But you also have the option of creating asymmetrical curvatures, for example, by rounding the top left and bottom right corners, while the other corners remain unchanged.

```
#myelement {
    -moz-border-radius: 5px 0 // for Firefox < version 4
    -webkit-border-radius: 5px 0 // for Safari < 5 and chrome < 5
    border-radius:5px 0;  // official standard for all supported
    ➥browser versions
}
```

box-shadow

With the statement `box-shadow` you can add a shadow to individual elements. This option offers a whole new range of design approaches that could previously be achieved only with a lot of effort.

The following statement adds a black shadow to the outside of a box, offset by 2 pixels in relation to the *x* and *y* axes of the element. The blur value—5 pixels in my example—specifies the shadow's blur.

```
#myelement {
    -webkit-box-shadow: 2px 2px 5px black; // iPhone & Android
    -moz-box-shadow: 2px 2px 5px black;  // FF 3.6
    box-shadow: 2px 2px 5px black; // official standard
}
```

You can now try some wonderful experiments with these specifications. The shadow can be added not just on the outside but also on the inside using the property inset, or you can change the spread of the shadow with the value spread.

To see an overview of the differences in how such box shadows are currently displayed in different browsers, have a look at this Web site: *http://thany.nl/apps/boxshadows/*.

linear-gradient

With linear-gradient you can implement color gradients via CSS. Until recently, we had to use repeating background graphics to achieve the same effect. At the time of writing (July 2012), none of the browsers support the W3C standard yet, but you can do quite a lot by using the vendor prefixes.

But this means the CSS statements are still rather bulky, so the question remains whether it might not be better to use the traditional method of background graphics instead.

Here is a brief example, creating a gradient from yellow to blue.

```
#myelement {
  background-color: yellow; /* Fallback Color */
  background: -webkit-gradient(linear,left top,left bottom,
  ↪from(yellow),to(blue));
  background: -webkit-linear-gradient(top, yellow 0%, blue 100%);
  background: -moz-linear-gradient(top, yellow 0%, blue 100%);
  background: -ms-linear-gradient(top, yellow 0%, blue 100%);
  background: -o-linear-gradient(top, yellow 0%, blue 100%);

  /* W3C Standard, */
  background: linear-gradient(to bottom, yellow 0%, blue 100%);
}
```

On the Internet you can find a useful tool that automatically generates the appropriate CSS code once you have selected the colors. Visit *www.colorzilla.com/gradient-editor/*.

The options that CSS3 will offer over the next few years promise to be truly groundbreaking in terms of designing Web sites. CSS3 animations in particular offer an enormous designer playground. Optimizing Web sites for different devices by using media queries will become much simpler with CSS3. To find out more, please read the Chapter 4, "Responsive Web Design."

4

Responsive Web Design

With the enormous array of Internet-capable devices in use today, *responsive Web design* has become a buzzword among developers. Responsive Web design attempts to solve a problem Web designers have faced for years: we do not know which device or which screen resolution a visitor will use to access our Internet site. In addition to desktop monitors with different screen resolutions, we now have a multitude of mobile devices: notebooks, netbooks, tablets, smartphones, and more—and you want your design to work on all of them.

The variety of devices, some of which have very low screen resolutions, makes it difficult to create a suitable design and requires a great deal of flexibility on the part of the designer. Designers who have already dealt with creating accessible Web sites are more familiar with this challenge than those who have always only implemented designs pixel by pixel. The previously used solution—floating elements that can be displayed below one another instead of next to one another in certain circumstances—is no longer a reliable means of presenting Web content.

The idea today is to design the page structure so that individual page elements can be automatically resized in case of low resolution or can be arranged differently on the screen. It is particularly important to ensure that the design stays consistent in order to maintain a high recognition value. This includes using graphics and videos that can be scaled to work with the different sizes and resolutions of the various devices.

There are great examples of responsive Web design at *http://designmodo.com/responsive-design-examples/*. Also, Ethan Marcotte covers this exciting topic well in his book *Responsive Web Design* (New York: A Book Apart, 2011).

But How Does It Work?

If you want to implement responsive Web design, you need to use CSS to specify the width in percentages for the individual page areas and combine it with the specification of a minimum or maximum width. It is also indispensable to use CSS3 media queries.

Let's illustrate the process with a little example. Suppose you have a two-column fluid layout. The column on the right is floated and is 30 percent wide. The column on the left has a width of 70 percent. If you now resize the browser window, both areas adapt flexibly to the new window size.

This works up to a very low window width. It is only a problem if the window is so small that the words in the columns are cut off. Here you could use the CSS statement `min-width` to ensure that the element cannot be pushed in any further than the specified minimum width.

The result of this approach is that, with very low resolutions, not all contents are still visible, so the browser displays scrollbars to accommodate the display. If you integrate photos or videos, their size can be annoying, especially on a smartphone, because they take up a lot of space. It would be nice if the presentation and arrangement of the content could be adapted in cases of low resolution. In our example, it would also be great if the column on the right could be positioned below the one on the left at a certain level of resolution. To achieve this, you need to use different CSS statements.

CSS3 Media Queries

Since the advent of CSS 2.1, you have the option of deploying CSS for certain media types. Media types enable you to assign the output of stylesheets to a specific media type.

If you have ever integrated a print stylesheet into your Web page, you are familiar with this concept.

```
<link rel="stylesheet" type="text/css" href="print.css"
 media="print" />
```

The attribute `media="print"` ensures that the stylesheet is used only in case of print output. `media="screen"` is responsible for output on the screen (any kind of screen).

The media queries in CSS3 also use this concept but add the function of determining properties of the output medium. With full browser support, you should be able to

- Recognize the width and height (of the browser window).

  WIDTH, HEIGHT

- Determine the width and height of the device.

  DEVICE-WIDTH, DEVICE-HEIGHT

- Find out if the device is currently in portrait or landscape orientation.

  ORIENTATION :PORTRAIT, ORIENTATION:LANDSCAPE

This function now enables you to react to the specific output medium. You have two options: you can save the targeted statements neatly in separate files, or you can integrate them directly into already-existing CSS files.

Option 1—Integration into the Main Stylesheet

Many designers who have dealt with this concept decide to build their main CSS file for the smallest of possible displays and load separate statements for the larger ones. This could also be done the other way around.

```
.right {width:30%; float:left}
.left {width:70%}
@media screen and (max-device-width: 480px) {
  .right {
    float: none;
    width:100%
  }
.left {width:100%}}
```

By using `max-device-width`, you can find out specific information on the output device and its size and then react accordingly. If you were to use just `width` instead of `device-width`, this statement would be applied to even a very small browser window, which may be useful in certain cases.

```
@media screen and (max-width: 480px) {
  .right {
    float: none;
    width:100%
  }
.left {width:100%}
}
```

Option 2—Integrating Separate Stylesheets

Integrating separate statements into the main CSS file is only practical if they are marginal adaptations. More comprehensive adaptations should be moved into separate CSS files for the sake of clarity. Doing so is not complicated, and it works with the same pattern.

```
<link rel="stylesheet" type="text/css"
 media="only screen and (max-device-width: 480px)"
 href="small.css" />
```

If you have a whole collection of different devices, than testing this statement won't be a problem for you. But most of us probably do not have so many different devices. Fortunately, ProtoFluid *(http://protofluid.com)* can help. This tool enables you to test the display on different end devices and in different widths. The greatest advantage is that you can even test local applications with it.

The little bookmarklet written by Frederic Hemberger is also useful. It gives you information on the return value of the currently used media query quickly and simply. You can find it at *http://fhemberger.github.com/mediaquery-bookmarklet/*.

Adapting Graphics and Videos

If you adapt graphics and videos to optimize pages for different devices, the content of the page remains the same in every case. It is just modified in terms of visual appearance.

However, the graphics are usually too tall to still look good if displayed on small monitors such as smartphones.

What can you do? The solution is to omit the `height` attribute of the image element in the source code of the document.

Let's imagine the following scenario in an HTML document with the following content:

```
<div id="test">
<img src="image.png"  alt="alternative Text">
</div>
```

The image used here has a width of 1000 pixels and a height of 600 pixels and is displayed in full size despite omitting the attributes `height` and `width`. The surrounding `div` element with the `id="test"` does not have any special CSS properties.

If you look at the page in the browser and minimize the browser window, there will be scrollbars because the image stretches out the page. If you want to stop this from happening, you tell the image that it can only have a maximum width that is the same as the surrounding element:

```
<style type="text/css">
<!--
#test img {max-width:100%}
-->
</style>
```

Because the image does not have the `height` attribute even in the HTML code, the height is conveniently rescaled along with it.

There are still some small disadvantages to adapting graphics and videos. The image is still loaded in its original size. Especially when building mobile applications, you should ensure that the loading times are as short as possible. Large graphics eat up unnecessary bandwidth. Also, scaled graphics sometimes lose quality, but you can't have it all.

This approach can also be applied to integrating videos. You can find further information at *www.alistapart.com/articles/fluid-images/*.

Using HTML5 Apps

Media queries provide a helpful method of influencing the display on different devices. However, a sensible alternative in some circumstances is to use HTML5 apps. Depending on how big the page is, it may make sense to output different content on mobile devices than on the normal Web site, because people (depending on their provider) may have different information requirements when they are on the move than at home on their personal computers.

5

PHP and Joomla!

Don't worry—you do not need to be a PHP: Hypertext Preprocessor expert to create templates for Joomla!. But a bit of basic knowledge will make it easier and give you considerably more creative range. PHP is a scripting language used mainly for creating dynamic Web sites or Web applications. PHP is involved in various stages of creating a template, such as in the index.php file, the control file of the template, and in the template overrides. I discuss these cases in more detail later. First, let's have a brief look at PHP.

PHP is integrated on the server side. The latest version of Joomla! requires at least version 5.2.4 of PHP. You can mix PHP and HTML in a file to create the desired output, which is the usual approach with templates. A file with integrated PHP code usually has the file extension .php. This extension tells the Web server that it has to process the file with the PHP processor. Joomla! is also written in PHP, and in addition to managing content, it has far more.

Joomla! is also a framework. Imagine a set of building blocks whose functions you can use without having to reinvent the wheel. For example, in your template you can easily display the current date or show which users are logged in. You determine the basic HTML frame of your site. Only dynamic content is output via PHP. You can control this output using a code mix of PHP and HTML. For these reasons, elementary knowledge of PHP is definitely an advantage.

Integrating PHP

You can mix PHP code with HTML, but you need to clearly mark the beginning and end of each code section. The PHP processor works its way through the files from top to bottom and only becomes active if it comes across a PHP instruction.

You have several options for integrating PHP into your Web site. The Joomla! standard suggests XML style, which opens with `<?php` and ends with `?>`. See the following example:

```
<?php
 // here is the PHP code itself, which, for example, fetches
 // the content of an article from the database.
?>
```

I strongly recommend that you follow this format because it results in a reliably more uniform overall effect. Table 5.1 lists some other methods some programmers use to get in and out of PHP.

When HTML code is mixed with PHP in Joomla!, the two are cleanly separated wherever possible. This means that in the overrides, you will frequently come across opening and closing PHP statements.

Template designers rarely deal with PHP. Usually they just want to change the HTML code. The strict separation of HTML and PHP ensures that the code is easier to handle and less susceptible to errors, even if it may seem a bit complicated at first. Following is an example of how to do this separation:

```
<?php
 // here is the PHP code
 ?>
<h1> This is my heading</h1>
<?php
 // here is the PHP code
 ?>
<p> and HTML again </p>
```

Table 5.1 **Methods Used to Get In and Out of PHP**

Start and End Tags	Description
`<? ... ?>`	SGML styles for lazy people; note that the PHP settings on the server have to be set to allow `short _ opentags`
`<?PHP ... ?>`	XML style with capital PHP
`<% ... %>`	ASP style: do not use because the PHP configuration has to have `asp _ tags` set to on; ASP is a Microsoft version of PHP

Comments

Good PHP code usually has comments to make it easier to understand. When you are diving into it later, you will certainly come across one comment or another.

A double slash introduces single-line comments:

```
//This is a comment
```

Multiple-line comments start with /* and end with */. You will probably recognize this syntax from CSS:

```
/*
This
is a
multiple line
comment */
```

echo

The function echo passes values or strings to the browser. You will see this function a lot because it is what you use to incorporate values calculated by PHP.

Outputting Strings

Strings are simply words or typed numbers:

```
<?php echo "This text will be output"; ?>
```

If you look at the code, you can see that the text to be output is enclosed by quotation marks and that a semicolon ends the instruction. Commands in PHP generally end with a semicolon. If you should forget this one day, you will get an error message: the parse error. Usually it includes a line number, but the error itself is usually one line above the specified number.

Outputting Variable Values

Variables are placeholders for dynamically changing content. Their values are saved during the script's runtime and are then available.

```
<?php $myvariable="This is the value of my variable"; ?>
```

To create a variable, you simply assign it a value using the equal (=) sign. The dollar sign ($) is used to tell PHP that a term is a variable:

```
<?php
 $myvariable="This is the value of my variable";
 echo $myvariable;
?>
```

The result in the browser is as follows:

```
This is the value of my variable
```

Please note: the variable is output without quotation marks. If you were to enclose it in single quotation marks, the result would be a text string:

```
<?php echo '$myvariable' ?>
```

and would result in this being displayed in the browser:

```
$myvariable
```

As you can see, there is a big difference between single and double quotation marks. Variables in double quotation marks are replaced with the variable's value. This substitution does not happen when the variable is enclosed in single quotation marks.

When you are dealing with the template overrides, you will frequently come across echo. In the layout for the article view (components/com_content/views/article/tmpl/default.php) you will see the following:

```
echo $this->item->text;
```

This line tells Joomla! to output the actual content of the article.

Conditions: if Statements

Often, you want to execute something only if a certain condition is fulfilled. You can use if and if/else statements to do this.

if Statement

Have a quick look at the back end of your Joomla! installation. Select the main menu and then click on the menu item Home. On the right-hand side, select the Page Display Options. You will see the parameter Page Heading.

The *Page Heading* today is what the *Pagetitle* was in Joomla! 1.5, and it outputs a heading above the content. Write something into it and activate the page heading by setting the parameter Show Page Heading to Yes.

Your specifications are saved in the parameter object and are now available. The content component of Joomla! responds accordingly and displays your heading on the homepage.

Following is the code that does the display:

```
<?php if ( $this->params->get('show_page_heading')!=0) : ?>
    <h1>
<?php echo $this->escape($this->params->get('page_heading')); ?>
    </h1>
<?php endif; ?>
```

This code displays the heading only if the parameter show_page_heading does not equal 0, that is, only if you have selected yes. This is an example of a simple if statement that you will probably come across frequently in the future.

The following example shows how Joomla! handles the logical separation of HTML and PHP code:

```
<?php if ( $this->params->get('show_page_heading')!=0) : ?>
```

The if statement is followed by a colon. The colon tells PHP that the following HTML code should be executed as long as the condition is fulfilled. After the HTML you will see:

```
<?php endif; ?>
```

This line indicates the end of the condition. The notation seems a little complicated, but it makes the code much clearer. Table 5.2 provides a brief overview of the most common relational operators.

Table 5.2 **Most Common PHP Relational Operators**

Description	Operator	Example	Condition
Equal	==	$a == $b	True if the two values are equal
Not equal	!=	$a!=10	True if the two values are not equal
Less than	<	$a<$c	True if the value on the left is less than the one on the right
Greater than	>	$a>$c	True if the value on the left is greater than the one on the right
Greater than or equal to	>=	$a>=$b	True if the value on the left is greater than or equal to the value on the right
Less than or equal to	<=	$a<=1	True if the value on the left is less than or equal to the value on the right
Identical	===	$a===$b	True if the two values are equal and the variables have the same type
Not identical	!==	$a!==$b	True if the two values are not equal or the variables have different types

else Statement

Sometimes you want to take one action if a condition is true and a different action if it is not true. For such relationships, you can add an `else` statement to your `if` statement:

```
<?php if ( $name=="Angie") : ?>
<h1> Angie </h1>
<?php else : ?>
<h1> You are not Angie </h1>
<?php endif ; ?>
```

Here is an example code snippet from Joomla!:

```
<?php
if ($params->get('link_titles')
[ca]&& !empty($this->item >readmore_link)) : ?>
<a href="<?php echo $this->item->readmore_link; ?>">
<?php echo $this->escape($this->item->title); ?></a>
<?php else : ?>
<?php echo $this->escape($this->item->title); ?>
<?php endif; ?>
```

For Pros: Accessing Objects and Their Values

When you start to dive deeper into the system and want to not only build a good template but also directly influence the code logic, you'll find it helpful to get information on the content of certain variables, arrays, or objects so you can respond appropriately to their values. This is an advanced topic, and you can create successful templates without using this functionality, so if you prefer to skip the rest of this chapter or come back to it later, you can safely move on to Chapter 6, "MooTools."

Parameter Basics

When you start to work with template overrides, you will come across the Joomla! parameters. Each menu item, each article, each category, and so on, has certain properties, and you can specify your preferences in the back end.

For example, under Article Options, for both articles and menu items, you'll find the following properties and some of the values you can assign to these properties:

- Show Title: Show, Hide
- Linked Titles: Yes, No
- Show "Read More": Show, Hide

The settings you choose are saved by Joomla! in an object. An object is simply a structured collection of data and functionalities.

The central object in Joomla! is $this, which contains all values and functions of the individual views. *Views* are the various views that you control via the menu items: article view, blog view, and so on. For example, if you are in article view, you can display properties, methods, and values of the object with:

```
<?php var_dump($this); ?>
```

You then get a very large structured list. You will see the parameters mentioned previously, along with many others, in this list.

If you are a PHP programmer, you may be used to displaying variables with the print_r function, like this:

```
<?php print_r($this); ?>
```

However, because this object can be very large in Joomla!, under certain circumstances, var_dump() is a better way of displaying the value. Here is just a brief extract of the result:

```
Object(ContentViewArticle)[180]
.....
    public 'show_title' => string '1' (length=1)
    public 'link_titles' => string '0' (length=1)
    public 'show_intro' => string '1' (length=1)
    public 'show_category' => string '0' (length=1)
    public 'link_category' => string '0' (length=1)
    public 'show_parent_category' => string '0' (length=1)
    public 'link_parent_category' => string '0' (length=1)
    public 'show_author' => string '0' (length=1)
    public 'link_author' => string '0' (length=1)
    public 'show_create_date' => string '0' (length=1)
    public 'show_modify_date' => string '0' (length=1)
    public 'show_publish_date' => string '0' (length=1)
    public 'show_item_navigation' => string '1' (length=1)
    public 'show_readmore' => string '1' (length=1)
....
```

Using Parameters

To access values of the object, Joomla! offers the function get of the object $this. The parameters mentioned previously are a property of this object. Another object, which contains the values themselves, is assigned to this property. But for dealing with the get method, this isn't important. You only need to know how to access it. This line gives you the value of the parameter Show Title:

```php
<?php echo $this->params->get('show_title') ; ?>
```

With this method, you can access all parameters in Joomla!.

If you have a parameter with values like Show/Hide or Yes/No, it returns 1 when the value is Show or Yes, and it returns 0 if the value is Hide or No. So if you include a parameter like this in an `if` statement, Show or Yes would meet the condition and Hide or No would be false.

6

MooTools

The significance of JavaScript has changed greatly in the last few years. When I started working with Web technologies in 1998, JavaScript was at a high point. Web sites were finally able to have moving parts. But the high did not last long because of the lack of security features in browsers. JavaScript suddenly had the reputation of being an unsafe technology. In Germany, the Federal Bureau for Data Protection even advised that people should avoid using JavaScript on public Web sites. System administrators were urged to turn off this feature in the browser configuration.

As a consequence, the use of JavaScript significantly dropped. It was not until the introduction of Web 2.0 that excitement once again surrounded JavaScript. A seemingly old technology experienced a new heyday. Today few of the old prejudices against Java-Script remain. Browsers have closed their security gaps, and JavaScript is, in many cases, a real gain. In the age of HTML5, JavaScript is essential to Web development. You can even increase accessibility with JavaScript.

With JavaScript it is possible to change the content of a Web site at runtime. The browser processes JavaScript commands and executes the changes within the Web site. The importance of this, above all, is speed. In some cases you can use PHP functions to achieve the same result, but it involves sending the page to the server, and that takes time.

With JavaScript you can, for example, manipulate HTML elements or output messages to the site user. This happens when the scripts directly influence the document object model (DOM). You have to imagine this DOM as a kind of tree structure. All elements are in the place provided for them within the hierarchy of that tree. If you know this structure, you can directly access individual elements of the tree.

But DOM in one browser is not necessarily the same as DOM in another. Each browser has its own concept in this respect. These concepts differ from each other by varying degrees. For example, to achieve the same result in Internet Explorer and Firefox, you would have to use a different approach for each. This behavior often causes confusion and more work, and it sometimes unjustly sheds a bad light on JavaScript.

In addition to providing many helpful functions, one of the most important tasks of any JavaScript framework is enabling a uniform use of JavaScript to compensate for the browser differences.

There are numerous JavaScript frameworks, and each has its advantages and disadvantages. Joomla! relies on MooTools. To use MooTools in your template, you need to ensure that it is integrated into your page. You can do so quickly in the index.php. Simply insert the following statement at the top of the page:

```
<?php JHTML::_('behavior.framework', true); ?>
```

Remember to remove this statement when you no longer need it because MooTools is not exactly small.

I am not necessarily the great MooTool expert, so I asked Peter Kröner to contribute this guest article. Kröner is an independent Web designer and frontend developer with a focus on JavaScript and HTML5. You can find him online at *www.peterkroener.de.*

Why MooTools?

By Peter Kröner

MooTools is one of many very good JavaScript frameworks and is available for free on the Web. Its beginnings lie in a plug-in called *moo.fx* for the framework Prototype. The author of moo.fx, Valerio Proietti, soon realized that Prototype was a nice framework, but it could not do everything the way he would have liked. This led him to create his own framework: *MooTools.* The name MooTools supposedly stands for *My Object Oriented Tools*, but as the author also has a Web site with the name "mad4milk," it is entirely possible that Valerio is simply a big fan of cows.

As mentioned, there are many different JavaScript frameworks—the best known is probably jQuery *(http://jquery.com).* Other common variations are Prototype *(www. prototypejs.org),* Dojo *(http://dojotoolkit.org),* and YUI *(http://developer.yahoo.com/yui/).* The difference between all these frameworks in terms of their functionalities is not so much what they make possible but how they do it. For example, jQuery is geared toward manipulating DOM elements with little effort, so that even beginners can easily integrate animations and Ajax functions. It is less suitable for programming gigantic Web applications—that is more a task for YUI, with its huge range of functions.

MooTools takes a middle path between simple DOM and powerful application framework. On one hand, it offers functions for DOM manipulation in the style of jQuery, and on the other hand, it offers tools for providing the foundations for more complex applications. MooTools is intended as an extension of the standard functions of DOM and JavaScript. Consequently, MooTools programming feels as if you are just writing normal JavaScript/DOM—minus the really nasty pitfalls. If you have already written a few lines of JavaScript, you will quickly feel at home in MooTools.

MooTools Quick Start—Dollar Functions and Events

MooTools consists of two parts. *Core* contains all basic functions for working with documents and for simple effects. In addition, it includes Ajax and other commonly used functions. The *More* component contains specialized plug-ins such as a form validator as well as tool tips. Both components are already integrated in Joomla!.

MooTools expands the standard objects of JavaScript and DOM with new methods. If, for example, you want to use `trim()` to remove the spaces from the beginning and end of a string, this works via a method particular to string. You can see this in action by going here:

```
// In action: http://jsfiddle.net/t88aD/
' Redundant spaces '.trim(); // Produces "Redundant spaces"
```

To be able to manipulate elements and attributes in DOM in this way, you first need to have access to them. MooTools offers two functions for this: the dollar function `$()` and the double dollar function `$$()`. The dollar function selects a single element using its ID, and the double dollar function selects several elements via a CSS selector:

```
// In action: http://jsfiddle.net/vUFp2/
$('foo');   // Returns the element with the ID "foo"
$$('div.bar'); // Returns all div elements with the class "bar"
```

Note that `$()` always returns exactly one element, and `$$()` always returns a list of elements, even if the selector has selected only a single HTML element. As an alias for `$()`, you can use `document.id()`, which is always useful when you want to use Moo-Tools along with other frameworks that also have a dollar function (for example, jQuery). This avoids inconvenient collisions. Also worth knowing is that when using MooTools, you *have to* select elements via `$$()` or `$()` or alternatively `document.id()`. `document.getElementById()` alone is not enough because the elements have to be prepared by MooTools before you can use them further in the framework.

We can apply the various MooTools methods to the elements or lists that we retrieve using this MooTools-compliant method. A more frequent task is creating animations, for which the `tween()` method is perfect. With it, you can let individual CSS properties merge fluently from one condition to another, allowing you to change the text color within an element:

```
// The element with the ID "foo" turns red
// In action: http://jsfiddle.net/UbnrR/1
$('foo').tween('color', '#F00');

// All div elements with the class "bar" turn red
// In action: http://jsfiddle.net/cMhxY/1/
$$('div.bar').tween('color', '#F00');
```

Usually you want to execute such an action only after certain events, such as after the user has clicked a button. The method `addEvent()` can help:

```
// In action: http://jsfiddle.net/gPbmn/1/
$('fooButton').addEvent('click', function(){ // If the button is
[c]clicked...
  $('foo').tween('color', '#F00'); // turn the element with the ID
[c]"foo" red
});
```

The dollar and double dollar functions can take effect only if the HTML of the Web site has been fully processed by the browser. So in most cases, it is necessary to move your own code to a special event known as the DOMReady event. This event fires on the `window` object as soon as the HTML is fully read in but before external resources such as images are downloaded. This is ideal for our little button script, which then looks like this:

```
// In action: http://jsfiddle.net/BNWPq/1/
window.addEvent('domready', function(){
  $('fooButton').addEvent('click', function(){
    $('foo').tween('color', '#FF0');
  });
});
```

Done! Producing the same effect without another framework would be a challenging task even for the most savvy JavaScript programmer because of the DOM problem (and animations are also not quite so easy), but thanks to MooTools, it becomes just peanuts. MooTools also has a suitable function for anything else you may need as a Web developer, such as more complex animations or Ajax requests. The comprehensive MooTools documentation at *http://mootools.net/docs/* explains how to use all of these little helpers, and the following section gives you a more concise overview.

The MooTools Core in Action

As mentioned earlier, the two components of MooTools are Core and More. More is a constantly growing plug-in collection, whereas Core contains the functionality you will need in almost any case. Besides useful extensions for the standard JavaScript building blocks (arrays, strings, and so on), Core offers tools for DOM operations, simple animations, and Ajax applications.

In addition to the dollar and double dollar functions, the element module of Core contains everything you need to insert elements into a Web page and manipulate them. You can create a new element with `new Element()` and simply specify the desired attributes in the form of a JavaScript object in addition to the tag name:

```
// In action: http://jsfiddle.net/Lbw3u/1/
var myNewDiv = new Element('div', {
        'id': 'newDiv',
        'text': 'Hello World',
        'styles': {
                'border': '1px solid red'
        }
});
var target = $('target');
myNewDiv.inject(target);
```

The newly created `div` is then inserted via `inject()` into another element that was previously selected via `$()` and is thereby integrated into the page. Once the element is in the Web page, you can use it to navigate easily through the entire DOM structure. Here are a few example functions.

- `el.getParent()` returns the parent element of the element `el`.
- `el.getNext()` returns the next sibling element of the element `el`.
- `el.getChildren()` returns all child elements of the element `el`.

To limit the selection, you can also add CSS selectors to all these functions and to the many more that exist. There are also methods for reading and setting attributes, deleting or moving elements, and an abundance of other things your heart may desire.

The first two central animation objects of MooTools are called `Fx.Tween` and `Fx.Morph`—the former allows you to create beautifully smooth animations of individual CSS properties; the latter changes several properties at once. Using `Fx.Tween` and `Fx.Morph` is practically identical. You create an effect object for one or more DOM elements of your choice, determine the animation parameters (for example, the duration), and start the effect via `start()`:

```
// In action: http://jsfiddle.net/LryMV/14/
var foo = $('foo');
var fooEffect = new Fx.Tween(foo, {
        'property': 'font-size',
        'duration': 'long'
});
fooEffect.start(60);
```

Here, the font size of the element `foo` is scaled via `Fx.Tween` in a slow animation to 40 units. The start value is usually the current style of the element at the start of the animation. `Fx.Morph` works similarly, only the properties to be animated are specified in `start()` and not the effect constructor:

```
// In action: http://jsfiddle.net/8p6nQ/12
var bar = $('bar');
```

```
var barEffect = new Fx.Morph(bar, {
      'duration': 'long'
});
barEffect.start({
      'font-size': 60,
      'color': '#FF0000'
});
```

Alternatively, you can add a configuration object to the `tween` or `morph` property of a DOM element and then start the animation via the `tween` and `morph` methods of this element:

```
// In action: http://jsfiddle.net/6dL89/
var foo = $('foo');
foo.set('tween', {
      'duration': 'long'
});
foo.tween('font-size', 60);
```

The next important block in the MooTools Core is *Ajax*. The classes `Request`, `Request.HTML`, and `Request.JSON` form a uniform interface for XML HTTP requests. The two latter also have directly integrated data processing on board. Using all three variations works in the same way: create the object, send the request, and get data in the success event:

```
// In action: http://jsfiddle.net/ErhKK/4/
var myRequest = new Request({
      'url': '/favicon.png',
      'method': 'get',
      'onSuccess': function(response){
            console.log(response);
      }
});
myRequest.send(null);
```

DOM functions, animations, and Ajax helpers form an important part of the Core of MooTools. With them it is easy to perform most of the daily frontend tasks. But the true power of MooTools is not that simple tasks become easier (all JavaScript frameworks can already do that quite well) but that it also has the right tools for challenging tasks.

The Class System

The MooTools class system—also a Core component—enables you to produce modular and reusable code in a very convenient way. Object orientation in JavaScript is really implemented via prototypes instead of via classes, which has various advantages and disadvantages. The only minus really worth mentioning is that this system causes confusion among many programmers who are used to classes from C++, PHP, or Java. To avoid this confusion, MooTools makes use of the fact that it is possible to put a class system on prototype-based code, so that everyone who is used to traditional object-oriented programming can feel at home right away.

You create a new class by calling the constructor function Class() with new and pass it a JavaScript object with the methods and properties of the class as argument:

```
var Chicken = new Class({
    peck: function(){
        alert('Peck, peck!')
    }
});
```

You could now use this Chicken class to create any number of completely identical chicken objects, which all have the method peck():

```
// In action: http://jsfiddle.net/8HcAD/4/
var myChicken = new Chicken();
myChicken.peck(); // Alert: Peck, peck!
```

You can create an extension to the Chicken class by adding a property Extends to the class constructor object, whose value is the name of the class you want to extend:

```
var Rooster = new Class({
    Extends: Chicken,
    crow: function(){
        alert('Cockadoodledo!');
    }
});
```

The class Rooster inherits all properties and methods defined for the class Chicken—in this case, the peck() method. Rooster also has its own crow() method, so our rooster can both crow and peck:

```
// In action: http://jsfiddle.net/nAwRk/2/
var myRooster = new Rooster();
myRooster.peck(); // Alert: Peck, peck!
myRooster.crow(); // Alert: Cockadoodledo!
```

If you want to copy properties and methods of a class into another without inheritance, you can use the Implements property of the constructor object. This is useful if you want to equip several classes with the same start values and functions. For example, you want your own class constructor function (for example, new Rooster()) to accept options objects:

```
var Hen = new Class({
    Extends: Chicken,
    Implements: Options,
    options: {
        startEggs: 2
    },
    eggs: 0,
    initialize: function(options){
        this.setOptions(options);
        this.eggs = this.options.startEggs;
    },
    layEgg: function(){
        this.eggs++;
    },
    countEggs: function(){
        alert(this.eggs);
    }
});
```

The Hen class extends the Chicken class, so it inherits the peck() method. It implements the options class and thereby takes on the setOptions() method. Also, Hen has a constructor function with initialize(), which processes the arguments passed when the class is created, in this case, the variable options. Hen has options.startEggs, which specifies how many eggs our chicken gets to start with. In the class itself, a default value (2) is specified but then is overwritten by setOptions() in initialize(). In practice, the effect looks like this:

```
// In action: http://jsfiddle.net/3GQrU/2/
myHen = new Hen();
myHen.countEggs(); // Alert: 2 (default value)

var myOtherHen = new Hen({
    startEggs: 5
});
myOtherHen.countEggs(); // Alert: 5
```

The number of eggs is saved in the internal variable eggs. With the method layEgg(), you increase the internal egg counter by one, while the start value can still be found under options.startEggs:

```
// In action: http://jsfiddle.net/XyTA3/2/
var myHen = new Hen({
    startEggs: 7
});
```

```
myHen.layEgg();
myHen.layEgg();
myHen.countEggs();          // Alert: 9
alert(myHen.options.startEggs); // Alert: 7
```

In each existing class, you can later implement additional methods using implement():

```
// In action: http://jsfiddle.net/hdDQV/2/
Chicken.implement({
    scratch: function(){
        alert('Scratch, scratch!');
    }
});
var myChicken = new Chicken();
myChicken.scratch(); // Alert: Scratch, scratch
```

This retrofitting also works with the standard classes of MooTools. Let's take an example without chickens for a change and implement a method into the element class (the class for all HTML elements) that completely replaces the content of the element concerned with the content of another element:

```
// In action: http://jsfiddle.net/Lznhj/4
Element.implement({
    swap: function(otherElement){
        var oldHTML = this.get('html');
        this.set('html', otherElement.get('html'));
        otherElement.set('html', oldHTML);
    }
});
// Replaces the content of the element with the ID 'myDiv' with
// the content of the element with the ID 'myOtherDiv'
$('myDiv').swap($('myOtherDiv'));
```

Because pretty much everything in MooTools consists of objects and classes, you can remodel everything to your taste in the framework or use it as basis for your own classes. Whether you use the class system to adapt MooTools or to create a completely new object hierarchy of your own, what comes out at the end is modular and portable code that can save you, the programmer, a lot of work.

The MooTools Principle

Thanks to the class system, you can write code pieces that build on one another. This saves work and makes it easy to transfer functionalities from project A to project B. All you need to do is keep your class code as general as possible. The Request.JSON class can serve as an example from MooTools itself. It starts an Ajax request and processes the result as JSON, which is a rather complicated affair if you take all the browser bugs and potential error messages into account. And yet, the `Request.JSON` class in MooTools 1.3.1 is only just over 20 lines long:

```
// https://github.com/mootools/mootools-core/blob/master/Source/Request/
➥Request.JSON.js
Request.JSON = new Class({
    Extends: Request,
    options: {
        secure: true
    },
    initialize: function(options){
        this.parent(options);
        Object.append(this.headers, {
            'Accept': 'application/json',
            'X-Request': 'JSON'
        });
    },
    success: function(text){
        var json;
        try {
            json = this.response.json = JSON.decode(text,
➥this.options.secure);
        } catch (error){
            this.fireEvent('error', [text, error]);
            return;
        }
        if (json == null) this.onFailure();
        else this.onSuccess(json, text);
    }
});
```

How is that possible? Where are all the other functions, such as `send()` and `cancel()`? The simple answer: they are in the `Request` class. Because `Request.JSON` is literally nothing but an extension of the normal request object, the MooTools developers have designed the request object in such a way that it fulfills a generalized function—it carries out an Ajax request. This makes it possible to simply attach variations of this functionality to the existing class with `Extends`. Although MooTools has three Ajax functions—`Request.JSON`, `Request.HTML`, and the normal `Request`—the core function has to be programmed only once. The variations simply derive from the existing form.

If you apply this principle to your daily Web developer work, you can save a lot of fiddling around in the long run. Quite often different projects have similar functions, and the naive approach is usually to just copy code from project A to project B and adapt it. This leads to an endless copy-and-paste chain, where the code is slightly changed in every project, which makes it longer, uglier, and more susceptible to errors. But if you stop and think before you program anew each time, if you generalize the problem and write an extendable and configurable MooTools class, you can create modular and portable JavaScript code that can be moved from project to project without hacks and adaptations. If you then need to make some changes and implement them as a class that expands the core function, the expansion is again a portable, expandable module. You can then use it in another project—but, unlike the copy-and-paste chain, you do not *have* to. That is why it is worth following the MooTools principle.

- If something has more than five lines, you should turn it into a class.

- You should generalize each problem and divide it into several small, also generalized class methods.

- New functionality should be implemented by expanding classes, not by changing the original code.

This does, of course, require a little bit more work by the programmer at the beginning in terms of thinking and typing, but in later projects, this extra work will no longer be necessary. Never again will you need ugly hacks and rampant copy-and-paste code—thanks to MooTools!

Related Links

Due to space constraints, this little MooTools overview has to remain somewhat superficial. I would therefore like to recommend selected links for further reading that are indispensable for finding out more about the MooTools universe.

- *http://mootools.net/docs/:* The official MooTools documentation is short and concise but comprehensive and easy to follow. Also available for MooTools More.

- *http://mootools.net/forge/:* The Forge is the plug-in directory of the MooTools community.

- *http://projswithmootools.com: Pro JavaScript with MooTools* by Mark Joseph Obcena (Dordrecht: Springer, 2010) is the best MooTools book for the current version 1.3.

- *http://blip.tv/file/3825733/:* MooTools developer Aaron Newton explains the MooTools principle with classes and reusable code in a 30-minute presentation.

- *http://jsfiddle.net:* JSFiddle is a playground for JavaScript experiments, including MooTools. Simply type in your HTML, CSS, and JavaScript, click on Run, and off you go!

7

Tools

Useful tools can make your everyday work significantly easier. For Web development in particular, you can choose from a whole smorgasbord of browser extensions and online offerings. The most important of these tools and helpers are listed in this chapter.

HTML Validator and CSS Validator

Web standards provide a common set of practices for hardware, software, and Web sites to follow when they come together to deliver Web content. Only if clients (the software for Web access) and the Web sites both adhere to these standards, as closely as possible, is there any chance that Web pages will appear to users as the designer intended. Some clients are error tolerant and can guess roughly what the designer intended even in cases of serious markup errors, but you cannot rely on the client to fix errors. Modern clients have to fulfill so many requirements that their developers are—quite rightly—concentrating more on following the standards and assuming that the developers of Web sites do so as well.

I usually use the validator provided by the W3C *(http://validator.w3.org)*, the international body that developed the Web standards themselves. You may notice that the standards are referred to as "recommendations." This term is used is for legal reasons, but you should consider them requirements because following them is mandatory for validation. This validator is not the only one, nor is it the only good one, but it is the one I usually choose because it is constantly being developed and brought up to the latest standards (see Figure 7.1). As of recently, it can even check the HTML5 specification, which I used in the Beez template.

Because you can use the HTML validator free of charge, there is no reason to put pages on the Internet without first checking them with this tool.

If you want to check the HTML validity of several sites at once, the validator of the Web Design Group at *www.htmlhelp.com* is useful because you can submit a list of Web site addresses.

The W3C also offers a CSS validator. It is very good at tracking down CSS errors that can cause display problems. You can find it at *http://jigsaw.w3.org/css-validator/*.

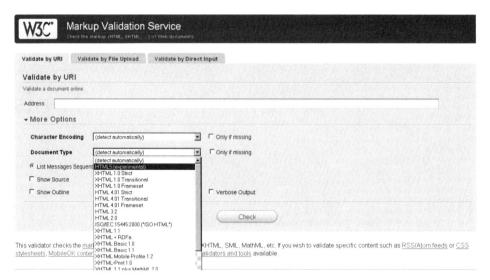

Figure 7.1   Result of the HTML validator in the W3C Markup Validation Service

Web Developer Toolbar

The Web Developer toolbar, an extension for Firefox, is one of the oldest and most useful tools in Web development. This little program offers numerous helpers, as you can see in Figure 7.2. You can selectively deactivate cookies, analyze CSS, validate Web pages, and even inspect forms. The highlighting function makes it much easier to look for errors.

You can download the Web Developer Toolbar from *https://addons.mozilla.org/en-US/firefox/addon/Web-developer/*.

The Web Developer toolbar menu has many features that you can use to analyze your Web page. Following is a list of the most common tasks.

- Deactivating colors, graphics, redirections, JavaScript, or various stylesheet elements
- Editing stylesheets directly in the browser
- Displaying and hiding all `alt` attributes of graphics
- Listing all graphics of a Web site with details of sizes and file size
- Displaying all colors clearly and with color code
- Showing guides in the browser
- Screen magnification for zooming in to different page elements
- Measuring tool for measuring Web site elements
- Highlighting frames, headings, links, and other elements
- Adapting window size quickly
- Checking dead links

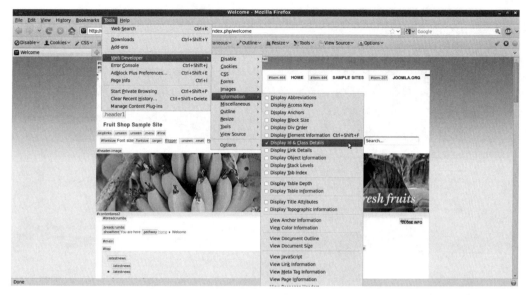

Figure 7.2   The Web Developer toolbar displays the internal structure of the Web pages. In this example, the id and class values are shown.

- Inspecting the document object model (DOM)
- Changing window size

Internet Explorer offers a similar tool. You can find it at *www.microsoft.com/downloads/en/details.aspx?FamilyID=95e06cbe-4940-4218-b75d-b8856fced535*.

Firebug

Firebug is one of the most glorious inventions for template designers. After its successful installation, you can use it to check Web sites live for their HTML and CSS code, simply by moving over them with the mouse. This is particularly useful if you want to adapt or change existing templates.

If you select an element, the corresponding CSS code, including line number, is displayed in a separate window. You no longer need to painstakingly search in the CSS files.

Firebug also has a live editing function. You can click on the corresponding instructions and change them. The result is displayed directly in the browser, as shown in Figure 7.3.

Here is an overview of the most important functions of Firebug.

- Inspecting HTML and modifying design and layout in real time
- JavaScript debugger/DOM inspector
- Performing precise analysis of links and the performance of Web sites

Figure 7.3   Firebug in action

If you are not using Firebug, you should deactivate it. Because it analyzes each site automatically, it can affect the performance of several sites. Activation and deactivation are extremely easy with just one mouse click.

You can download Firebug at *https://addons.mozilla.org/en-US/firefox/addon/firebug/*.

Helpful Tools for Accessibility

Helpful tools for accessibility include the Colour Contrast Analyser, accessibility extensions for Internet Explorer and Mozilla Firefox, Wave, the WCAG 2 checker of the University of Toronto, and Tilt 3D. Here is a brief overview of these tools.

Colour Contrast Analyser

Pleasant colors are not easy to see in all cases. The hue and brightness contrasts are very important, especially in the context of accessibility. The Colour Contrast Analyser (CCA) by Nils Faulkner is a useful tool (see Figure 7.4).

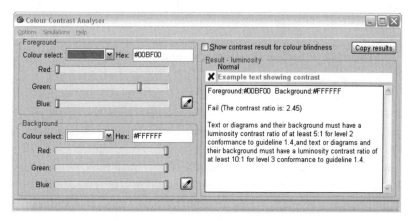

Figure 7.4   Colour Contrast Analyser 1.2

An interesting property of the CCA is that it can also analyze values for how color differences will appear to people with different vision impairments.

The new version analyzes the color following the guidelines of the WCAG 2 and is therefore better than the previous version. You can download it from *www.paciellogroup. com/resources/CCA-2.2.zip.*

Alternatively, you can use the Juicy Studio Accessibility extension, which is based on the same algorithm and also gives you information on the Web Accessibility Initiative–Accessible Rich Internet Applications WAI-ARIA elements used. We discuss these elements further in Chapter 17, "The Default Templates and Their Features." You can find the add-on at *https://addons.mozilla.org/en-US/firefox/addon/juicy-studio-accessibility-too/.*

Accessibility Extensions for Internet Explorer and Mozilla Firefox

The Mozilla Accessibility toolbar and the AIS (accessible information solutions) toolbar for Internet Explorer are important additional tools that can help you automatically check your Web sites for accessibility.

For Internet Explorer, you can use the AIS Web Accessibility toolbar *(www.visionaustralia.org.au/ais/toolbar/).* It was developed by a team for accessible information solutions at the National Information and Library Service (NILS) in Australia. It offers functions such as the following:

- Validating the code with the W3C validator
- Validating the CSS code by using the CSS validator of the W3C
- Integration of W3C HTML Tidy
- Link checker

- Quick access to setting browser window size for the most frequently used resolutions
- CSS functionalities such as hiding and showing
- Displaying deprecated HTML attributes
- Image functions such as creating an image list and replacing the `img` elements via your `alt` text
- Color functions such as grayscale, integration of color contrast analyzer by Juicy Studio, and a display of colors used
- Display of document structure (headings, lists, document titles, form elements, acronyms, abbreviations, JavaScript event handlers, access keys, tables, and much more)
- Redirection to external checking programs (Wave, Cynthia Says, Webxact, etc.)
- Simulations (disabled plug-ins, disabled mouse, vision impairments, etc.)
- The Firefox extensions also offer a function that allows you to check WAI ARIA code (see Chapter 17)

The installation is simple. Once you download the accessibility toolbar file, you simply execute it and the toolbar appears in your browser panel.

The Accessibility Evaluation Toolbar for Mozilla Firefox *(https://addons.mozilla.org/en-US/firefox/addon/accessibility-evaluation-toolb/)* offers similar functions for the Firefox browser. At the time of writing, it even offered more than AIS, including

- A high-contrast CSS
- Turning off images altogether
- Analysis of document structure
- Linearization of table contents
- A focus inspector to check focus issues
- Helpful functions for creating accessible JavaScript
- Listing the WAI ARIA attributes

Once you download the extension, the automatic installation takes place easily without any complications. After a successful reboot, you will find the toolbar in your browser panel.

Wave

On the Web you can now find the checking tool Wave in version 4 *(http://wave.webaim.org)*. It does not produce long lists with error messages but shows you at a glance how important accessibility rules have been followed. Because of its visual nature, Wave is not very accessible: visual and textual presentation are two fundamentally different things and cannot be transposed on one another.

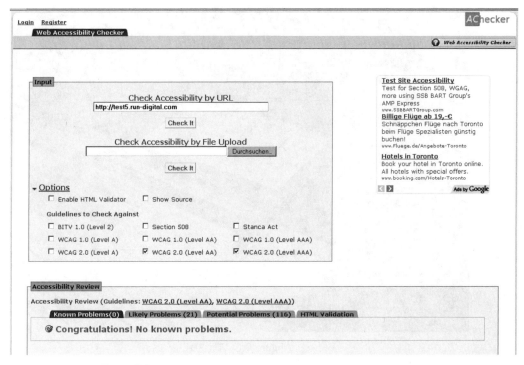

Figure 7.5   Web Accessibility Checker of the University of Toronto

WCAG 2 Checker of the University of Toronto

This nice little tool is an online application from the University of Toronto, which tests Web sites for compatibility with the WCAG 2 *(http://achecker.ca/checker/index.php)*. Potential errors or problems are listed clearly and explained (see Figure 7.5).

Tilt 3D

The Firefox extension Tilt 3D is relatively new and a great tool especially for those who like to have some fun while inspecting Web pages (see Figure 7.6).

Tilt 3D lets you see at a glance the nested structure of your Web page. The tree structure allows you to easily display the HTML for each section. This extension creates a three-dimensional visualization of a Web page based on WebGL (Web Graphics Library). Among other information, it indicates how deeply the HTML code is nested and displays it on request.

Tilt can be found at *https://addons.mozilla.org/en-US/firefox/addon/tilt/*.

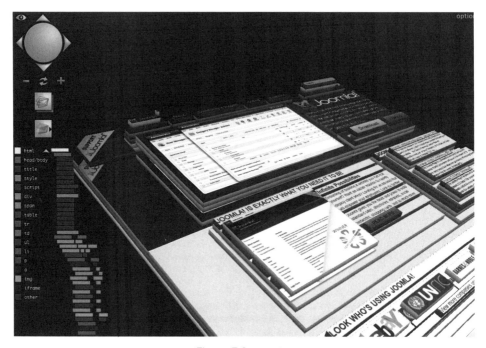

Figure 7.6   Tilt 3D

8

Now for the Details:
A First Look at Templates

You are using Joomla! now and would like to know more about its template functions. This chapter gives you an overview of the structure of the templates—knowledge that will help you develop your own individualized template based on the default templates.

Templates determine the general structure of a page. Apart from the design, they determine where the content is within the document, where and when certain modules are shown or hidden, whether to use your own error pages, and which HTML version you should use.

The standard version of Joomla! currently contains three templates for the front end and two for the back end. The frontend templates are two versions of Beez and one Atomic template. In the back end are the standard template Bluestork and the accessible template Hathor by Andrea Tarr. We are going to ignore the backend templates for now.

First and foremost, the frontend templates should be captivating. You can adapt templates according to how you want your Web site to look and feel to the outside world. All templates differ not just in their visual design but also in their range of technical functions. Here is a brief overview of the frontend templates.

Atomic

The focus of the Atomic template is on using the Cascading Style Sheet (CSS) framework Blueprint. Prepared CSS classes help you create complex layouts. If you select this template in the back end and look at the page, it initially seems to have no design. It only appears this way, though, because it is not designed to work with the current sample data. Once you adapt it, you will have a very nice design. More on Atomic a bit later.

beez_20 and beez5

A template usually contains more than you can see at first glance. Apart from the design, it distinguishes itself by how it is implemented in technical terms.

You may be familiar with the Beez template version 1.5. When I created it, I wanted to build a standards-conforming, easily accessible and adaptable template. I chose to use the color purple to make it obvious that you were meant to customize the template to fix your style rather than use it as it was. I hoped that many designers would use the code, modify it creatively, and make it available for free use. I was counting on a multitude of new templates. Sadly, this has not happened. Many users did not understand how to modify the template, and many others did use the code but did not publish their templates.

I made another mistake in not communicating clearly what I had in mind. The output was structured in such a way that almost any design could be achieved with it, simply and without complications. Easy modifications could also be made in the CCS code. I have kept to this principle with each new version of Beez, while making some important changes. There is now more accessible JavaScript. beez5 has a small portion of HTML5, and beez_20 manages without template overrides because the default output has been adapted to the output of the old Beez templates, so overrides are not required.

In beez5 you will find HTML5 code in the overrides.

The Template Manager: Styles

The Template Manager in the back end has the task of managing existing templates in an organized way. It shows you the installed and available frontend and backend templates in a clear list. You can find the template manager in the back end at Extensions → Template Manager.

If you open the Template Manager, you will first notice the selected (in-use) styles of the installed templates, as shown in Figure 8.1. Styles are variations of the same template.

Figure 8.1   Template Manager in the back end

The term *style* is probably confusing for some people. Style here refers to different versions of the same template. These versions may differ in both CSS styling and HTML markup. The use of styles is further explained in Chapter 11, "The XML File and the Template Parameters." But let's get back to the Template Manager.

In addition to viewing the selected styles, you can use the Template Manager to see whether it is a frontend or backend style, which template the selected style relates to, or if it has been assigned to specific page areas. The gold star indicates the selected, and therefore currently active, default style.

By clicking on the checkbox in front of each style and selecting Make Default at the upper right, you can change the default style.

At the top right are also two checkboxes for filtering styles. This function is helpful if you are using many different styles and different templates. The styles can be filtered through the front end or back end or by the template they belong to.

Each template can have different properties, called parameters, that can be configured. By copying a style, you can assign it to different pages or areas with different properties. You can do it both in the Template Manager and via the menu items.

Here is a little example to make things clearer. In the beez_20 template you can choose between two different design variations: *Personal* and *Nature*. Personal is the default display option with the blue header image. Nature is in all green. Both variations differ only in that they use a different CSS file for certain elements of the template.

If you want to use the default variation on some pages and the green version on others, you can do so very easily. You can copy the styles from the Template Manager and save them under a different name.

If you then click on the style beez_20, you will see the image shown in Figure 8.2.

Tip

Creating multilingual content was not yet possible in Joomla! version 1.5. Now, Joomla! offers a small but smart method of managing content even in different languages. The solution offered is not appropriate for all cases. Sites with a lot of content must fall back on external solutions. But for smaller pages, it is a simple and quick solution.

On the right you can see the parameters, here called Advanced Options. The selection of parameters actually constitutes a style. You have a range of selection options. At the bottom under Template color are the styles *Personal* and *Nature*. Here you can make your selection and choose the desired display variation.

Under Details you will find the name of the relevant style. You can choose any name, but you should make sure it's a meaningful title to avoid confusion later. The name will help you distinguish between styles, especially if you are using several copies of a style.

You can also see which template the selected style relates to, which unique ID it has, and whether it should be used only when a certain language is selected.

Below the Details panel you will find the Menus assignment panel. Each menu item is listed there, and the style can be assigned to the relevant menu item by enabling

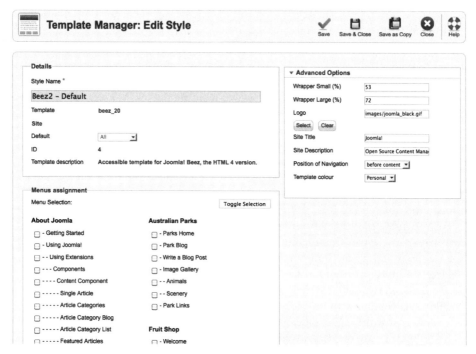

Figure 8.2   Default style beez_20

the corresponding checkbox. By selecting Toggle Selection, you can disable all the checkboxes.

Once you have made your selection, you can save your style by clicking on Save as Copy at the top right. Joomla! automatically creates a copy of the default style with the options you have selected. And that's it!

Here is a summary of all the steps.

1. Select default style.
2. Change title or name of style.
3. Adapt parameters to your preferences.
4. Assign menu items.
5. Save template as copy.

The Template Manager: Templates

If you select the tab Templates in the horizontal navigation, you will get straight to the installed templates, as shown in Figure 8.3. At first glance, this view does not seem very spectacular, but it is clearly a very different picture than in Joomla! version 1.5.

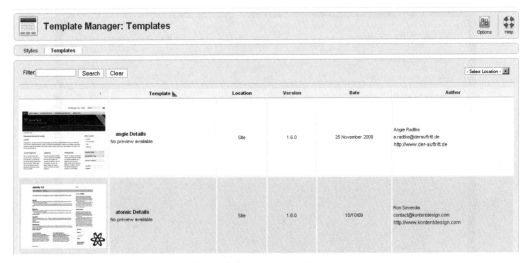

Figure 8.3   Template Manager

The templates are still listed with a screenshot, their name, their location (site for front end or Administrator for back end), their date of creation, and their author. By clicking on the template name, you get to the really interesting information.

The Template Preview

You will notice that under the template name in Figure 8.3 there is a note that says "No preview available." If you have already been working with Joomla!, you know that you can assign modules, which usually output dynamic contents, to certain positions. In the template itself you control where a module should be placed within the document. Its position is then determined by using CSS. The template preview gives you an overview of the position used for the module.

For security reasons, you have the option of enabling or disabling the preview. You can find the Template Options in the top right corner. When you click on the Options icon, you will see the screen shown in Figure 8.4.

Here you can enable the preview function and configure the permissions management. Once you enable the preview function, you will see, as shown in Figure 8.5, that the preview is now available.

Where in Figure 8.3 it said "No preview available" under the template name, you will now see "Preview," which is a link that takes you directly to the preview (if Preview does not appear after you change the options, try reloading the page). If you then click on Preview, a new window pops up with the preview. All module positions assigned in the template are displayed clearly.

Figure 8.4   Template Manager Options

Figure 8.5   The preview is now available.

The latter part of the URL is particularly important: *tp=1&template=beez5*. This helpful function can be used not only in the back end but also in the front end, where it is even more helpful. See Figure 8.6.

Particularly with large sites, you may see a module displayed in the front end but, for the life of you, cannot remember which module position it uses. In the Module Manager, modules can be sorted by type and position, but sometimes you still cannot find a specific module.

If you now go the relevant page in the front end and append *?tp=1* to the URL, you get a preview (of the assigned template) of the corresponding page, which tells you the position of the module you are interested in. This is shown in Figure 8.7.

You may wonder why you can enable and disable this rather useful function. Wouldn't it be great if it was available all the time? The flexibility of the function makes it necessary to have the option of enabling and disabling it, because anyone who knows about

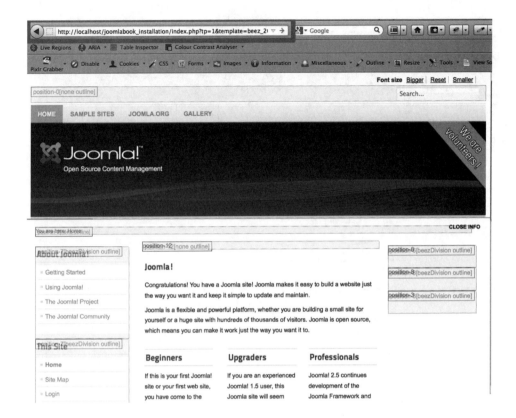

Figure 8.6   Template preview

this method can look up this information. And only rarely would you want them to. So, if you require this function: *enable, look it up, disable!*

Template Details

As you can see in Figure 8.8, the Template Details view also differs slightly from the previous version of Joomla!.

On the right is a list of all CSS files used in the template.

With just one click, you can edit from the administrator back end. The same goes for the internal control files in the template. Here you can edit the index.php file, the heart of the template, the error page, and print preview.

This function is useful while running the operation if you want to change something quickly. But I have to admit that I prefer editing these files directly in an editor and then uploading them to the server via FTP.

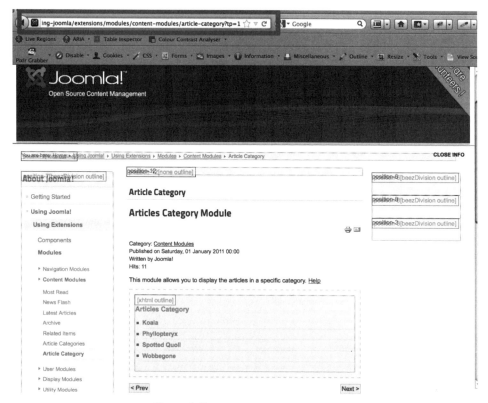

Figure 8.7   Preview in the front end

Figure 8.8   Template Details gives access to template page HTML and CSS files.

Installing Templates

When people start getting into Joomla!, they often do not build their own template right away but instead use one of the many templates available on the Internet and adapt it to their needs. Quite a number of templates are now available. In addition to free templates, various templates can be purchased on the Web. The templates differ not just in their design but also in their range of functions, quality, and price.

If you are considering one of these, you should look at the templates very closely. Most of them offer a whole range of functions in addition to the pure design and try to be as generic as possible to fulfill as many wishes as possible. For that reason, these templates are often very hard to adapt, because the more complex they are, the more complicated they are to change.

Now that Joomla! 2.5 has been out for a while, the number of templates offered is extensive.

Templates are managed by Joomla! in the same way as any other extension; that is, they are installed in the same way as any other extension, via the extension manager. Your template is probably in the form of a ZIP archive. You can install this archive, as is, via the extension manager. Joomla! takes care of unzipping the archive. How to create such archives yourself and which rules you need to follow are explained in Chapter 11, "The XML File and the Template Parameters." So to install a template you go to Extensions → Extension Manager on the Install tab, as shown in Figure 8.9.

If the template is well formed and follows all the Joomla! guidelines, there should not be any problems in the installation, and the template should appear in the Template Manager.

Starting with version 1.6, there has been a considerable change in template handling: they are now stored in the database. In version 1.5 you were still able to simply copy templates into the Joomla! template folder. They were fully functional and automatically detected by the system. This is no longer possible, which does not necessarily mean that it is more complicated. The Extension Manager's *Discover* function, shown in Figure 8.10, is available to help.

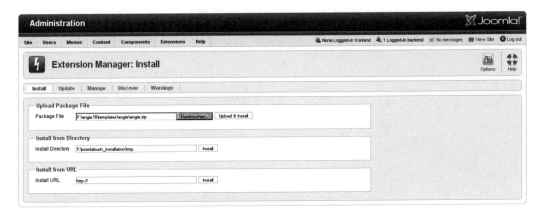

Figure 8.9   Extension manager

Figure 8.10   The Template Manager's Discover function

Once you have manually inserted the template into the Joomla! template directory, go to the Extension Manager on the Discover tab. Click the Discover icon, and the system will detect your template. Check the box in front of your template and click the Install icon. It will then be listed in the Template Manager next to the default templates.

Of course, the question is why the templates are now saved in the database. Templates have, as previously mentioned, parameters: properties that can change under certain circumstances. Like the template name, these properties are also saved in the database, which in turn enables extensions such as modules or components to directly access these properties. This method of storage makes it possible to design a very flexible template.

9

The Underlying Structure

You can find the default templates in the Joomla! back end, but how do you get there? Which conventions do you need to follow? How are they structured in terms of technology and content? Which commands do you use to change or adapt them? These are some of the many questions answered in this chapter.

Let's leave the Joomla! administration interface and move on to the data level so we can look at the directory structure of Joomla! (see Figure 9.1). All contents of the template are arranged below a single directory, as you can see in Figure 9.2.

The frontend templates are located in the folder *templates* directly in the root directory of Joomla!. The backend templates can be found in the folder *administrator/templates*.

I am going to give you an initial overview of the individual components of the templates using the default template. Some are simple and easy to explain, but others require their own chapter.

Let's start with the simple components of a template (see Figure 9.3).

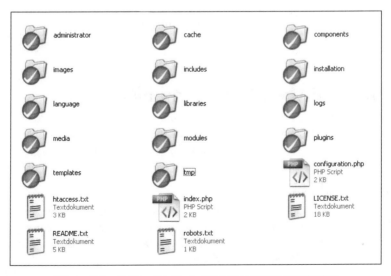

Figure 9.1   Folder structure after successful installation

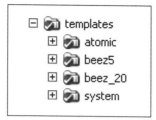

Figure 9.2   Default templates in the Joomla! directory structure

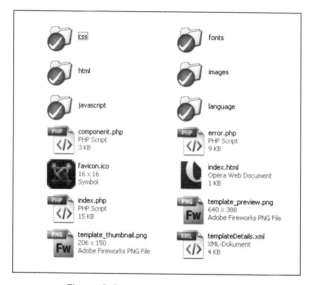

Figure 9.3   Structure of a template

The Heart of the Matter, the index.php

The index.php file is the heart of the Joomla! template. It controls the structure and display of your Web site, and it brings together all the files used. How this works is described in detail in Chapter 10, "The index.php: The Heart of the Matter."

The css Folder

Not surprisingly, the css folder contains the CSS files used by the template. You can rename this folder as you wish because it does not follow any naming convention. In the Beez templates you will find a separate CSS file for printing (print.css) in addition to the files responsible for the presentation on the screen.

templateDetails.xml

This file is basically the table of contents of the template. All contents—from the author to the graphics files—are listed in XML format here. Joomla! needs this file to be able to install the template, so it is important to handle this file with great care. More on this in Chapter 11, "The XML File and the Template Parameters."

The images Folder

As the name indicates, the images folder contains all graphics used in the template. This folder also does not follow any naming convention, so you can give it an individual name. Just make sure you reference it correctly when you later use graphics in your template. But if you decide to replace the system graphics of Joomla! you should ensure that the folder keeps its name.

The html Folder

This folder has magical significance: it enables the template developer to adapt practically the entire default output of Joomla! to his or her individual wishes. Here is where overrides happen: code in this folder, adapted for Joomla!, overwrites the default output of Joomla!. More on this topic in the next few chapters, particularly in Chapter 14, "Designing Default Output Individually."

The javascript Folder

This folder contains the scripts used in the template. You can save your scripts in any folder and then simply reference them later as you need them.

The language Folder

This folder contains the template language files. Joomla! uses language files to allow the same text to be displayed in any language. Templates can contain language constants such as those used for skip links. You can also make the administration interface available in several languages. When you want to assign a module to a position, you will find a description of this position in the Module Manager. The text of the description is stored in the template's language file. More on the language files in Chapter 12, "The Language Files."

component.php

In Joomla! you can display content without browser navigation or header information in a separate window. This display option is available, for example, in print preview and e-mail. It is also applied when you set a link to open in a new window without browser navigation.

In principle, the component.php file is like the little sister of index.php, the actual template control file. You usually want to add a separate design for this view, which is easily done by adapting this file. In this case, a strict naming convention applies. You can adapt the contents of this file as you wish, but you may not change its name. More information on the component.php file can be found in Chapter 15, "The System Template: Adapting and Modifying Output."

error.php

You can use this file to design custom error pages, such as a 404 page (File not found). This file is also subject to the naming convention and should not be renamed.

template_thumbnail.png and template_preview.png

Remember the Template Manager in the back end? Each template is represented by a little thumbnail using *template_thumbnail.png*.

If you want to display your own template thumbnail in the back end, you can easily do so. Just create a screenshot of your template and give it a size of 206 × 105 pixels. Then save it under the name *template_thumbnail.png* in your own Template folder, and tada!

The larger preview image works along the same principle. Click, in the back end, on the small preview to open a window with an enlarged preview image. This image (template_preview.png) should have a size of 800 × 600 pixels.

favicon.ico

Warning

If you decide to use one of the Joomla! default templates as the starting point for your own template, please make sure you adapt or remove the favicon.

Favicons are little icons that are inserted in the browser bar next to the URL. These icons originate from Microsoft. They used to be icons for the Favorites in Internet Explorer. Nowadays almost all browsers can display these 16 × 16 pixel–sized icons. If there is not a file with the default name favicon.ico, nothing will be displayed.

Favicons can be easily created with Photoshop and saved in the file format .ico. The popular Irfan-View and other converters are also saved in .ico format. If you need further information or guidance on favicons, these online tools can help:

- *www.favicongenerator.com*
- *www.favicon.cc*

On both of these sites, you need to upload an image, which is then converted into a favicon.

The fonts Folder

The font folder is present only in the Beez templates. The Web font used in these templates is stored in different file formats. I described what Web fonts are and how to use them in Chapter 1, "The Basis: Designing the Content and Visual Concept."

The index.html

In the template folder you will see an empty index.html file, as in every Joomla! folder. This file should not be deleted and should also be present in the templates you create yourself. The reason for this is security. This file prevents people from being able to view the contents of a folder via the browser, provided the Web server is properly configured.

10

The index.php:
The Heart of the Matter

Throughout the last few chapters I have repeatedly mentioned that the index.php file is the central control file of a Joomla! template. It takes on the task of setting patterns for the content created by the system and is the first template file used by the system.

The index.php file integrates the actual content, controls which modules are positioned where and when, combines the CSS files, and gives the template its unique look. It has the file extension .php, but it actually contains a mixture of HTML elements and PHP code. The HTML is responsible for the general page structure. The PHP integrates dynamic content.

Every Web designer who knows HTML will quickly be able to see the structure of a page by looking soley at the HTML code and ignoring the PHP code. But unfortunately, you cannot get by without PHP.

The code of the beez_20 template is quite complex, but I'm going to explain it to you from top to bottom. Please open the index.php file in the templates/beez_20 folder and have a look at it in an editor with syntax highlighting.

The Document Head

We start deconstructing the beez_20 template by looking at the document head in the index.php file, that part of the HTML that comes in the `<head>` section. Before we get to the actual `<head>` section, we have some Joomla! housekeeping to take care of as well as the task of defining the type of HTML we will use.

Safety First: Security

Even if you are Web designer who would rather work with HTML and CSS than PHP, believe me, a little bit of PHP can actually be fun. So let's have a go at it.

In every Joomla! file with a name that ends with .php, you will see this at the beginning:

```
<?php
// no direct access
defined( '_JEXEC' ) or die;
```

This is a security feature internal to Joomla!. Specifically, it checks whether or not the constant JEXEC is set. As soon as someone surfs to a Joomla! site, this constant is set and checked repeatedly. This check prevents someone from outside gaining direct access to this file.

Which Document Type?

The Web speaks HTML. The first statement in each HTML document is the specification of the markup language used; its grammar is determined by the doctype declaration.

If you do not change the HTML output in the template (as described in Chapter 14, "Designing Default Output Individually"), but use the default output of Joomla!, you should choose XHTML Transitional:

```
<!DOCTYPE html PUBLIC "-//W3C//DTD XHTML 1.0 Transitional//EN"
  "http://www.w3.org/TR/xhtml1/DTD/xhtml1-transitional.dtd">
```

From version 1.6, you can also use Strict:

```
<?xml version="1.0" encoding="utf-8"?>
<!DOCTYPE html PUBLIC "-//W3C//DTD XHTML 1.0 Strict//EN"
  "http://www.w3.org/TR/xhtml1/DTD/xhtml1-strict.dtd">
```

beez5 even enables you to use HTML5 with the nice and simple declaration:

```
<!Doctype html>
```

As mentioned in Chapter 3, "CSS and HTML—Getting the Basic Structure into Shape," it makes sense to use XHTML Transitional because of the editors packaged with Joomla!.

HTML Language Indicator

After the document specification, you will find further details on HTML itself:

```
<html xmlns="http://www.w3.org/1999/xhtml" xml:lang="<?php echo
  $this->language; ?>" lang="<?php echo $this->language; ?>"
  dir="<?php echo $this->direction; ?>"
```

xmlns refers directly to the markup language used, and xml:lang specifies the language used in the document. dir, the abbreviation for *direction*, indicates the Western reading direction, from left to right: ltr (**l**eft **t**o **r**ight).

Joomla! can also display Arabic or Hebraic sites, for example, which have content written from right to left. These would need the specification **r**ight **t**o **l**eft: rtl.

The language used is determined in the Language Manager. Since Joomla! can manage multilingual content, the language itself is stored as a variable and can adapt dynamically to the language you enable.

jdoc: include type:head

> **Tip**
>
> jdoc is the abbreviation for *Joomla! document* and part of the Joomla! language range. If you want to know more, `<jdoc:include type="head" />` integrates the functions of the file *libraries/joomla/document/html/renderer/head.php*.

The first line in every Joomla! template directly after the opened <head> area is this:

```
<head>
<jdoc:include type="head" />
```

With the statement `<jdoc:include />` you can integrate not only the page head into the template but also the modules used and the actual content. The statements differ only by the specified type. I discuss them in more detail later.

What does `<jdoc:include type="head" />` actually do? It automatically integrates a large part of the document head, so that you barely need to do anything to the design at this point. These are the statements that are added by the jdoc statement.

base

```
<base href="http://localhost/joomlabuch_installation/index.php" />
```

This information in the href attribute helps Joomla! generate search engine–friendly URLs. The base element is almost as old as HTML itself. It generally refers directly to the root directory. In Joomla! it is not used completely cleanly, for technical reasons, because it is part of the Joomla! routing. If you are in a category view for example, the base does not always refer to the root directory but to the category that the system is currently in.

> **Tip**
>
> The base element appears in the document head only if the search engine–friendly URLs are enabled in the Joomla! configuration.

The Character Set: UTF-8

```
<meta http-equiv="Content-Type" content="text/html; charset=utf-8" />
```

This statement indicates the character set used in the document. Joomla! uses UTF-8. The browser needs to know which character set it should use to correctly display the characters.

For a long time, character sets could contain only a maximum of 256 characters. There are so many different character sets because the different languages of the world use different characters. Just think of umlauts in German or accents in French: characters that do not appear in many other languages. Depending on the language used, you need to specify a different character set in the head of the HTML file.

Because this is complicated and laborious, UTF-8 was developed. UTF-8 is a universal character set that can process up to 1,114,112 characters.

Some Web servers still have problems with displaying UTF-8, but it is the character set of the future. Joomla! uses UTF-8, and so it is well prepared for this future.

Metadata for Google and Company

As you probably know, you can include global details regarding the metadata in the Joomla! configuration; they are then added, automatically, in the document head. Individual articles can also contain these details.

```
<meta name="robots" content="index, follow" />
```

This data refers to the behavior of the search engine robots that frequently scan your pages for relevant information. The keyword index gets the robots to index a page. follow permits them to follow all links on the page. But if these statements were not present in the document head, the robots would still behave in the same way, so using these statements makes sense only if you want to stop the robots from indexing the page. You stop them with the keywords noindex and nofollow.

```
<meta name="description" content="Joomla! - the dynamic portal engine
  and content management system" />
```

Describing the content of your site can pose a challenge even for a professional copywriter. It should be as precise and descriptive as possible, should not contain more than two or three sentences, should contain relevant keywords, and should attract future visitors with its wording. Some search engines display up to 250 characters, and others cut off the text after just 80 characters.

```
<meta name="keywords" content="joomla, Joomla" />
```

The relevance of the meta keywords has rapidly decreased in recent years. Opinions among search engine experts on the significance of the keywords currently vary greatly.

While some believe the keywords should be the same on every page, others think that Google judges this negatively.

The experts agree that *keyword spamming* (using a great number of keywords) has a negative effect. You will not go wrong if you pick keywords carefully and make sure they are relevant to the contents of your page.

Generator

```
<meta name="generator" content="Joomla! 2.5 - Open Source Content
Management" />
```

The information generated by this statement is of little or no interest to the person looking at the Web site. Its purpose is to help people search the Web more easily and to find out how many pages were created with Joomla! and where they can be found.

Document title

```
<title>Joomla!</title>
```

The document title (`title`) is one of the most important pieces of information in the document head. The browser displays it at the very top of the browser bar and tells the user where he or she currently is. It should be descriptive and clearly worded because, for example, this document title is the first thing a blind person will hear when surfing with the appropriate software.

For Google it also has special significance. If someone searches for a specific term, Google first looks for Web sites that have this term in the URL. Then the search engine uses the contents of the document title and later the actual content of the site.

Joomla! generates the document titles dynamically. Depending on whether you have enabled or disabled search engine–friendly URLs, the document titles are composed of the page `title`, and the category and/or the heading of the article. In version 1.6 you can set this document title for each menu item individually—a new feature that many developers will certainly appreciate.

RSS Feeds

Joomla! makes the contents of a page available as RSS (Really Simple Syndication) feeds as well. It is done in the index.html file by the statements:

```
<link
 href="/joomlabuch_installation/index.php?format=feed&amp;type=rss"
 rel="alternate" type="application/rss+xml" title="RSS 2.0" />
```

and:

```
<link
 href="/joomlabuch_installation/index.php?format=feed&amp;type=atom"
 rel="alternate" type="application/atom+xml" title="Atom 1.0" />
```

RSS is a platform-independent, XML-based format that exchanges information in a very simple way. Unlike HTML pages, RSS files are structured purely logically. Content is output without any formatting and can be taken over by other applications depending on how you want to use it.

With RSS readers you can simply subscribe to news from different providers in an application. You can find an overview of different RSS readers at *http://blogspace.com/rss/readers*.

Atom is also a platform-independent, XML-based, exchange format in competition to be the successor to RSS. Whereas the contents of the RSS feed can contain pure text and HTML without having to specify clearly that it is HTML, Atom offers the option of marking contents as HTML code. The advantage is that the processing program knows what it is dealing with and can react accordingly.

Favicon

The favicon referenced in the following link is also added automatically. It appears as the little icon next to the URL in the browser address bar:

```
<link href="/joomlabuch_installation/templates/beez_20/favicon.ico"
 rel="shortcut icon" type="image/vnd.microsoft.icon" />
```

Integrating CSS and JavaScript

Each template needs one or more CSS files to design its content. Almost all modern sites also integrate JavaScript or whole JavaScript libraries to enable certain behavior of individual elements. The following statement integrates the CSS file layout.css, which is located in the CSS folder:

```
<link rel="stylesheet" href="<?php echo
 $this->baseurl ?>/templates/beez_20/css/layout.css"
 type="text/css" media="screen,projection" />
```

This statement does the same as those you may have used to call external CSS files in static Web sites. The only difference is that it uses PHP variables to create the right address to the CSS file. The following code always references the current base path of the relevant Joomla! installation, which makes the template more flexible:

```
$this->baseurl
```

If you integrate JavaScript files, you will also use this code. Here's an example from an early Beez template:

```
<script type="text/javascript" src="<?php echo $this->baseurl ?>
 /templates/beez_20/javascript/hide.js"></script>
```

You simply refer to the template via the template name. If you like, you can also use the Joomla! variable $this->template, which is particularly useful if your template is also intended to serve as a pattern for other templates. The current Beez templates use this variable so that if you copy the file to use as a base for your template, you don't need to change the folder name to your template folder name.

```
<link rel="stylesheet" href="<?php echo
 $this->baseurl ?>/templates/<?php echo
 $this->template; ?>/css/layout.css"
 type="text/css" media="screen,projection" />
```

Integrating MooTools

MooTools is a JavaScript framework with a multitude of functions that can save you a lot of work when programming your own scripts (see Chapter 6, "MooTools").

The MooTools framework is not exactly small, so loading it does not make sense if you do not really need it. But if you do want to use it in your template, you can easily do so by inserting a line of PHP code:

```
<?php JHtml::_('behavior.framework', true); ?>
```

You may still remember this statement:

```
JHTML::_('behavior.mootools')
```

It has now been replaced by `<?php JHtml::_('behavior.framework', true); ?>`.

Reading Direction from Right to Left

As mentioned previously, Joomla! can manage multilingual content. Depending on the target group and area of use, it can be necessary to optimize your template and its display for use, say, in Arabic-speaking countries. For designers from the West, this is not easy, because in most cases, you cannot actually read what you can see. We are so formed by our Western direction of reading that our creativity can desert us in such cases.

If you need to adapt your CSS for a right-to-left language, it can sometimes help to place a mirror in front of the monitor so you can get a feel for the proportions.

Technically, the integration is simple: the Joomla! framework automatically provides the currently used reading direction in the variable $this->direction. You just have to fetch it and then adjust accordingly.

```
<?php if ($this->direction == 'rtl') : ?>
<link rel="stylesheet" href="<?php echo
 $this->baseurl ?>/templates/beez_20/css/template_rtl.css"
 type="text/css" />
<?php endif; ?>
```

And Off We Go: The Body

The basic framework of our template is still the HTML code that we determine. It is the basis for the organization of the content and, together with the CSS files, determines the visual design.

You can build your HTML here as you are used to and use dynamic content only in certain places. With PHP you can deal with the presence of certain elements and page components and then adapt the source code accordingly. A number of templates use this option because it is significantly more flexible.

So what can be dynamically inserted?

- The actual content (the Joomla! component)
- Modules
- Error messages/system notices

Perhaps I should add a quick side note on how components and modules actually differ: while both are extensions, components are significantly more complex and have a lot more program logic. Modules are usually responsible for outputting some content. The exception is the login, because it expects input.

As mentioned before,

```
<jdoc:include.... />
```

is part of the Joomla! internal language range and integrates both components and modules.

```
<jdoc:include type="component" />
```

is of central importance and integrates the actual content. Depending on the menu structure, the text content can be output here (com_content) or, for example, in the form of the contact component.

The statement type="component" may be used only once in a file.

With the following statement you can integrate modules:

```
<jdoc:include type="modules" name="position-12" />
```

This code loads all modules to be displayed on position-12.

Integrating modules is discussed in Chapter 13, "Modules—Dynamics within the Presentation."

The last types of dynamic content that can be added are the error messages and notices. Anyone who uses Joomla! will certainly have come across error messages or notices. If not, try logging in to the front end with an incorrect password. You will see a screen similar to that shown in Figure 10.1.

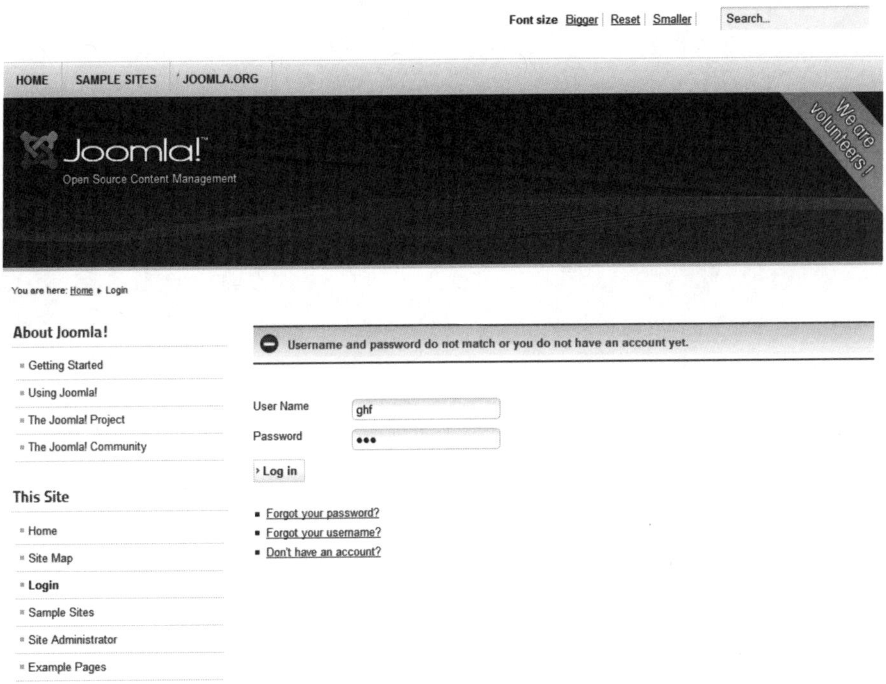

Figure 10.1   Notice displayed when using an incorrect password

You will see an error message. The following statement is responsible for the error message:

```
<jdoc:include type="message" />
```

The visual design of the error messages is done using CSS. The CSS instructions can be found in the general.css file of the included templates. You can easily inspect them with Firebug and adapt them as you wish. For more information, see Chapter 15, "The System Template: Adapting and Modifying Output."

The XML File and the Template Parameters

The templateDetails.xml file is a central part of the template. All content is deposited here in XML format. Without this XML file, a template would not run. In principle, it is something like a table of contents for your template. Among other information, it contains the name of the template, its author, the license, the files it contains, the module positions, a brief description, and of course the template parameters. If this file is missing, the template cannot be installed later.

Template parameters significantly increase the flexibility of templates. For example, they enable you to choose between different display versions of the same template without having to create different templates. If you want to develop your own template later, the easiest method is to adapt one of the existing templates according to your wishes. One of the first steps necessary to do so is adapting the XML files, which is described in the following section.

templateDetails.xml: General Information

Joomla! uses the XML format to automatically integrate content into the system. XML is a markup language, similar to HTML, with which you can manage, hierarchically, structured content. The names of the structuring elements are not predefined as with HTML but rather can be chosen freely. The naming of the structuring elements described in the following are part of the Joomla! defaults and should not be changed.

XML is less error tolerant than HTML. Anything you open also needs to be closed again. A missing closing element or other syntax error invariably results in an error notice.

Please open templatedetails.xml of the beez_20 template. You will find the file under templates/beez_20/templateDetails.xml.

Right at the top, you can see the XML prologue, which simply records the XML version and character set used. Leave this section unchanged:

```
<?xml version="1.0" encoding="utf-8"?>
```

Next comes the Joomla! internal document type, which contains instructions on the file structure:

```
<!DOCTYPE install PUBLIC "-//Joomla! 2.5//DTD template 1.0//EN"
 "http://www.joomla.org/xml/dtd/1.6/template-install.dtd">
```

Then the type of the extension is defined:

```
<extension
 version="2.5"
 type="template"
 client="site">
```

As you can see, it is an extension for version 2.5. The attribute `type` informs you that it is a template, and `client="site"` tells you it is a frontend template.

XML documents are nested, just like HTML documents. You can see that at the end of the file, `</extension>` is closed again. Then the following statements are embedded in it:

```
<name>beez_20</name>
<creationDate>25 November 2009</creationDate>
<author>Angie Radtke</author>
<authorEmail>a.radtke@derauftritt.de</authorEmail>
<authorUrl>http://www.der-auftritt.de</authorUrl>
<copyright>Copyright (C) 2005 - 2012 Open Source Matters, Inc. All
[ca]rights reserved.</copyright>
<license>GNU General Public License version 2 or later; see
[ca]LICENSE.txt</license>
<version>2.5.0</version>
<description>TPL_BEEZ2_XML_DESCRIPTION</description>
```

The preceding statements define the following information:

- Name
- Creation date
- Author's e-mail
- Copyright
- License
- Version
- Description

All this information is output in the Template Manager in the back end. Have a go and change the author of the template to Author, just for fun, and then save the file. If you now go to beez_20 in the Template Manager in the back end and look at the details listed there, you will see that Author is now listed instead of my name (see example in Figure 11.1). Isn't that easy?

```
<author>Author</author>
```

Customizing Template Names

But watch out! If you think that it's now just as easy to change the name of the template, then you are not quite right. See what happens if you try to change:

```
<name>beez_20</name>
```

to:

```
<name>your_name</name>
```

At first, nothing at all happens, neither in the front end nor in the back end. If you had done the same in version 1.5, the template would no longer have been able to run in the front end. This does not happen in the new version. This change in behavior is due to a change in version 1.6. From this version forward, the templates themselves are written into the database. In version 1.5 they were still integrated into the system via the file system.

If you want to make beez_20 run under your name, you need to do go to the folder Your Installation/templates and rename the folder beez_20 to your name. Ensure that all files of the template are closed, otherwise the file cannot be renamed.

Then go to the front end. You will get the error message "The template for this display is not available," as shown in Figure 11.2.

The reason for this error is that the Joomla! internal database has not yet recognized your template, and the system is still looking for a template with the name beez_20. You need to ensure that your template is actually saved in the database by opening the Extension Manager in the back end, going to the Discover tab, and clicking on the Discover icon, which will look for any uninstalled extensions. The result is shown in Figure 11.3.

Figure 11.1   Edited author

Error
  • **The template for this display is not available. Please contact a Site administrator.**

Joomla!

Congratulations! You have a Joomla site! Joomla makes it easy to build a website just the way you want it and keep it simple to update and maintain.

Joomla is a flexible and powerful platform, whether you are building a small site for yourself or a huge site with hundreds of thousands of visitors. Joomla is open source, which means you can make it work just the way you want it to.

Beginners

If this is your first Joomla! site or your first web site, you have come to the right place. Joomla will help you get your website up and running quickly and easily.

Start off using your site by logging in using the administrator account you created when you installed Joomla.

Read more: Beginners

Upgraders

If you are an experienced Joomla! 1.5 user, this Joomla site will seem very familiar. There are new templates and improved user interfaces, but most functionality is the same. The biggest changes are improved access control (ACL) and nested categories. This release of Joomla has strong continuity with Joomla! 1.7 while adding enhancements.

Read more: Upgraders

Professionals

Joomla! 2.5 continues development of the Joomla Framework and CMS as a powerful and flexible way to bring your vision of the web to reality. With the administrator now fully MVC, the ability to control its look and the management of extensions is now complete.

Read more: Professionals

Figure 11.2   Error message

Figure 11.3   Discover and Install

Then you need to install the template. Select the template by checking the checkbox for the template and then click on the Install button in the top right corner. The installation process will save the template with the new name in the database.

Before it will work in the front end, you need to take care of a few more things. Open the Template Manager in the back end and navigate to the styles. You will find your style there. Now you need to tell Joomla! that this is going to be the default style. To do this, enable the checkbox in front of it and click on Make default at the top right. Then click on the name itself to go to the configuration of this style.

As you can see in Figure 11.4, the parameters on the right are empty except for the top two, and the labels are strangely written in capital letters. This is because Joomla! can no longer find the associated language file for the translation because you have renamed the template. More on this later.

Be creative and try to fill in the fields, then save the style. This should not be too difficult because you can see from the cryptic labels which information you need to enter here. Once you finish, these values will also be saved in the database.

Now you need to think about how to name your CSS and JavaScript files. In older versions of Joomla! none of your CSS or JavaScript files would be named because they would still be naming the beez_20 files.

If you go to the front end and look at the source code there, you will see that the path to the CSS and JavaScript files matches your template name. This is determined by the name of the template (`$this->template`). If you were copying a template that specified a particular name, instead of looking to see what the current template was and using that, then you would need to change the template name to your new one.

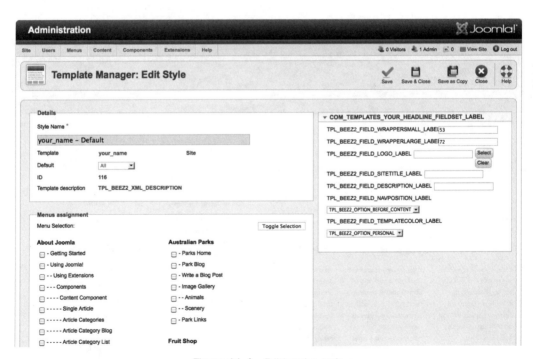

Figure 11.4   Editing the style

You can see this in the index.php file in your renamed folder (templates/your_name/index.php). Here is an example:

```
<link rel="stylesheet" href="<?php echo
$this->baseurl ?>/templates/<?php echo
$this->template; ?>/css/<?php echo htmlspecialchars($color); ?>.css"
type="text/css" />
```

You now have beez_20 running under the different name. There are still some small display errors related to the use of the language files (see Figure 11.5).

If you want to fix this problem quickly, just go to the language folder of the template (templates/your_name/language) and rename the language files.

```
en-GB.tpl_beez_20.ini
en-GB.tpl_beez_20.sys.ini
```

should be renamed to

```
en-GB.tpl_your_name.ini
en-GB.tpl_ your_name.sys.ini
```

If you have carried out all the steps correctly, it should all be working now.

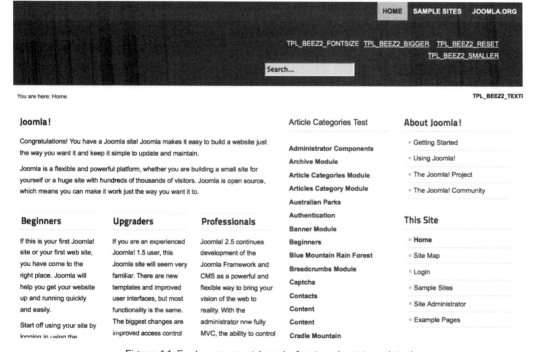

Figure 11.5   Language strings in front end not translated

Here is a summary of the individual steps.

1. Customize the names in the XML file.
2. Rename the template folder.
3. Execute Discover and Install in the Extension Manager.
4. Make the template style the default style.
5. Select parameters to enable them.
6. Adapt the path to CSS and JavaScript files in index.php if necessary.
7. Rename the language files.

Integrating Files and Folders

To install your template properly, Joomla! needs to know what folders and files your template has. In older versions, you had to list every single file individually, even when it was in a folder. Depending on the size of the template, this task could be quite laborious. Now it is no longer necessary. You only need to list the folders and files in the root directory. Joomla! detects the rest itself.

```
<files>
<folder>css</folder>
<folder>html</folder>
<folder>images</folder>
<folder>javascript</folder>
<folder>fonts</folder>
<folder>language</folder>
<filename>index.html</filename>
<filename>index.php</filename>
<filename>templateDetails.xml</filename>
<filename>template_preview.png</filename>
<filename>template_thumbnail.png</filename>
<filename>favicon.ico</filename>
<filename>component.php</filename>
<filename>error.php</filename>
</files>
```

As you can see, the information is listed in the <extension> element in the <files> element. There is an element, <folder>, where you can specify the individual folders, and the element <filename> with which you can mark the individual files.

Defining Module Positions

The module positions used by Joomla! are also defined here:

```
<positions>
...
<position>position-10</position>
<position>position-11</position>
```

```
<position>position-12</position>
<position>position-13</position>
<position>position-14</position>
</positions>
```

The element `<positions>` encloses the actual module positions. Within `<position>` you can then insert your desired name, which will later be listed automatically in the Module Manager in the back end.

Chapter 13, "Modules—Dynamics within the Presentation," explains in more detail how to use the module positions.

The Language Files

The path to the language files is very important for the installation so that the system can later integrate these files correctly. When you customized the template name, you also renamed the language files. Now you should do this here too:

```
<languages folder="language">
<language tag="en-GB">en-GB/en-GB.tpl_beez_20.ini</language>
<language tag="en-GB">en-GB/en-GB.tpl_beez_20.sys.ini</language>
</languages>
<languages folder="language">
<language tag="en-GB">en-GB/en-GB.tpl_your_name.ini</language>
<language tag="en-GB">en-GB/en-GB.tpl_your_name.sys.ini</language>
</languages>
```

Template Parameters: config

Template parameters increase the flexibility of templates and make it easier for us to design our templates more dynamically. We reviewed them briefly in Chapter 8, "Now for the Details: A First Look at the Templates"; now let's look at them in more detail.

Before we discuss their actual use, we ought to think about why you might need such parameters in the first place. The simplest case is if you want to offer your template with different color variations. Especially in large Web sites, the need may arise to design different areas of the content in different colors to make it easier for the user to navigate around the site. Or you may want to offer your template for sale and enable your customers to select the color scheme to match their business.

Another reason to use template parameters is to integrate the width of the template as an option. Some clients may prefer a fixed page width, and others prefer flexible widths that adapt to the screen width.

It is also possible that you could directly integrate the logo of the site provider via the template parameters. This makes sense if, for example, a company has a daughter company and both want a joint Web site. You can then assign the daughter company a template style with a different logo.

In beez5 you can even choose between different HTML versions.

We explore this rather technical topic with some practical examples. The first question that arises is, How on earth do the form fields you see in the Template Manager get there, and how can you access their values later? The answers are easier than you might think and clearly show how flexible the template engine of Joomla! really is. This engine is controlled by the file templateDetails.xml.

Let's have a go and look at the structure to start with. All necessary statements are present in the <config> element:

```
<config>
Statements
</config>
```

Like all other elements, the <config> element is a child element of the <extension> element.

So that you can integrate the template parameters, Joomla! offers predefined form fields whose values are automatically saved in the database. This system applies not only to the templates but also to all Joomla! extensions. Wherever form fields appear in the back end, there is an XML file somewhere in which these fields are defined. It is a really simple system, and it makes it easier for programmers to use parameters, because just specifying them here automatically adds them to the Template Style Editor and makes them available for use in the frontend layouts. The following code shows the basic framework that will contain the parameters you want to create:

```
<config>
<fields name="params">
<fieldset name="advanced">

</fieldset>
</fields>
</ config>
```

The following explains the preceding code in more detail. With

```
<fields name="params">
```

you group a set of fieldset statements. The name attribute tells Joomla! how to use the subsequent fields. In this case the name defines them as parameters.

Then there is a fieldset with the name advanced. By using the element fieldset, you can group statements, which then appear under the headline advanced in the back end (see Figure 11.6).

The term *advanced* is not obligatory here: you can choose whichever headline you want. But you should avoid special characters because the system cannot handle them:

```
<fieldset name="YOUR_HEADLINE">
```

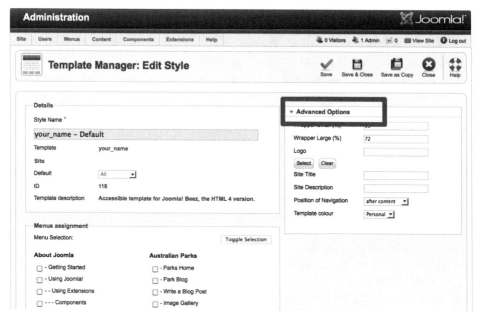

Figure 11.6   Localization of parameters

I used capital letters for the name because it is a translatable language string. In the back end you will see the result, as shown in Figure 11.7.

The name you assigned is integrated into a predefined construct. You can now simply translate it in the language file of your template. For example, go to the English translation of your template (templates/your_name/languages/en-GB_tpl_your_name.ini) and insert the following string at the end:

```
COM_TEMPLATES_YOUR_HEADLINE_FIELDSET_LABEL="Your Headline"
```

Of course, later you can also directly write into any language file. But more on this in Chapter 12, "The Language Files."

If all went well, the result should look like the one shown in Figure 11.8.

Adding Your Own Form Fields and Accessing Them

JForm is a very useful class in the Joomla! framework. It enables you to create your own form fields in the back end very easily.

The values of the fields defined in the XML file are saved directly in the database and are therefore also available in the index.php file of the template. There you can access and work with them accordingly. A simple example is the option of choosing different stylesheets.

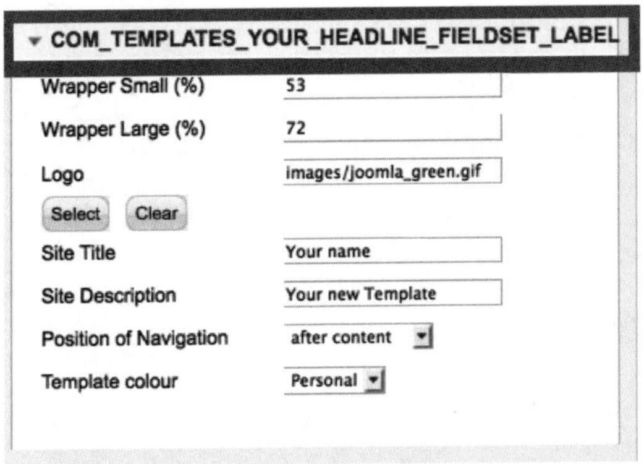

Figure 11.7   Result after changing the name

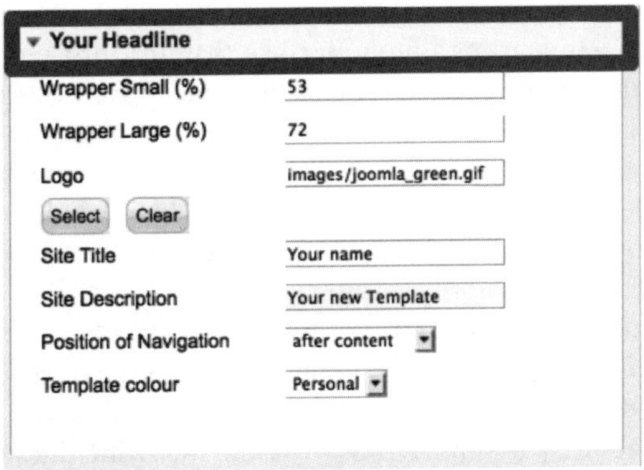

Figure 11.8   Headline after the translation

As previously mentioned, in the beez_20 template you can choose between the Nature and Personal styles. Personal is the default display with the blue header image. Nature is used in the default installation (with example data) for the site of the Australian National Park.

The template now just sees which style is currently selected and then loads the appropriate CSS file.

Open the index.php file of the beez_20 template. You can find it under templates/beez_20/index.php or templates/your_name/index.php. Around line 56 you will find the following statement:

```
<link rel="stylesheet" href="<?php echo
 $this->baseurl ?>/templates/<?php echo
 $this->template; ?>/css/<?php echo htmlspecialchars($color); ?>.css"
 type="text/css" />
```

This is a normal integration of a CSS file, as any Web designer knows it. The only difference is that parts of the path use PHP variables. The name of the file is in the PHP variable $color; it is output there with echo.

If you go to the front end and look at the source text of the site, you will see a classic call of a CSS file:

```
<link rel="stylesheet"
 href="/joomlabook_installation/templates/your_name/css/personal.css"
 type="text/css" />
```

or respectively,

```
<link rel="stylesheet"
 href="/joomlabook_installation/templates/your_name/css/nature.css"
 type="text/css" />
```

The value of the variable is not output just like that. It is first sent through the PHP filtering function htmlspecialchars(). This function converts special characters into HTML codes. This is not absolutely necessary here, as the value comes from a preset checkbox, so you can be fairly sure that the template user has not inserted any special characters. If the values came from a non-preset text field, it would be a different story. But now the question is where the variable $color comes from. It gets a bit more technical now, but don't worry, it's not that hard.

In the template, the Joomla! framework offers the global object $this. This object contains quite a lot of data regarding the template, including information on the template parameters, the site title, the site name, and the language used. If you want to find out exactly what it's all about, you can try this: write the following line somewhere into the index.php file of your template, maybe directly before the doctype to make it clearer:

```
<?php var_dump($this) ;?>
```

Then go to the start page. You will see that the entire object with all its values is output. Our params are a component of this object:

```
public 'params' =>
object(JRegistry)[476]
protected 'data' =>
object(stdClass)[477]
public 'wrapperSmall' => int 53
public 'wrapperLarge' => int 72
public 'logo' => string 'images/joomla_green.gif' (length=23)
public 'sitetitle' => string 'Your name' (length=8)
public 'sitedescription' => string 'Your new Template'
(length=18)
public 'navposition' => string 'left' (length=4)
public 'templatecolor' => string 'personal' (length=8)
```

Now you can access these parameters via the function get() by passing it the name of the parameter:

```
$color = $this->params->get('templatecolor');
```

Here I assigned the value of the currently selected template CSS style to the variable and can simply output its value, if I need it, with <?php echo $color; ?>. You can access all other template parameters via the same mechanism.

Adding Form Elements

To keep the parameters of the template dynamic, we have a range of form elements available that can be integrated easily and simply. Following are the elements that are really significant for developing a template.

- type="text": simple text fields
- type="list": select boxes
- type="radio": radio buttons
- type="media" : display and selection in the Media Manager
- type="spacer": optical separator

Other useful elements are:

- type="folderlist"
- type="editor"
- type="menuitem"
- type="timezone"
- type="modal_article"

You can find a complete overview in libraries/joomla/form/fields.

type="text" Adding Simple Text Fields

A good example for this field type is the site title in the beez_20 template. It is displayed directly below the logo, as you can see in the example in Figure 11.9.

In the XML file you will find:

```
<field name="sitetitle" type="text" default=""
 label="TPL_BEEZ2_FIELD_SITETITLE_LABEL"
 description="TPL_BEEZ2_FIELD_SITETITLE_DESC" filter="string" />
```

The field has the unique name 'sitetitle'. This is mandatory because you use this name later in index.php to access the value of the field.

In this case, that would be:

```
<?php echo $this->params->get('sitetitle'); ?>
```

Figure 11.9   Example of type="text"

The attribute default is empty here, which means no default value is output. You can enter a default value if you wish.

The label is the describing title of the element, which you can see to the left of the input field. The description is the tool tip that shows up when you move the mouse over the label.

You can see that both the description and the title are written in uppercase letters. As you already know, this ensures that your templates can be used in multiple languages.

Figure 11.10 shows the field for entering the site title in the back end.

In addition to the attributes used here, the attributes size, class, autocomplete, filter, and required are also available. With size you can determine how many characters should be saved in the text field. With the class attribute, you can validate the field, via JavaScript, as well as use it for your CSS.

The class attribute can have the following values:

- validate-numeric, which checks if the field has only numeric characters. If not, an error message is displayed.

- validate-email does not make much sense here because it checks whether the entered data is an e-mail address.

Figure 11.10   Site title in the back end

- `validate-username` also makes little sense here because it checks whether the entered value corresponds to the standards for a valid user name.
- `validate-password`, the validation rules for a valid password, is also superfluous here but listed for the sake of completeness.

With `autocomplete` you allow (or disallow) the field to be autocompleted. This is an optional attribute that is used only rarely. Its possible values are:

- `autocomplete="off"`
- `autocomplete="on"`

The `filter` attribute filters the input in accordance with your value. If you use this attribute, the data entered into this field is processed according to the specified filter before the data is saved. The most important possible values are:

- `filter="string"`, which converts the entered data into a string.
- `filter="integer"`, which converts the entered data into a number. If you enter only letters, the field is filled with the value 0. If you enter letters and numbers, the letters are filtered out.
- `filter="alnum"`, which allows both letters and numbers.
- `filter="word"`, which converts the entered data into a word. This means that if you enter, for example, three words, the space between them will be removed, and it will be output as one word.

If you add `required="true"` to your field, the field cannot be empty. It has to contain a value, or else the whole form cannot be saved and the field itself will be bordered in red.

A field that has `type="text"` can also be a `readonly` field. This, of course, makes sense only if you previously assigned it a `default` value. Here is an example of a `readonly` field:

```
<field name="angie" type="text" default="Joomla is great"
 readonly="true"
 label="TPL_BEEZ2_FIELD_ANGIE_LABEL"
 description="TPL_BEEZ2_FIELD_ANGIE_DESC" />
```

type="list": Select Boxes

Sometimes it is necessary to offer fields with different selectable options. This is where select boxes come in handy. At the beginning of the chapter, I mentioned the CSS style options of the Beez template. This selection is realized via such a select box:

```
<field name="templatecolor" type="list" default="nature"
 label="TPL_BEEZ2_FIELD_TEMPLATECOLOR_LABEL"
 description="TPL_BEEZ2_FIELD_TEMPLATECOLOR_DESC" filter="word">
<option value="nature">TPL_BEEZ2_OPTION_NATURE</option>
<option value="personal">TPL_BEEZ2_OPTION_PERSONAL</option>
</field>
```

Just as with the `type="text"` field, the `type="list"` field has a unique `name`. It has a `default` value of nature, as well as `label` and `description` attributes. The `filter` word does not really make much sense here. Perhaps someone thought it best to be on the safe side (it wasn't me), because the value of the select box is fixed and defined in the `options` and cannot be changed by the user. Such a select box always has to have at least one `option`. The value of the variable to be processed is determined in the `value` attribute of the `option` element and is mandatory. The language string within the `option` element is only responsible for the readability of the value.

type="radio" Radio Buttons

Using radio buttons makes sense if you want to offer several options from which the user can choose only one. This is recommended for yes-or-no questions. You could imagine the following scenario for using radio buttons within a template:

Do you want to display the logo? Yes/No

The corresponding field would look like this:

```
<field name="displaylogo"
 type="radio" default="1"
 label=" TPL_BEEZ2_FIELD_DISPLAYLOGO_LABEL "
 description="TPL_BEEZ2_FIELD_DISPLAYLOGO_DESC">
<option value="0">JNO</option>
<option value="1">JYES</option>
</field>
```

where the `default` value is set to 1 and therefore *yes*. In the index.php file, you can access its value with

```
$this->params->get(' displaylogo ');
```

and respond accordingly.

type="media" Display and Selection from the Media Manager

This type is the really useful kind. It opens the Media Manager directly and allows you to choose an image from there. You can view its use in the Beez template, as shown in Figures 11.11 and 11.12.

The following code creates a media type parameter called `logo` that lets you select an image and/or upload an image file from your computer:

```
<field name="logo" type="media" label="TPL_BEEZ2_FIELD_LOGO_LABEL"
 description="TPL_BEEZ2_FIELD_LOGO_DESC" />
```

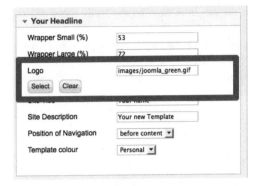

Figure 11.11   Selecting logo in Beez template

Figure 11.12   The opened Media Manager

type="spacer" Optical Separator

The spacer is basically nothing other than a separator between the individual parameters. This separator can either be a visual line or any text that you specify.

The following code merely inserts a horizontal line:

```
<field name="separator" type="spacer" class="spacer" hr="true" />
```

If you were to omit the attribute hr="true", only the word separator would be inserted.

But this method would not necessarily be the right one to insert text, because the name="separator" could then not be translated.

With the corresponding label, you can easily have the text translated in the language files, as shown in Figure 11.13.

```
<field name="spacer1" type="spacer" class="text"
 label=" TPL_BEEZ2_FIELD_SEPARATOR_LABEL "/>
```

Other Field Types

The following field types can also be useful, depending on your project.

- type="filelist" lists files from a predefined folder in a select box.
  Code: <field name="filelist" type="filelist" directory="images" />

- type="folderlist" lists folders within the specified folder in a select box.
  Code: <field name="myfolder" type="folderlist" directory="images" />

- type="editor" integrates a text area with the default editor.
  Code: <field name="mytextarea" type="editor" />
  Example attributes: filter="safehtml", buttons="false", editor="none", rows="3", cols="40", default="", label="MYAREA", description="MYAREADESCRIPTION"

- type="menuitem" creates a select box with the existing menu items.
  Code: <field name="mymenuitems" type="menuitem" />

- type="timezone" creates a select box with the available time zones.
  Code: <field name="mytimezone" type="timezone" />

Figure 11.13   Spacer text

12

The Language Files

It is frequently a requirement to offer a Web site in several languages. We touched on this topic briefly in earlier chapters. Now let's learn more about the language files.

If you want to offer your template in several languages, you have the option of defining language constants in both the front end and the back end so that they can be translated into several languages. Examples of these constants, which are often called *language strings*, are "Next" and "Prev," used in pagination.

In the back end you will find language strings in the XML file of the template.

In the Beez template are invisible skip links and subheadings, which make the navigation within the site easier for people with disabilities. If a template is to be offered in multiple languages, these elements should also be set up as language strings.

But before we get into the details, let's first have a look at how Joomla! solves this problem.

Tip

A new feature in Joomla! is that you can now create content in different languages, both in the articles and in modules, categories, and menu items. This feature is not a replacement for the already existing Joomla! extensions, which are devoted entirely to this topic. But for smaller sites in particular, it is a very useful innovation if, for example, you want to offer only certain parts of the content in another language. If you want to use this feature, you should select the corresponding module for the language selection and enable the relevant plug-in. In the default installation, both are enabled. This has little to do with the language files themselves, which deal with constants; it is only meant to explain to you why it can be necessary to set up your template for multilingual use.

How Joomla! Translates Constants to Multiple Languages

For each extension in Joomla! there are anywhere from one to several language files where corresponding language constants are translated. Generally, you will find them in the system's language folder. This folder contains subfolders that are named after the relevant languages. The naming follows the official Iso Code scheme. Here are some examples.

- en_GB stands for British English.
- de_DE stands for German.
- es_ES stands for Spanish.

The language files of the template should be saved directly in the template itself because then you have everything that has to do with the template combined in one place. This function was not yet available in Joomla! 1.5, where all language files had to be stored in the main language folder. In version 1.6 you can put a language folder in the template itself and in it the corresponding files sorted by language.

If you look at the template you have been creating, you will find only the files for the English language in the template language folder. Go to the directory tree and open the following folder: templates/_your_name/language/en-GB/. This currently contains two files:

- en-GB.tpl_your_name.ini
- en-GB.tpl_your_name.sys.ini

The .ini files contain all the language constants specific to the template, and you will find all language constants used by the system in the sys.ini files. You may remember that you can save a description on your module positions there.

Adding Your Own Languages

Tip

If you open a language file, please use a UTF-8 capable editor; otherwise there will be display problems.

If you already know Joomla! quite well, you know that the language files for the Joomla! default output can be installed via the back end. Let's assume you have decided to use German as your default language.

All available language files can be found at *http://extensions.joomla.org/extensions/languages/translations-for-joomla*.

Once you have installed the German language file and selected German as the default language, you can prepare your template for this new language.

You need to carry out the following steps:

1. Navigate on the file level to the folder templates/_your_name/language and create a folder for the German language in addition to the English folder: templates/_your_name/language/de-DE.

2. Copy the language files from the English language folder into this folder.

3. Translate the language strings used there by replacing the content within the quotation marks accordingly.

Joomla! Conventions for Using Language Strings

To make sure the translation works, you must comply with a few requirements.

- Always write the language constants in uppercase letters.
- Separate the translation from its constant with an equals sign (=).
- Always enclose the translation within quotation marks.
- Avoid using {}, |, &, ~, !, [], (), ^ and the words `Null`, `Yes`, `No`, `True`, `False`, `on`, `off`, and `none`, because they are reserved symbols and expressions.

The constant must not include umlauts.

In addition to these rules, the Joomla! team has also agreed on a convention regarding the content:

```
TPL_BEEZ2_ADDITIONAL_INFORMATION
```

This is not obligatory, but using it makes life a lot easier for all concerned.

If you look at the language files of the Beez template, you will see that all language strings start with `TPL_`. If you read this abbreviation, you can tell right away that it is a template. (The language strings of modules, for example, always start with `mod_com`, and those of components with `com_`.) Next follows the template name and then title. It has become a convention to separate words with an underscore.

Language Files in index.php Using the Examples of Skip Links

You may remember Chapter 2, "Accessibility: What Is It?," in which we discussed the problem people with impaired vision have when trying to navigate a Web site. The content is read out to them or output to the braille display linearly, from top to bottom. Depending on the page structure, it may take a long time to reach content at the lower end of the page.

But on the screen, several areas can start at the top in a three-column layout, and the eye can immediately skip to where it suspects the most interesting information will be (supported by visual clues). Skip links can provide help. They offer a nonvisual counterpart to the graphic layout and enable users or linear display units to identify significant content areas at the beginning of the page. Users can then jump directly to where they expect to find the information they are interested in.

In the index.php file of the Beez template is a list with the skip links to the content area, the navigation, and—if present—the additional information.

Via Cascading Style Sheets, their display is suppressed for visual devices by pushing them outside of the visible area. They will appear in the foreground only when they have the focus: in other words, if they are currently active. This makes it easier for people with vision impairment and for others who, for whatever reason, can navigate only via the keyboard to find their way through your Web site.

```
<ul class="skiplinks">
<li><a href="#main" class="u2">
    <?php echo JText::_('TPL_BEEZ2_SKIP_TO_CONTENT'); ?></a></li>
<li><a href="#nav" class="u2">
    <?php echo JText::_('TPL_BEEZ2_JUMP_TO_NAV'); ?></a></li>
    <?php if($showRightColumn ):?>
<li><a href="#additional" class="u2">
    <?php echo JText::_('TPL_BEEZ2_JUMP_TO_INFO'); ?></a></li>
    <?php endif; ?>
</ul>
```

If you now want to offer a multilingual page, it makes sense to be able to translate the text content of these skip links. As you can see, the actual text content is output via PHP function:

```
<?php echo JText::_('TPL_BEEZ2_SKIP_TO_CONTENT'); ?>
```

The Joomla! method JTEXT::_('STRING') always knows which language is currently enabled and fetches the translation from the appropriate language file. If the corresponding string is not present, it will output whatever is within the round brackets—in our example, TPL_BEEZ2_SKIP_TO_CONTENT.

In the Joomla! configuration you have the option of enabling the function Debug Language. This helps you find missing translations quickly and easily.

Modules—Dynamics within the Presentation

Modules are a central component of Joomla! and are integrated into the page layout in the template's index.php file. They are really nothing more than content elements that can be placed around the actual content. They usually do small dynamic tasks. If you have been using Joomla! for a while, you probably know the number and type of the different modules. Joomla! currently has 23 different module types (in version 1.6) that can be easily integrated into any template.

Some of these modules are almost indispensable to the design and usability of a Web site. The most important module is the one for the navigation, because without it you could not use a Web site. The search field also makes a Web site significantly more usable. For my part, I like to use Most Read Content, especially for large sites, because this way you can direct the attention of new users quickly and easily toward the most interesting topics. But there are many other useful modules. The most important and most widely used modules are probably these:

- Menu
- Search
- Articles - Newsflash
- Articles Category
- Breadcrumbs
- Custom HTML
- Login
- Most Read Content

jdoc:include

This method is available to integrate the modules into the index.php file:

```
<jdoc:include type="modules" name="position-12" />
```

With `jdoc:include` you can integrate not just modules but also the actual content, system messages, or the document head. It is not the statement itself but the value of its attributes that determines what is integrated. The attribute `type` controls what is to be loaded: in this case, the modules. In addition to the `type` attribute, the statement also has a `name` attribute that allows you to clearly allocate the modules.

The name Attribute

Via the module's name, you can control its use—that is, its position—in the template. You can position the statement

```
<jdoc:include type="modules" name="position-12" />
```

anywhere in your index.php file. All modules that are assigned to the position with the name `position-12` will be output in this position. All modules are managed in the Joomla! back end in Extensions → Module Manager. There you can create new modules and assign them to the positions and pages. If you open the Module Manager and create a new module, you can see where you specify the `position` (see Figure 13.1).

This selected position always refers to the `name` attribute of your `jdoc:include` statement in the index.php file. If you leave the position blank in the module, it can't be displayed by a `jdoc` statement.

A new feature in version 1.6 was an overview of the usable module positions in the Module Manager. Sorted by template and with a brief description, you can see all

Figure 13.1   Module Manager

positions listed clearly here. If you click the button Select position, it opens a new window with this useful feature (see Figure 13.2). It is easy to lose track of things, especially with very large pages and many modules, so this feature helps a lot.

The default templates use generic names that tell you nothing about their use: from `position-0` up to `position-xx`. They are very flexible in their use and offer many options. You cannot tell in advance which user will position which module where, so we use generic names. In practice, this method is not very suitable because the names are not meaningful. To avoid losing track of things, you should rename your own templates with more meaningful names, such as `Mainmenu`, `Search`, or `Breadcrumbs`.

The names are stored in the file templateDetails.xml and are available in the back end. Try opening the templateDetails.xml of the template, then insert your own module position and save the document. You will find the positions starting around line 30.

```
<positions>
...
<position>position-10</position>
<position>position-11</position>
<position>position-12</position>
<position>position-13</position>
<position>position-14</position>
<position>mainnavigation</position>
</positions>
```

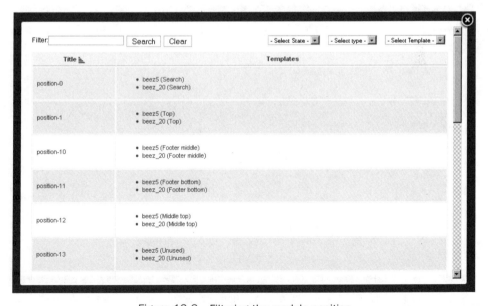

Figure 13.2   Filtering the module position

XML requires well-formed documents and is absolutely not error tolerant. You must make sure that all opening elements are also closed again; otherwise, you will get an error notice in the Module Manager.

Once you have done this, open the Module Manager, and you will see that your position has been added to the already existing positions, as shown in Figure 13.3.

Unfortunately, a corresponding description is missing, such as "horizontal navigation below logo." This information can be added via template-internal language files. The English language file, for example, can be found in the beez_20 template under languages/en-GB/en-GB.tpl_beez20.sys.ini.

Add the following line at the end, and you will see that the explanation (position main menu = horizontal navigation below logo) appears behind the displayed module position, as shown in Figure 13.4.

```
TPL_BEEZ_20_POSITION_MAINNAVIGATION="horizontal navigation below logo"
```

Tip

If this does not work for you, it is probably because you have a duplicate set of English beez_20 language files in the language folder at the root of your installation. For the purposes of this example, delete languages/en-GB/en-GB.tpl_beez20.sys.ini; then you will see the language file in your template folder.

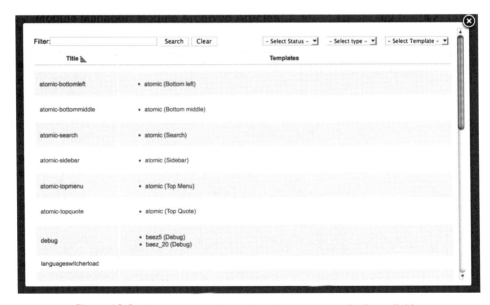

Figure 13.3   The new module position is now automatically available.

Title ≜	Templates
atomic-bottomleft	• atomic (Bottom left)
atomic-bottommiddle	• atomic (Bottom middle)
atomic-search	• atomic (Search)
atomic-sidebar	• atomic (Sidebar)
atomic-topmenu	• atomic (Top Menu)
atomic-topquote	• atomic (Top Quote)
debug	• beez5 (Debug) • beez_20 (Debug)
languageswitcherload	
mainnavigation	• beez_20 (horizontal navigation below logo)

Figure 13.4   The result with visible description

The language files also follow certain rules.

- Language constants should always be written in uppercase.
- The translation is separated from its constants with an equals sign (=).
- The translation is always enclosed by quotation marks.
- Avoid using { }, |, &, ~, !, [], (), ^ and the words Null, Yes, No, True, False, on, off, and none, because they are reserved symbols and expressions.

Tip

You can also create a new position directly via the Module Manager, without writing it into the XML file first. You just need to write it into the field for the position and then save the module. The system remembers this position, and you can use it in the template's index.php file. But watch out—there is a big drawback: if you later want to package your template for installation, this position is missing because it is only saved in the database, not in your XML file.

If you now integrate

```
<jdoc:include type="modules" name="mainnavigation" />
```

into the index.php file of your template, all modules assigned to this position are loaded and output at that place.

The style Attribute and the Default Styles

Modules usually output content. Depending on what you would like to do with this content later and how you want to design it, it can make sense to embed it into HTML code as well, for example, in a div or in a table. The different ways of embedding of modules are called *styles* in Joomla!, probably because you can style them. Please note that these styles initially have nothing to do with the styles from the stylesheet. Instead, they concern the display style of the document on the finished page.

Joomla! has some styles by default:

```
<jdoc:include type="modules" name="mainnavigation" />
```

If you do not specify any particular style, the module is output without surrounding HTML code. The module heading is not displayed either, even if it is set to visible in the module:

```
<jdoc:include type="modules" name="mainnavigation style="none" />
```

Once again, you get the same effect: the pure module is output.

div.moduletable

```
<jdoc:include type="modules" name="mainnavigation style="xhtml" />
```

If you choose style="xhtml", you surround the module with a div element with the class moduletable. The module headline, if enabled, is output above the module content as a third-level heading (h3).

```
<div class="moduletable">
<h3> Headline</h3>
Module content
</div>
```

Rounded Corners

```
<jdoc:include type="modules" name="mainnavigation" style="rounded" />
```

For a while there was nothing cooler in Web design than rounded corners. To integrate them in a standard conforming way without using CSS3, you need to use four divs, which have background images added and surround the module. These four surrounding div elements are always required if you are using a flexible width and want to have the boxes grow simultaneously with the font when the font size is enlarged.

You can find plenty of general instructions on how to do this on the Web. For example, have a look at *www.devWebpro.com/25-rounded-corners-techniques-with-css*.

When using style="rounded", the module is output in this form:

```
<div class="module myclass">
<div>
<div>
<div>
<h3>Headline</h3> Module content
</div>
</div>
</div>
</div>
```

With this HTML frame you have everything you need (and even a bit more) for displaying the rounded corners with background images.

Nowadays you can create rounded corners beautifully with CSS3. Unfortunately, not all browsers support this function yet. Once again, Internet Explorer (through version 8) does not play along. For Firefox, Safari, and Opera, the solution is easy:

```
.myclass
{
-webkit-border-radius: 4px; // Safari
-moz-border-radius: 4px; // Firefox
border-radius: 4px; // CSS3 Standard
}
```

To get Internet Explorer into line, you need to work a bit harder. Fortunately, CSS3 Pie can help. Pie is the abbreviation for Progressive Internet Explorer and is nothing more than a JavaScript that expands Internet Explorer by the missing functions. To find out more, go to *http://css3pie.com*.

Perhaps you would like to have a table around the actual module output? That is possible, too. The line

```
<jdoc:include type="modules" name="mainnavigation" style="table" />
```

outputs the following code:

```
<table cellpadding="0" cellspacing="0" class="moduletable myclass">
<tr>
<th>headline</th>
</tr>
```

```
<tr>
<td> Module content</td>
</tr>
</table>
```

At least the headline is within a `th`. This display method is hardly used today. It is a relic from the past.

Beez Styles

In the Beez template I have tried to demonstrate what you can do with the styles. In Joomla! version 1.5, the style `beezDivision` enabled you to control the heading hierarchy of the modules. This was and still is a simple application that will help explain the functionality of the Chrome concept rather well. Other styles are `beezTabs` and `beezHide`.

The term *Chrome*, in this context, is a metaphor for diversity (in the sense of multi-chrome, perhaps). Diversity is exactly what the concept is all about: being able to design the output of the modules yourself in many different ways. It is not just the surrounding HTML code that you can change. The contents of the modules can also be manipulated. Using the example of the style `beezDivision`, I explain this concept in more detail.

The Problem

If you choose the style `XHTML` for a module, the module heading is automatically output as a third-level heading (`h3`). This may not make sense in the semantic structure of your page: sometimes you may prefer to have an `h1` or even an `h6`. Of course, you can eventually solve this manually, but it is easier and more comfortable if you write your own style.

The Solution

The HTML file of the template is responsible for outputting the template-specific code. In the HTML folder of the Beez template, there is a file named modules.php. The contents of this file are processed by the Joomla! framework, and the module output is influenced directly. The line:

```
<jdoc:include type="modules" name="mainnavigation"
 style="beezDivision" headerLevel="5" />
```

calls the function `modChrome_beezDivision()` in modules.php and renders the module accordingly.

As you can see, the module `jdoc::` now has the attribute `headerLevel` added to it. The value of the attribute corresponds to the desired heading hierarchy. This approach shows that the attributes of the methods are not fixed. You can expand them as you wish and then access them later in the corresponding PHP function.

The attribute `headerLevel` is passed to the function as a parameter and is then available within the function.

If you would like to write your own function, it is important that your function name always starts with modChrome_. The name of the style is simply added to the back of the name with an underscore: modChrome_*yourFunctionname*.

The approach is enough to make the new style come into effect. The entire function then looks like this:

```
function modChrome_beezDivision($module, &$params, &$attribs)
{
$headerLevel = isset($attribs['headerLevel']) ?
↪(int) $attribs['headerLevel']: 3;
if (!empty ($module->content)) { ?>
<div class="moduletable<?php echo
 htmlspecialchars($params-> get('moduleclass_sfx')); ?>">
<?php if ($module->showtitle)
{ ?> <h<?php echo $headerLevel; ?>> </h<?php echo $headerLevel; ?>>
<?php }; ?>
<?php echo $module->content; ?></div>
<?php };
}
```

The method joc:include makes sure that the function is given the attributes and the module with all its properties.

Within the function you can then access the attributes with $attribs and the module with $module. The $attribs is an array of values within a variable. $module is an object whose properties you can access with ->.

If you would like to know which properties this object has, you can find out by using var_dump($module).

But let's get back to the function itself. The first line of the code ensures (if there is no attribute headerLevel) that the level is set to the default value 3; in other words, that the headings are still output as third-level headings (h3). Then it is verified whether the module has content at all. If yes, a div container with the heading and the actual content is output. Done!

beezTabs

With the style beezTabs, all modules loaded on that position are automatically arranged in tabs. Tabs are usually helpful in structuring content clearly, as seen in Figure 13.5.

Previously, you needed additional modules to make this display type possible.

If you want to present content in tabs, you have the big task of accessibility in designing the output of the HTML code. The modules offered are generally not usable for people with impaired vision in particular. Beez Tabs relies on the new Web Accessibility Initiative–Accessible Rich Internet Applications (WAI-ARIA) technology to provide greater accessibility.

```
<jdoc:include type="modules" name="mainnavigation"
 style="beezTabs" headerLevel="2" id="3" state=0 />
```

Figure 13.5   Presenting modules within tabs

BeezHide

BeezHide enables you to initially display only the heading (as in Figure 13.6) and then show the module content by clicking on the heading (see Figure 13.7). beezHide is also based on WAI-ARIA.

```
<jdoc:include type="modules" name="position-4"
 style="beezHide" headerLevel="3" state="0 " />
```

Both styles are discussed in more detail in Chapter 17, "The Default Templates and Their Features."

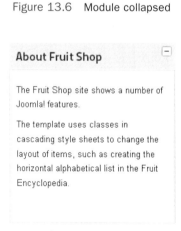

Figure 13.6   Module collapsed

Figure 13.7   Module open

Integrating the Module Flexibly into the Layout

One of the dynamic features of Joomla! is the use of modules. They are integrated in the index.php file at the place where they are intended to go within the markup.

Imagine you want to implement a three-column layout. The navigation is in the left column, the actual content in the middle, and important additional information in the right column (see Figure 13.8).

The contents of the right column are put together from the modules Articles - Newsflash and Most Read Content. Now you want to assign these modules not to all subpages but only to individual areas. In such cases and depending on the structure of index.php, the right column would then be empty:

```
<div id="navigation">
Navigation
</div>
<div id="content">
Content </div>
<div id="information">
<jdoc:include type="modules" name="right" style="xhtml" />
</div>
```

But it would be better if the right column disappeared and the content was stretched over the whole available width. You would need the three columns to become two columns:

```
<div id="navigation">
Navigation
</div>
<div id="content">
Content
</div>
```

This can be achieved using the function countModules().

Via the function $this->countModules('right'), you can check whether a module is output in the specified position. If so, the number of modules is output; otherwise the return value is 0.

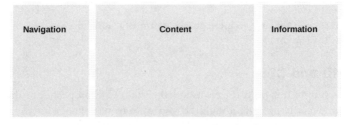

Figure 13.8   Three-column design

Tip

PHP always interprets the value 0 in an `if` statement as false!

With this information, you now have the option of only displaying the right column if it does indeed have content in it:

```
<?php if ($this->countModules('right')): ?>
<div id="information">
<jdoc:include type="modules" name="right" style="xhtml" />
</div>
<?php endif; ?>
```

If you want to have this kind of check more frequently in your index.php file, you can also use a more elegant solution. To do this, at the very top of index.php, define the following variable:

```
$showinformation=$this->countModules('right');
```

and then access this variable only within the HTML code:

```
<?php if ($showinformation): ?>
<div id="information">
<jdoc:include type="modules" name="right" style="xhtml" />
</div>
<?php endif; ?>
```

In the rarest cases, you would position only one module in the right column:

```
<?php if ($this->countModules('right')): ?>
<div id="information">
<jdoc:include type="modules" name="right" style="xhtml" />
<jdoc:include type="modules" name="right2" style="xhtml" />
</div>
<?php endif; ?>
```

To get the same effect, you now need to check both variables:

```
$showinformation=($this->countModules('right') or $this->
countModules('right2'));
```

Adapting ID and CSS

With a three-column design, you have assigned certain CSS properties to the content area—for example, it has a certain width. If you were to not change anything in the CSS now, you would end up with a big gap where the right column used to be. To close this gap, you need to ensure that the content area stretches over the whole width. To achieve this, assign it another `id` and format it accordingly with CSS.

We can use the variable `$showinformation` to assign the `id` within the `div` element dynamically:

```
<div id="<?php echo $showinformation ?
↪'content': 'contentmaxwidth'; ?>"
```

If the right column is not present, this code snippet sets the `id` to `content`. Otherwise, it sets it to `contentmaxwidth`.

Via this `id`, you can now format appropriately in the CSS.

The Module Class Suffix

The customized formatting of individual page areas is one of the most important tasks of the template designer. To provide the flexibility necessary for this design, Joomla! offers integration of individual CSS classes for the modules. This principle is also present in the formatting of the actual content.

With all modules, you will find the tab Advanced Options in the administration interface in the back end (see Figure 13.9). Here you can make individual entries in the text field Module Class Suffix. The suffix you enter is saved by Joomla! and automatically appended to the classes of the predefined HTML elements.

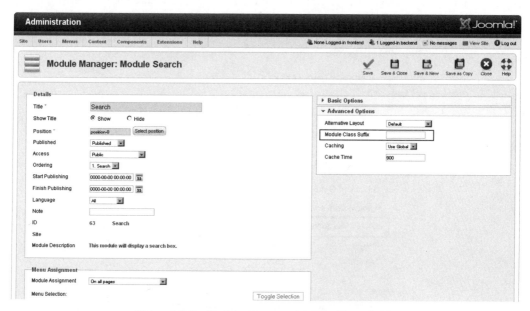

Figure 13.9   Module Manager, Module Class Suffix

The elements this suffix is ultimately appended to depends on:

- the module used and
- the style by which it is integrated into the page.

You may recall that if you add a module with the style `style="xhtml"` or the beez style `style="beezDivision"`, it is automatically enclosed by a `div` container with the class `moduletable`:

```
<div class="moduletable">
<h3> Headline</h3>
Module content
</div>
```

If you assign a suffix in the Module Manager, it is automatically appended to the class `moduletable`. The result looks like this:

```
<div class="moduletablemysuffix">
<h3> Headline</h3>
Module content
</div>
```

This approach allows you to choose your individual formatting via CSS.

In Chapter 3, "CSS and HTML—Getting the Basic Structure into Shape," I mentioned that it is also possible to assign two different classes to an element. This method allows you to assign general properties in the first class and define the particularities in the second class. It is simple and easy to do. Just make sure you insert a space before the actual text within the module in the field for the suffix, as shown in Figure 13.10.

The result looks like this:

```
<div class="moduletable mysuffix">
<h3> Headline</h3>
Module content
</div>
```

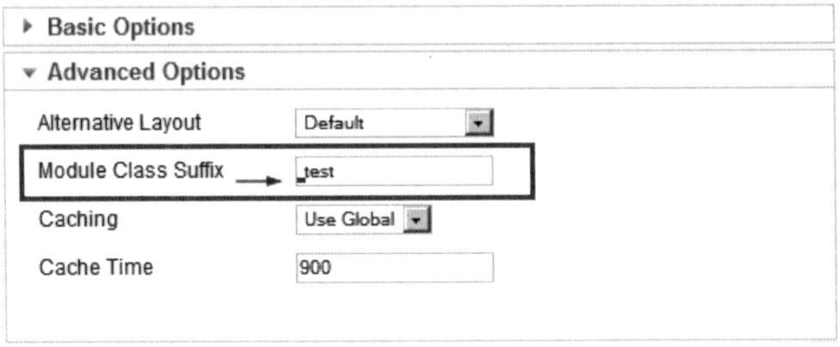

Figure 13.10   Space before the suffix

This suffix affects not only the surrounded `div` element provided by the selected style but also the HTML elements that are provided by the modules.

Generally, we always append this class to the first element of the module output, so the element encloses the actual module content. At first glance, this seems to produce an unnecessary duplication. But if you integrate the module without a surrounding `div` element—in other words, without a style—you still have the option of individually formatting it.

Perhaps a specific example will make it easier to understand. Try adding the module Articles Category to your page via the Module Manager and then add a suffix. Next choose a position that uses the style `xhtml`. In the Joomla! default installation, this can be `position-6`. Save the module. Then use Firebug to look at the generated source code. You will see this result:

```
<div class="moduletablesuffix">
<h3>News</h3>
<ul class="category-modulesuffix">
<li> ... </li>
<li> ... </li>
</ul>
</div>
```

If you now set the used style in the template's index.php to `none`, the surrounding `div` element and the module heading will have disappeared.

```
<jdoc:include type="modules" name="position-6" style="none" />
```

The result is:

```
<ul class="category-modulesuffix">
<li> ... </li>
<li> ... </li>
</ul>
```

Via the class of the list, you still have the option to format your CSS files individually. For example:

```
.category-modulesuffix ul li
{background:#000}
```

Joomla! offers you a multitude of different module types. Table 13.1 provides a list of all modules with the elements that can have a suffix added to them.

Table 13.1 **Core Modules Showing Where Added Class Suffixes Will Be Added**

File	Element
Module Archived Articles: `mod _ articles _ archive`	
`default.php`	`<ul class="archive-module<?php echo $moduleclass_sfx; ?>">`
Module Article Categories: `mod _ articles _ categories`	
`default.php`	`<ul class="categories-module<?php echo $moduleclass_sfx; ?>">`
Module Article Category: `mod _ articles _ category`	
`default.php`	`<ul class="category-module<?php echo $moduleclass_sfx; ?>">`
Module Latest Articles: `mod _ articles _ latest`	
`default.php`	`<ul class="latestnews<?php echo $moduleclass_sfx; ?>">`
Module Articles Newsflash: `mod _ articles _ news`	
`default.php`	`<div class="newsflash<?php echo $moduleclass_sfx; ?>">`
`horizontal.php`	`<ul class="newsflash-horiz<?php echo $params->get('moduleclass_sfx'); ?>">`
`vertical.php`	`<ul class="newsflash-vert<?php echo $params->get('moduleclass_sfx'); ?>">`
Module Popular Articles: `mod _ articles _ popular`	
`default.php`	`<ul class="mostread<?php echo $moduleclass_sfx; ?>">`
Module Banners: `mod _ banners`	
`default.php`	`<div class="bannergroup<?php echo $moduleclass_sfx ?>">`
Module Navigation path: `mod _ breadcrumbs`	
`default.php`	`<div class="breadcrumbs<?php echo $moduleclass_sfx; ?>">`
Module Custom Content: `mod _ custom`	
`default.php`	`<div class="custom<?php echo $moduleclass_sfx ?>">`
Module Feed Display: `mod _ feed`	
`default.php`	`<ul class="newsfeed<?php echo $params->get('moduleclass_sfx'); ?>">`
Module Footer: `mod _ footer`	
`default.php`	`<div class="footer1<?php echo $moduleclass_sfx ?>">`
	`<div class="footer2<?php echo $moduleclass_sfx ?>">`
Module Language Selection: `mod _ languages`	
`default.php`	`<div class="mod-languages<?php echo $moduleclass_sfx ?>">`
Module Login: `mod _ login`	
	No suffix
Module Random Image: `mod _ random _ image`	
`default.php`	`<div class="random-image<?php echo $moduleclass_sfx ?>">`
Module Articles Related Items: `mod _ related _ items`	
`default.php`	`<ul class="relateditems<?php echo $moduleclass_sfx; ?>">`

Table 13.1 **Core Modules Showing Where Added Class Suffixes Will Be Added** (*continued*)

File	Element
Module Search: mod _ search	
default.php	`<div class="search<?php echo $moduleclass_sfx ?>">`
Module Statistics: mod _ stats	
default.php	`<dl class="stats-module<?php echo $moduleclass_sfx ?>">`
Module Syndication Feeds: mod _ syndicate	
default.php	`<a href="<?php echo $link ?>" class="syndicate-module<?php echo $moduleclass_sfx ?>">`
Module Latest Users: mod _ user _ latest	
default.php	`<ul class="latestusers<?php echo $moduleclass_sfx ?>" >`
Module Weblinks: mod _ Weblinks	
default.php	`<ul class="Weblinks<?php echo $moduleclass_sfx; ?>">`
Module Who is Online: mod _ whosonline	
default.php	`<ul class="whosonline<?php echo $moduleclass_sfx ?>" >`
Module Wrapper: mod _ wrapper	
	No suffix
Module Menu: mod _ menu	
Special case: can also have a unique ID in addition to the class	
default.php	`<ul class="menu<?php echo $class_sfx;?>"<?php $tag = '';`
	`if ($params->get('tag_id')!=NULL) {`
	`$tag = $params->get('tag_id').'';`
	`echo ' id="'.$tag.'"';`
	`}`
	`?>>`

The Menu Module

A Web site cannot function without a navigation menu. It determines the page structure and leads the visitors directly to content on lower levels. Knowing how to operate and use this module is part of the basic knowledge required for all those who want to design Joomla! pages. I mention it briefly here and explain things that may not be obvious at first glance.

Displaying a menu on the front end is a two step process. You need to create a new menu in the Menu Manager in the back end. Your menu will remain invisible in the front end until you have created a new menu module in the Module Manager and selected your menu under the module's Basic Options. See Figure 13.11.

Then you need to give the module a significant title and position it on the page where the menu should appear. This approach probably seems unremarkable to you. As you would expect, the menu will be positioned in the spot you assigned.

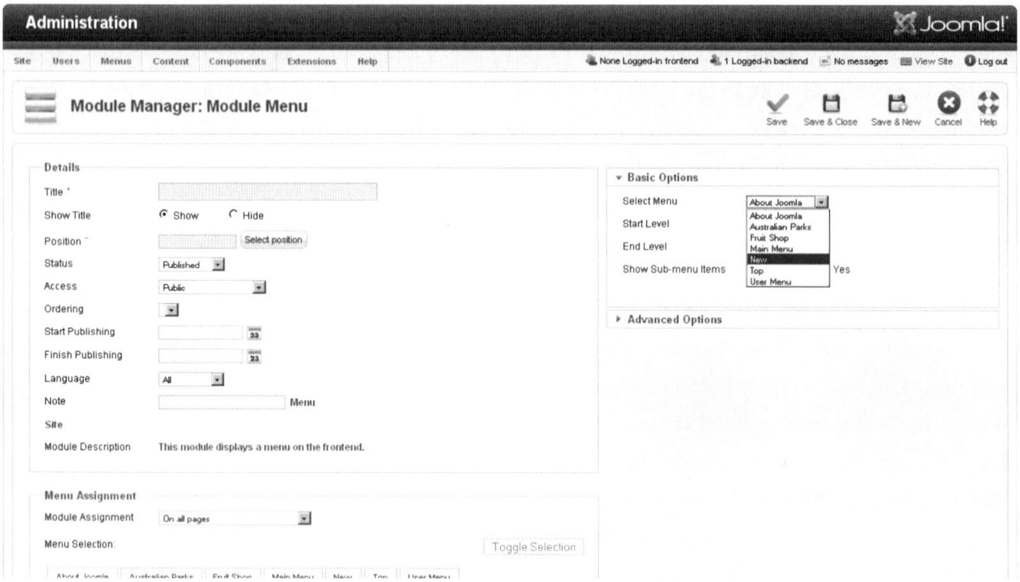

Figure 13.11   Creating a menu module

But what makes dealing with the menu really exciting are the display variations that you can achieve through correct configuration of the module options and the settings under the relevant module item.

Horizontal Navigation with Subnavigation

On many Web sites, you initially find a horizontal navigation with a maximum of six to seven main navigation items. If you click your way deeper into the site via one of these items, a submenu often becomes visible on the left or right, depending on the design.

If you want to use this type of display, you do not need two navigations, as many people think, but only one that can be nested as deeply as you want it. Joomla! offers the option of specifying the levels of the selected menu within the menu module, as shown in Figure 13.12.

If you want to display only the first level of your module, select Start level: 1 and End level: 1. If you decide you want to show the lower levels of your navigation in other places, follow these steps:

1. Copy the existing menu module or create a new one that points to the same menu (menu name).

2. Position it where you want it.

3. Choose the levels you want to show. In most cases this will be Start level: 2, End level: your last level.

4. Position the module on all pages.

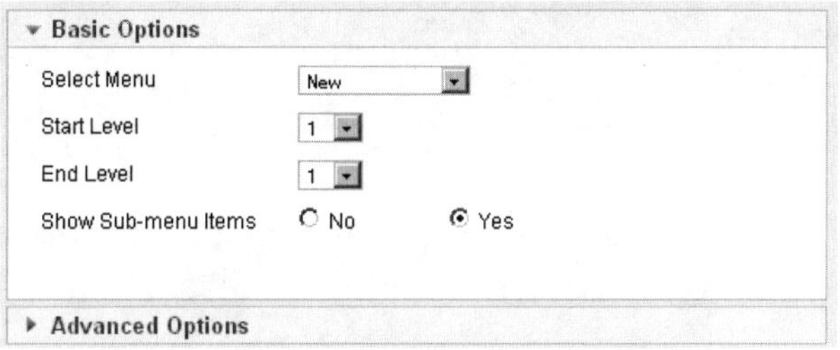

Figure 13.12   Start- and end-level options of the menu module

Once you have done all of this, you will see that it's working beautifully. But what is the advantage in doing this? We could just use separate menus for the different levels and then position them on the correct pages independently of one another.

Because this is only a single menu, the individual elements know who their children and parents are. This may sound somewhat technical, but it leads to the system being able to visually connect parent and child elements by using predefined CSS classes and to highlight the currently active menu item. This approach is essential to designing a Web site that is easy to navigate.

The menu is output in the form of a list that can be nested if necessary. The classes to be formatted are linked to the relevant list item. For example, the list element of the active menu item is equipped with the class `active`.

```
<li id="item-464" class="active"><a href="/joomlabook_installation/">
 Home</a></li>
```

If the menu is open and the active menu item contains child elements, it also gets the class `.parent`. If it is an active menu item without child elements, it gets the additional class `.current`. Using these classes makes a flexible menu design possible. You can see an example in Figure 13.13.

Folded Out Menu

Sometimes you want the lower levels of the navigation to be displayed immediately. You can do this by selecting the option Show Sub-menu Items in the module. This function is particularly helpful if you want to offer a drop-down menu along the lines of Sucker-fish—a menu whose subitems open automatically when you move the mouse over them. You can see an example of a drop-down menu in Figure 13.14.

Such menus are very trendy at the moment; unfortunately, you often cannot use them without a mouse and just a keyboard. This can be remedied, though. A functioning example can be found using the Hathor template in the back end of Joomla!. Go to Extensions → Template Manager and make Hathor your default template for the administrator to see an accessible drop-down menu.

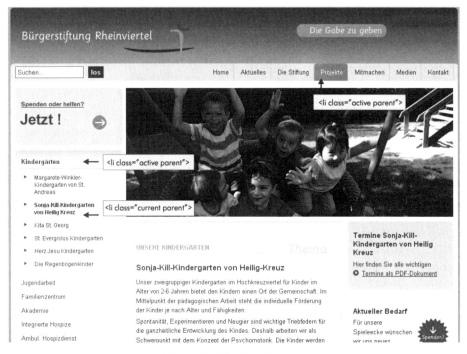

Figure 13.13   A split menu

Figure 13.14   A drop-down menu

The basis for these types of menus is usually a unique id of the menu list. Apart from the Module Class Suffix, the menu module is the only one that you can assign an additional unique id to. The id that you assign in the Module Manager will be assigned only to the top list element. For example: `<ul class="menu" id="your_id">`.

Styling Individual Menu Items via Individual Classes

New in Joomla! 1.6 was the option of assigning each menu link its own individual class. This can be applied effectively if, for example, you want to work with color guidance systems. Color guidance systems can help provide better orientation, especially if there is a lot of content.

In the Menu Manager, you can find the text field Link CSS Style under Link Type Options (see Figure 13.15). Here you can directly enter your desired class name, which has the following result in the source text:

```
<li id="item-464" class="active"><a class="home" href="/
 joomlabook_installation" >Home</a></li>
```

Now nothing stands in the way of your individual menu design.

Link Image

Menu items are often displayed not as normal text but as graphics. In Joomla! you have the option of integrating clickable graphics into your menu using the option Link Image. You can then select an image directly via the Media Manager, and the image is automatically integrated into the link. The result is the following:

```
<a class="home" href="/joomlabook_installation/" >
<img src="/joomlabook_installation/images/joomla_black.gif"
 alt="Home" />
<span class="image-title">Home</span>
</a>
```

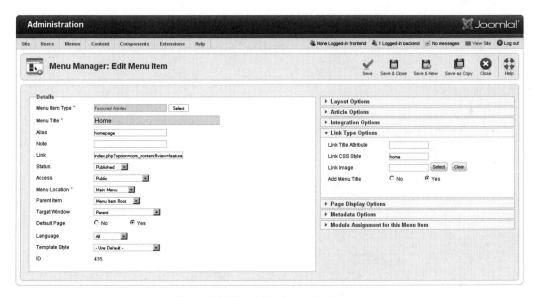

Figure 13.15   CSS class of reference

The image is integrated within the link and automatically assigned an alternative text. The link title is used as alternative text. A span element with this link text is positioned below the graphic. You may be surprised by this—you were probably expecting only the graphic. The span element below it has two distinct advantages: On one hand, you have the option of integrating topical images into the navigation and at the same time presenting the link as a normal text link below each image. On the other, it gives you the option of designing the menu accessibly, despite the graphics. If you do not want this text link to be displayed, you can remove it from the viewport via CSS, so it is no longer visible but is still present for nonvisual devices.

Allocating Individual Link Titles

If you like, you can allocate an individual link title for each link. You should be cautious when choosing the content of the link titles. It may be very helpful to integrate additional information about the link target into it. The link titles are generally displayed as tool tips when you move the mouse over the links. This information can also be helpful for users of screen readers. But you should not rely on the title functioning properly.

I know many users of screen readers who have disabled the display of the title attribute by default in their screen reader. They do so because it is often misused. Many content management systems generate the link title automatically and fill it with the link text, which can result in annoying redundancies.

14

Designing Default Output Individually

Content management systems have the task of managing content in a structured way and outputting it in the same organized form. On the Web, we need HTML code for this output. Now, you know which parts of the code you can determine yourself. But the actual content is output by the system with predefined code. If you are not happy with this output, you can it by using template overrides. Even if you do not want to do so, the default output is part of the template, and it too must be formatted via CSS.

Inspecting the Default Output

To be able to directly influence the design of the default code using CSS, you should know its structure, setup, and the CSS classes used. So you need to have a closer look at the automatically generated code. Thanks to Firebug, this should not be difficult. Joomla! focuses on a well-structured, semantically correct HTML code and therefore offers a good basis for conforming to standards and creating accessible Web sites featuring neat structures.

During the development phase, this structure was closely scrutinized. In addition to accessibility, an important aim was to keep the design as flexible as possible using CSS without unnecessarily inflating the code. The CSS classes usually have descriptive names to make them easy to use.

In naming classes, the words should be separated by a dash to achieve a uniform convention of usage—for example, .items-more. The appendix contains a list of the CSS classes used and a brief description of their functions.

You will get a first impression of the default code if you look at the HTML structure of the article columns on the homepage. In older Joomla! versions, this multicolumn design was achieved using tables. Starting with the Beez template in version 1.5, the display was controlled using positioning div containers. As of version 1.6, there are no longer table layouts. The design is now up to the template designer—a very sensible approach, even if it requires slightly more knowledge of CSS.

The Page Class Suffix

I mentioned the Module Class Suffix in Chapter 13, "Modules—Dynamics within the Presentation," when discussing the modules. The Page Class Suffix is basically an extension of this system.

Joomla! offers a number of ways to vary the display content, such as the blog view, the article view, and the featured view. All these views can be formatted using CSS. Despite these options, you sometimes have to display a few in a different way. Many Web developers solve this problem by assigning a body id.

Let's build a simple example to illustrate this concept.

Normally, all second-level headings (h2) should be displayed in red. Only in very special cases is black preferable for a heading. For technical reasons, it is not possible to assign an individual CSS class to this heading, but in this special case, we can assign an id to the body element of the page.

This gives us the option of accessing the h2 via context selectors:

```
...
<body id="black">
<h2> My black heading</h2>
...
```

For displaying the red heading on all other pages, we simply note in our CSS:

```
h2 {color:#990000} start page
```

And via

```
#black h2
{color:#000}
```

we achieve the special formatting for the page with the black heading.

Since version 1.5, Joomla! offers a similar method. Using the Page Class Suffix you can assign individual class names for certain page areas. The Page Class Suffix is assigned via the menu item of the page you want to design. You can find it under Page Display Options.

Open the back end, navigate to the main menu, and open the homepage link. In Page Display Options, enter the word *test* in the Page Class field (see Figure 14.1). Then save the link.

To see what happens to this parameter, you need to look at the source code of the homepage. The simplest way to do this is to use Firebug.

As you can see in Figure 14.2, the suffix you chose is appended to the class of the div container that surrounds the content of the homepage.

Without this suffix, the container would only have the class .blog-featured. With the suffix, this class becomes .blog-featuredtest. All contents in this container can now be styled individually via the context selector .blog featuredtest.

For example:

```
.blog featuredtest h2
{color:#000}
```

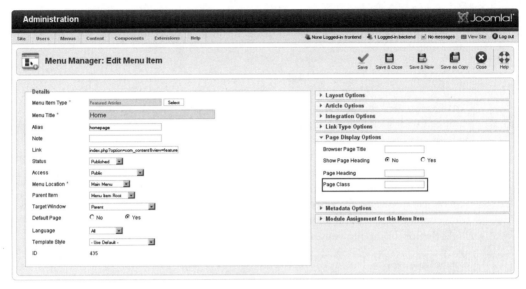

Figure 14.1   Localizing the parameter in the Menu Manager

```
☐ <div id="all">
    ¶ · · · · · · · ·
    ☐ <div id="back">
        ¶ · · · · · · · · · · · · · · ·
        ⊞ <div id="header">
        ¶ · · · · · · · · · · · · · · · · · · · · · · · ·
        ⊞ <div class="custom_image">
        ¶ · · · · · · · · · · · · · · · · · · · ·
        ☐ <div id="contentarea2">
            ¶ · · · · · · · · · · · · · · · · · · · · · · · · · · · · · · · · · · · · · ·
            ⊞ <div id="breadcrumbs">
            ¶¶ · · · · · · · · · · · · · · · · ... · · · · · · · · · · · · · · · · · · · · · · · ·
            ☐ <div id="wrapper">
                ¶¶ · · · · · · · · · · · · · · · · · · · · · · · · · · · · · · · · · · · · · · · · · · · · · · ·
                ☐ <div id="main" role="main">
                    ¶¶ · · · · · · · · · · · · · · · · · · · ... · · · · · · · · · · · · · · · · · · · ·
                    ☐ <div class="blog-featuredtest">
                        ¶¶
                        ☐ <div class="items-leading">
                            ¶└┴┘
                            ☐ <div class="leading-0">
                                ¶└┴┘¶
                                <h2> ¶└┴┴┘Relax·and·enjoy·your·favorite·music!·└┴┘</h2>
                                ¶¶¶¶¶→¶¶
                                <p> In·our·store·you·will·f...1,·Rhythm·and·Blues·...</p>
                                ¶¶└┴┘
                            ⊞ <p class="readmore">
                                ¶¶¶
                                <div class="item-separator"></div>
                                ¶└┘
                            </div>
                            ¶└┴┘
                        </div>
                        ¶¶└
                        ☐ <div class="items-more">
                            ¶└
                            <h3> More·Articles...</h3>
                            ¶¶
                            ☐ <ol>
                                ¶└
                                ⊞ <li>
                                ¶└
```

Figure 14.2   Generated HTML code after assigning suffix

If you do not want the suffix to be appended directly to the existing class, but instead you want to create a new class, you need to ensure that your suffix starts with a space. The result would be:

```
<div class="blog-featured test">
```

All views used in Joomla! are integrated into the page via the menu and can be equipped with such a suffix. Usually we add a suffix to the HTML elements that enclose content and can therefore be styled using context selectors.

The technical basis for this behavior can be found in the views of the individual components. In our case, the content component com_content is responsible. If you want to use template overrides later on, you will certainly come across this suffix.

The featured view described here can be found under Your_Installation/components/com_content/views/featured/tmpl/default.php.

At the top of the file you can see how the suffix is integrated into the code:

```
<div class="blog-featured<?php echo $this->pageclass_sfx;?>">
```

Table 14.1 shows an overview of all views including HTML elements that can get a suffix.

Table 14.1 **Layout Views Showing Where Page Suffixes Are Added**

View	File	Element That Can Get the Additional Class
The content component: com _ content		
Featured	default.php	`<div class="blog-featured<?php echo` ↪`$this->pageclass_sfx;?>">`
Category	default.php	`<div class="category-list<?php echo` `$this->pageclass_sfx;?>">`
	blog.php	`<div class="blog<?php echo $this->pageclass_sfx;?>">`
Categories	default.php	`<div class="categories-list<?php echo` ↪`$this->pageclass_sfx;?>">`
Article	default.php	`<div class="item-page<?php echo` ↪`$this->pageclass_sfx?>">`
Archive	default.php	`<div class="archive<?php echo` ↪`$this->pageclass_sfx;?>">`
The contact component: com _ contact		
Featured	default.php	`<div class="blog-featured<?php echo` ↪`$this->pageclass_sfx;?>">`
Categories	default.php	`<div class="categories-list<?php echo` ↪`$this->pageclass_sfx;?>">`
Category	default.php	`<div class="contact-category<?php echo` ↪`$this->pageclass_sfx;?>">`
Contact	default.php	`<div class="contact<?php echo $this->pageclass_sfx?>">`

Table 14.1 Layout Views Showing Where Page Suffixes Are Added (*continued*)

View	File	Element That Can Get the Additional Class
The newsfeed component: `com_newsfeed`		
Categories	default.php	`<div class="categories-list<?php echo` `↪$this->pageclass_sfx;?>">`
Category	default.php	`<div class="newsfeed-category<?php echo` `↪$this->pageclass_sfx;?>">`
Newsfeed	default.php	`<div class="newsfeed<?php echo $this->pageclass_sfx?>`
The Weblinks component: `com_Weblinks`		
Categories	default.php	`<div class="categories-list<?php echo` `↪$this->pageclass_sfx;?>">`
Category	default.php	`<div class="Weblink-category<?php echo` `↪$this->pageclass_sfx;?>">`
The user component: `com_user`		
Login	default_login.php	`<div class="login<?php echo $this->pageclass_sfx?>">`
	default_login.php	`<div class="logout<?php echo $this->pageclass_sfx?>">`
Profile	default.php	`<div class="profile<?php echo $this->pageclass_sfx?>">`
Registration	default.php	`<div class="registration<?php echo` `↪$this->pageclass_sfx?>">`
Remind	default.php	`<div class="remind<?php echo $this->pageclass_sfx?>">`
Reset	default.php	`<div class="reset<?php echo $this->pageclass_sfx?>">`
The search: `com_search`		
Search	default.php	`<div class="search<?php echo $this->pageclass_sfx; ?>">`
The wrapper: `com_wrapper`		
Wrapper	default.php	`<div class="contentpane<?php echo` `↪$this->pageclass_sfx; ?>">`

Template Overrides

Up to Joomla! version 1.5, template designers were only able to determine the output of the frame document—that is, the HTML code specified in the template's index.php file. The contents of the system were output with surrounding HTML code whose design you were unable to influence. Most of the contents were stuck in a table design.

It was a huge drawback because Web designers had very little influence on the code. This changed with Joomla! 1.5 with the introduction of the template override system, which allowed direct manipulation of the default output without affecting the system itself. The template contained its own HTML folder whose content was processed and circumvented the actual Joomla! output.

At that time, this feature was particularly relevant, because the default code generated by the system was obsolete and not very standards conforming. The Beez template in version 1.5 demonstrated how you could use template overrides. The result was a standards-conforming, clean, and semantically correct code.

With version 2.5, the default output of all components and modules was significantly improved. Now you can build a XHTML Strict or HTML5 template without having to touch the code.

If you have a close look at the Beez template code in version 1.5 and compare it to the Joomla! default output, you will see immediately that the structure is very similar. Only a few CSS classes have been renamed, and the output has been expanded with a few useful parameters. This means that a template from version 1.5 based on Beez can be integrated relatively easily into newer Joomla! versions. You just have to adapt a few CSS statements.

Despite the new and improved HTML concept, it can sometimes be necessary to overwrite the default output. I have done this myself in the beez5 template in order to use HTML5 elements on the lower levels.

Model-View-Controller

The system of template overrides is possible only because it uses the model–view–controller principle. This approach ensures that the application logic and the presentation of contents are cleanly separated. Each component and each module in Joomla! follows this system. This principle consists of three components:

1. The *model* contains the data to be represented and the logic itself.

2. The *view*, the presentation layer, takes care of the actual presentation.

3. The *controller* controls it all.

The template designer is really only interested in the view, because that is where the output of contents is located. I explain the override system using the example of the most important component, the com_content. The overrides control the output of the content.

If you create a menu item in the Joomla! back end, you can choose among different views. The com_content has the following views:

- *Featured Articles:* special view for display on the homepage
- *Category Blog:* displays articles of a selected category
- *Category List:* displays a table with contents of a selected category
- *List All Categories:* lists all available categories
- *Archived Articles:* displays archived articles
- *Single Article:* direct article view
- *Create Article (Form):* form for creating an article

You can influence these views directly using the template overrides.

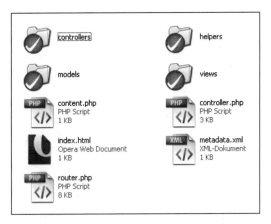

Figure 14.3   Structure of com_content

Have a quick look at the file level now and navigate to the components and from there to the com content: your_Installation/components/com_content. You will see the picture shown in Figure 14.3.

The folder we are interested in is, as mentioned earlier, the one with the name views, because it contains the actual output of the content. Please navigate directly to this folder (see Figure 14.4).

In the views folder you will once again find a folder for each view. The term *form* indicates it is the form for creating and editing an article. Let's first look at the folder article, which is a less complex presentation (see Figure 14.5).

This time, we are interested in the folder tmpl, because it contains the file we may want to change (see Figure 14.6).

Regardless of which view you want to edit later, the first file called by the system is always the default.php file. References to other files, where necessary, always start there.

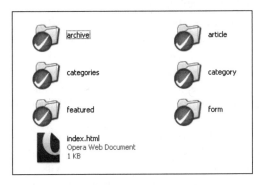

Figure 14.4   com_content/views

Figure 14.5   com_content/views/article

Figure 14.6   com_content/views/article/tmpl

In the article view you will find only this one file because the display of this view requires relatively little code.

Imagine the following scenario: in the default display, the article heading has an h2, but we would like to use an h3 in that place. The page heading should be output as h2, but the default is h1. As you may know, you can enable or disable this page heading via the menu items. This is then displayed in the article heading. To achieve this, you need to shift the output to the template.

Shifting Output to the Template

If you look at the structure of the Beez template you have renamed, you will find a folder with the name html. It specifies, among other things, the output for the module. This folder is also the place where the overrides are saved.

Go to this folder and create a subfolder with the name com_content. Then create a subfolder with the name article and copy the default.php and index.html files from com_content/views/article/tmpl/ into it. You may recall that the index.html file is empty and exists only for security reasons.

Once you have done this, Joomla! will automatically know that it should no longer use the default output but instead the article/default.php from the template for the article view display. Now you can adapt the file as you wish. The result will be immediately visible.

With this method it is particularly important that you arrange the folder structure correctly. The actual com_content also contains the intermediate level tmpl, which you will not find in the overrides. You should copy the contents of tmpl directly into the article folder.

Structure com_content
com_content
article
tmpl
   default.php
      default.xml
         index.html
metadata.xml
view.html.php
index.php

Structure template
html
   com_content
      article
         default.php
            index.html

Adapting Output

If you now open html/com_content/article/default.php from your template, you will see that the file contains a mixture of HTML and PHP code, which you can easily adapt. At the top you will find the following code:

```
<?php if ($this->params->get('show_page_heading', 1)) : ?>
<h1>
<?php echo $this->escape($this->params->get('page_heading')); ?>
</h1>
<?php endif; ?>
```

If the option show_page_heading is active, the pageheading is output, enclosed by an h1. You select this option when you create a menu item.

As soon as the parameter Show Page Heading is enabled (as in Figure 14.7), the text specified in the Page Heading field is output. If the field provided for this is empty, the system uses the title of the menu item and outputs it.

If you now want to replace the h1 with an h2, you can go ahead and do it. Then save the file, and you are done.

```
<?php if ($this->params->get('show_page_heading', 1)) : ?>
<h2>
<?php echo $this->escape($this->params->get('page_heading')); ?>
</h2>
<?php endif; ?>
```

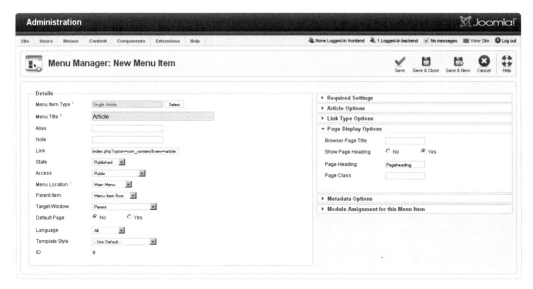

Figure 14.7   Creating an article in the back end

You can proceed in the same way with the article heading. Just replace the h2 with an h3:

```php
<?php if ($params->get('show_title')|| $params->get('access-edit'))
: ?>
<h3>
<?php if ($params->get('link_titles') && !empty($this->item->
readmore_link)) : ?>
<a href="<?php echo $this->item->readmore_link; ?>">
<?php echo $this->escape($this->item->title); ?></a>
<?php else : ?>
<?php echo $this->escape($this->item->title); ?>
<?php endif; ?>
</h3>
<?php endif; ?>
```

The scenario is very simple, and you could probably think of far more complex cases, up to a complete restructuring of the content. But this would exceed the scope of this book.

New—A View with Different Output

You may sometimes want to use more than one override for a view. This is absolutely possible. The aim is to design the output as flexibly as can be done. To do this, all views and modules should have the parameter Alternative Layout available. Let's use an example to make the function easier to illustrate.

First, we will stay in article view. If you create an article in the Joomla! back end, you will find the parameter Alternative Layout at the bottom of the category Article Options on the right (as shown in Figure 14.8).

Thanks to this parameter, you can choose between several layouts.

The folder Your_Name/html/com_content/article/ currently contains only the default.php file. If you copy this file and rename it as you wish, the file will be available for selection in the article view, as shown in Figure 14.9. You can edit the content and individually adapt the output of the contents.

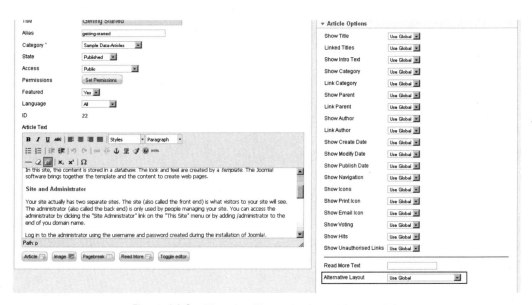

Figure 14.8   Choosing Alternative Layout in an article

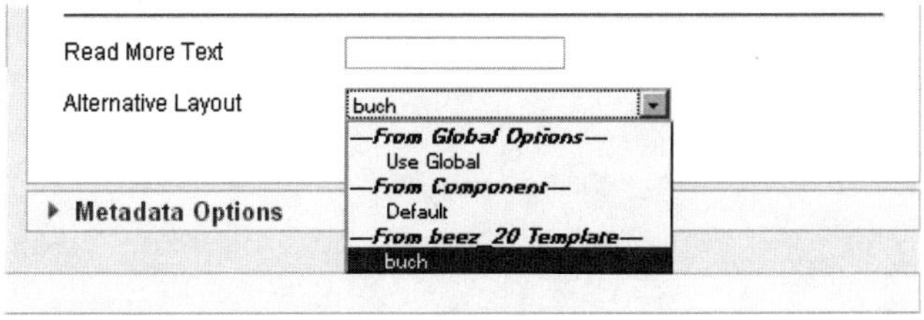

Figure 14.9   The new file is shown in the overview and is available for selection.

Now you can assign the customized view to your article. This means that the normal override file (default.php) will not be used for the output; the file you just customized will be used instead.

I named the file buch.php (*buch* is German for "book").

Easy, isn't it? This useful concept not only works in article view but can also be applied in the categories, the contact component, the Web links, the newsfeed, and all other modules.

15

The System Template: Adapting and Modifying Output

The system template is responsible for, among other things, the layout of Joomla!'s system messages, error notices, and offline notifications. Whenever the assigned template does not specify a style for messages, the system template ensures that they look good and the application remains usable. In other words, if you have not designed these views in your template, they will be automatically formatted in accordance with the system template. You will find the system template in its own folder: your_installation/templates/system. The system template is structured in exactly the same way as the other templates.

System Notices

When a user interacts with the system, the system is supposed to support user actions and point out possible sources of errors or give direct feedback in reaction to the actions. For example, the user should be notified if trying to log in with an incorrect username or password (see Figure 15.1), if all required fields are not filled in correctly during registration, or if a form was successfully submitted.

Joomla! distinguishes between three different types of messages that differ not only in their text content but also in their visual design:

- *Errors* (for example, failed login)
- *Warnings* (for example, if a form has not been completed correctly)
- *Notices* (for example, if your e-mail has not been sent)

When system messages or errors are output, Joomla! uses the system template to present them if the currently selected template does not offer a way to do so. Both Beez templates use this option and demonstrate quite well how the whole process works.

To modify the visual presentation of messages, you have to make only small changes in the template Cascading Style Sheet (CSS).

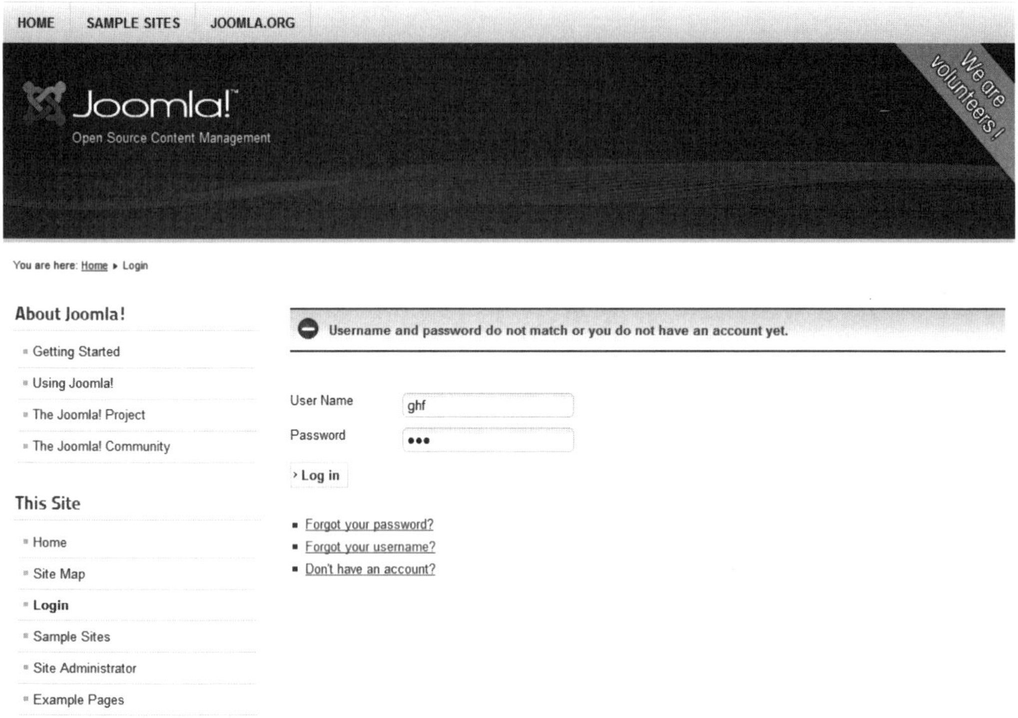

Figure 15.1   Error messages during login

Open the index.php file of the Beez template you have already modified: templates/_ your_name/index.php. As you can see, the CSS file of the system template is integrated into the existing template in line 38:

```
<link rel="stylesheet" href="<?php echo $this->baseurl ?>
 /templates/system/css/system.css" type="text/css" />
```

So, among other things, it serves as the basis for formatting the system messages. In this example, you do not want to modify the entire presentation, but only parts of it. Altering the system.css file directly is not recommended because it could be overwritten again in the next Joomla! update. Instead, because this file is integrated into the template at the very top of the document, directly following the head information, you can overwrite the formatting by including a file below it. In the Beez template this happens in CSS/general.css, where it is inserted around line 43 using PHP:

```
$files = JHtml::_('stylesheet', 'templates/'.$this->template
↪.'/css/general.css ', null,false,true);
```

This may seem like a strange way to add the file; the reason for doing it this way is explained later. You may also add the file in the "normal" way, with a link tag without affecting the functionality.

```
<link rel="stylesheet" href="<?php echo $this->baseurl ?>
 /templates/your_name/css/general.css " type="text/css" />
```

Open the file in an editor and have a quick look at it. As you can see, various kinds of formatting are stored in the file, including that for the editor in the front end, for the tool tips, and for the system messages. This is where the formatting from the system template can be modified.

To make things clearer, let's customize the red message that is displayed after a failed login. Suppose you are not happy with the background image with the gradient and would prefer a red background with white writing. Using Firebug, you can quickly find out in which line of the file you need to start.

Open the page with Firefox and log in with an incorrect password. The expected error notice should appear. Then open Firebug and inspect the code in the appropriate place (see Figure 15.2).

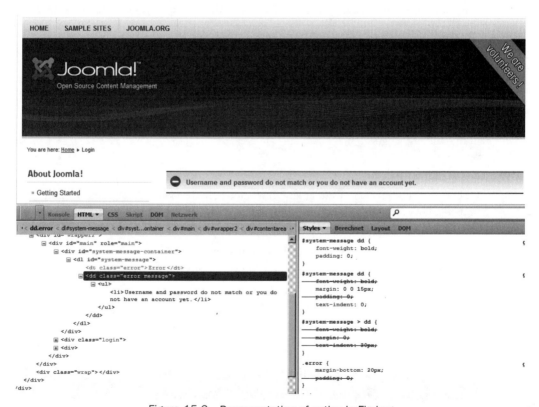

Figure 15.2   Representation of notice in Firebug

As you can see, the error notice is output as a list enclosed by a definition list. The formatting for it is in line 226 of the CSS file. You can now make your individual changes here:

```
#system-message dd.error ul
{
background:#990000;
padding-left:40px;
padding: 10px 10px 10px 40px;
border-top: 2px solid #990000;
border-bottom: 2px solid #990000;
color:#fff
}
```

If all goes well, your error notice should now look like the one shown in Figure 15.3. Following the same method, you can adapt all other messages as you wish.

Integrating the Messages into the index.php File

Error messages can be easily integrated into the index.php templates via the statement:

```
<jdoc:include type="message" />
```

It does not matter where you put the statement.

Adapting the Language

You can adapt the language via the system's language files. The error texts can be found in the relevant language file.

Error Messages

Of course, real errors can occur at any time and cause the system to stop functioning properly. They are usually server messages, such as the following:

- *401 Unauthorized:* The user did not have authorization for this access.
- *403 Forbidden:* The type of access is forbidden.
- *404 Not Found:* Page was not found.
- *500 Server Error:* There is an internal server error.

If one of these errors occurs, the server generally sends an error message to the browser. Usually the design of these messages is not very attractive or individualized.

Username and password do not match or you do not have an account yet.

Figure 15.3   Adapted error notice

With Joomla!, you can directly change the design using the error.php file, which is in the template's root directory.

As it does for other messages, if Joomla! does not find the error.php file, it automatically loads the corresponding file in the system template and uses that for the representation instead (see Figure 15.4).

Both Beez templates have error pages. For example, to force a 404 error message, you only have to enter a nonexistent URL from your domain in your browser. If you test for this error, based on your already modified template, the result should look like the one shown in Figure 15.5.

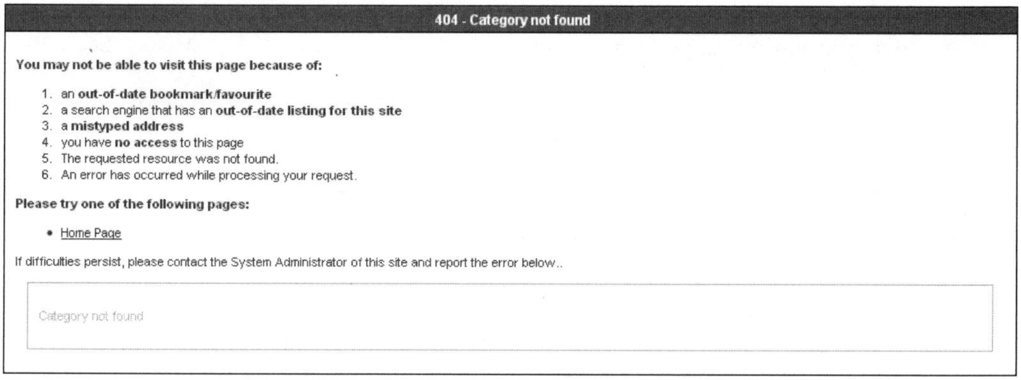

404 - Category not found

You may not be able to visit this page because of:

1. an **out-of-date bookmark/favourite**
2. a search engine that has an **out-of-date listing for this site**
3. a **mistyped address**
4. you have **no access** to this page
5. The requested resource was not found.
6. An error has occurred while processing your request.

Please try one of the following pages:

- Home Page

If difficulties persist, please contact the System Administrator of this site and report the error below..

Category not found

Figure 15.4   Error message based on system template

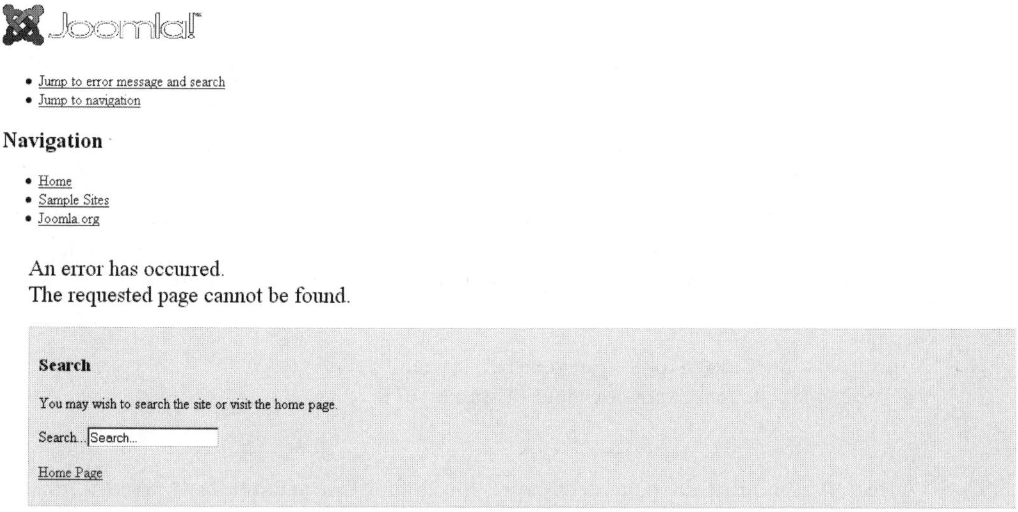

- Jump to error message and search
- Jump to navigation

Navigation

- Home
- Sample Sites
- Joomla.org

An error has occurred.
The requested page cannot be found.

Search

You may wish to search the site or visit the home page.

Search... | Search... |

Home Page

Figure 15.5   Error message without CSS

As you can see, the page is lacking CSS because you have not yet changed the paths to the files there. But this is easily done. Look at the links to all the CSS files and change the paths to your template name.

The error.php file is structured similar to index.php and therefore calls the same CSS files. If you want a less complex design, you could create a single CSS file that is responsible for all of the design of this page and call it instead of the existing CSS files.

The file has a relatively complex structure, especially due to the large bandwidth of error messages that load using this page. Also, many functions that can be used in the index.php file are not available here. Therefore, to get the same results, you have to dive a bit deeper into the PHP box of tricks.

The page is divided into two individual designs. All server messages with an error code of 400 to 500 get layout A, and all others get layout B. First, the current error code is retrieved and the output is designed accordingly:

```php
<?php if ($this->error->getCode()>=400 && $this->error->getCode() <
  500) { ?>
// output we are interested in
<?php } else { ?>
// other output
<?php } ?>
```

The only really interesting bit for our purposes is that it controls only the display of error messages with error codes from 400 to 500, which are the most commonly seen error codes. All the others appear infrequently.

The output of the error is defined by only a few lines of code:

```php
<h2><?php echo JText::_('JERROR_AN_ERROR_HAS_OCCURRED'); ?><br />
<?php echo JText::_('JERROR_LAYOUT_PAGE_NOT_FOUND'); ?></h2>
<?php echo $this->error->getCode() ; ?>
<?php echo $this->error->getMessage();?>
```

All the rest is just decoration.

Via the template parameters, you add the logo, the page description, and the page title. To make the page more user friendly, you can also add the main navigation and the search using the statement `<jdoc:include ... />` in the error.php file. But for technical reasons, modules do not load automatically in this file, so you need to load the module directly with PHP. You can simply copy and paste the following code:

```php
<?php
  $module = JModuleHelper::getModule( 'menu' );
  echo JModuleHelper::renderModule( $module);
?>
```

Keep in mind that the parameter passed to the function `getModule()` refers to the name of the relevant module.

Replacing System Graphics

The system has its own little graphics or icons in various places. For example, you can configure Joomla! in such a way that each article automatically gets a print or e-mail icon. The graphics for this feature can be found in the media/system folder.

If you would like to use your own custom graphics, you can do so very easily. Simply create a subfolder in the images folder and name it system, then insert your custom graphics into that folder. Important: you must comply with the naming conventions! For example, the print button uses the graphic printButton.png. If you save your custom graphic under exactly the same name in templates/your_name/images/system, Joomla! will use your graphic. You have successfully overwritten the default output. Easy, isn't it? With Firebug you can quickly find out the file names of the graphics.

component.php and How to Do Magic with It

The component.php file is almost like the little sister of the index.php file. It is used when the content is to be displayed without navigation and head. This type of display appears in the window for the print preview or when you click the e-mail icon to e-mail the link to a friend. The whole thing is controlled by the fact that the link in the URL contains the additional information tmpl=component. It will make more sense to you if you inspect a page with an inserted Print button using Firebug.

Let's assume you want to create a link in the main menu to an article that opens in a new window and does not integrate the logo and the navigation. It can easily be done via a little detour (see Figure 15.6).

First you need the article's URL. You can find out what the URL is by creating a link to the relevant article in the menu. Once you have selected an article there and saved your selection, the necessary URL appears in the field Link.

Now copy this URL to the clipboard and change the link type from Article link to External URL by clicking on the Select button. The field for the link is now empty and you can insert your copied URL there.

In my example, the URL is `index.php?option=com_content&view=article&id=1` (see Figure 15.7).

If this link should now use the output of the component.php instead of the default output, you only need to append `&tmpl=component` to this URL.

But because the link of the type *url* requires an absolute URL, you still need to insert the domain name at the beginning. The link then looks like this:

```
http://localhost/joomlabook_installation/index.php?option=com_content&
↪view=article&id=1&tmpl=component
```

If you want the link to open in a new browser window, you can specify so under Target Window. Save your menu item and have a look at what happens in the front end. If you click on the link, the page display should now appear in a new window (see Figure 15.8).

Figure 15.6   Using Firebug to display the tmpl link

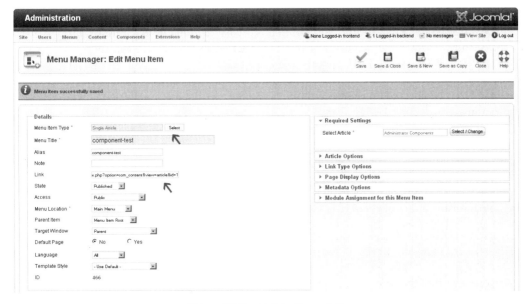

Figure 15.7   Link to the article

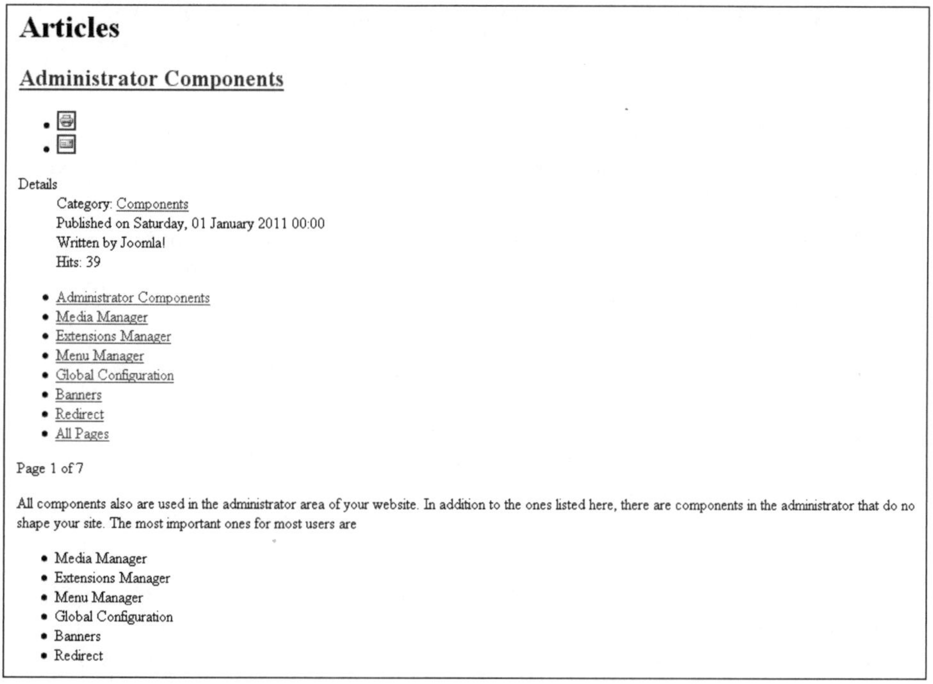

Articles

Administrator Components

- ⊟
- ⊟

Details
    Category: Components
    Published on Saturday, 01 January 2011 00:00
    Written by Joomla!
    Hits: 39

- Administrator Components
- Media Manager
- Extensions Manager
- Menu Manager
- Global Configuration
- Banners
- Redirect
- All Pages

Page 1 of 7

All components also are used in the administrator area of your website. In addition to the ones listed here, there are components in the administrator that do no shape your site. The most important ones for most users are

- Media Manager
- Extensions Manager
- Menu Manager
- Global Configuration
- Banners
- Redirect

Figure 15.8   Component view

However, there are now display errors because the paths to the integrated CSS files are no longer correct. You should adapt them in the component.php file using your template name.

Component View with Search Engine–Friendly URLs

One little problem still remains: the URL we have created is not very search engine–friendly. To remedy this, you need to create a URL that really exists, so Joomla! itself can convert it to a search engine–friendly URL. In other words, you need to have a menu item somewhere. But the problem is that this menu item cannot appear anywhere in public, so you need to create an invisible menu.

In this context, an invisible menu means that the menu is visible in the back end but is not displayed anywhere in the front end. You do this by setting the menu on a module that is not assigned to a position so it is never displayed. Follow these steps:

1. Create a new menu in the Menu Manager, and give it the name invisible.

2. Create the link to the view you want to be represented in the Component view. I usually use an article link because it's easy.

3. Go to the Module Manager, create a menu module, and assign it to a visible module position.

4. In the front end, go to this menu item and click on the link.

5. Copy the URL from the browser bar.

6. In the back end, go to your normal main menu and create a link with the type *External URL*.

7. Paste the copied link into it and add ?tmpl=component at the end; for example, http://localhost/joomlabook_installation/index.php/article-invisible.html?tmpl=component.

Warning

Careful: In this case, you do not use & to append the value to the URL; instead, you use ?. The reason is that this is now the only parameter in the URL, and the first parameter is always preceded by a question mark.

If you click on this new link, everything seems to be working fine, but the invisible menu is still visible on the page at the moment, which you did not want to happen. Don't be tempted to unpublish the menu or the link. If you do, the link will be totally gone, and the link to the *component* view will thus be broken.

8. The right way to suppress the display of the invisible menu is to remove the module position. If the module position is blank, that menu module will not display on your site, but it will still be used to calculate search engine–friendly URLs.

Once this is done, it should all work as you want it to.

The component.php File as the Basis for Custom Views

The flexibility of Joomla! becomes noticeable in cases such as this one. You are free to create your own custom views. If you copy the component.php file and save it under a new name directly in the root of your template directory, you can use the same mechanism to access these views. You simply need to replace *?tmpl=component* with *?tmpl=yourfilename*.

You may wonder why this is useful, and I can think of two cases right away: the iPhone and offline PHP.

The iPhone

Let's assume you want to design a separate view for display on the iPhone or the iPad. You simply need to start a query in the index.php file right at the top. If the page is then accessed from an iPhone, a redirect to the iPhone view is executed.

```
if(strstr($_SERVER['HTTP_USER_AGENT'],'iPhone') ||
strstr($_SERVER['HTTP_USER_AGENT'],'iPod'))
{
JFactory::getApplication()->redirect($this->base.'?tmpl=iphone');
}
```

Integrating Parts of Your Web Site into Another Joomla! Page

Suppose other Joomla! users want to integrate the news from your site into their own
site. Using a menu item of the type *wrapper*, they could load another Web site into the
content area of their Joomla! page. But this approach would lead to the entire page being
integrated with the logo and navigation menu which would not be desirable

If you offer a separate news view, it becomes possible to integrate only the pure content. You can do this by reducing your view to a minimum and making only the actual
content available via `<jdoc:include type="component" />`. Using the link www.
your-site/index.php?tmpl=news, this view will become available in the other system.

offline.php

In the global configuration, you have the option of switching the page to offline mode.
This can be very useful, particularly for maintenance tasks. You control the design of this
view via the offline.php file of the system template. You will find this file in the root
directory. Copy it into your own template, and then you can customize the design.

16

Advanced Template Customization Tricks

Let's finish exploring customization with a few techniques that do not require separate chapters but should be mentioned because they can be important when building templates. This information is partly technical in nature but can help you efficiently solve certain problems. You will find out how you can prepare your template for use in countries where the reading direction is right to left, how to use the Joomla! internal PHP browser switch, how to design the homepage differently than the rest with simple methods, and how to output the current date.

When the Reading Direction Changes: Right-to-Left Languages

Joomla! is a content management system used all over the world, including in many countries whose language is read from right to left. If you look at the Joomla! statistics, you discover many Joomla! sites in countries such as Egypt and Israel where languages are read from right to left. For this reason, the Joomla! default templates are prepared for use with languages read from both left to right and right to left.

Designers from the Western-language sphere must rethink their designs, because when the reading direction changes, the design has to change, too. It sounds simpler than it really is. We—and therefore our designer eyes—are not used to thinking in the opposite direction. Once we start switching everything around, the result often appears unbalanced to us. In most cases, we cannot read or understand the language, which is an unfavorable condition for building a template and invariably results in an unsatisfactory design. We can only try to imagine, and can never really be certain, how our design will be perceived in those countries with reading directions opposite to ours. I am very glad to have had helping hands that were able to sort out my mistakes in this book.

To adapt the design for right-to-left (RTL) languages, you only need to adapt the Cascading Style Sheet (CSS) and change lefts to rights and rights to lefts. If you want to see what it is like to see your design differently, try holding a mirror in front of the screen, as shown in Figure 16.1. Using the mirror, you get an approximate impression of how your design will behave in RTL mode.

Integrating RTL CSS

If you open the index.php file of your modified template, you will find this statement in the head of the document:

```
<?php if ($this->direction == 'rtl') : ?>
<link rel="stylesheet" href="<?php echo $this->baseurl ?>
/templates/your_name/css/template_rtl.css" type="text/css" />
<?php if (file_exists(JPATH_SITE. DS .
'/templates/your_name/css/'
. $color . '_rtl.css')) :?>
<link rel="stylesheet" href="<?php echo $this->baseurl ?>
/templates/your_name/css/<?php echo $color ?>_rtl.css"
type="text/css" />
<?php endif; ?>
<?php endif; ?>
```

This statement basically adds two additional CSS files for the RTL view into the page. The template_rtl.css file is responsible for positioning in RTL mode. Recall that in the Beez template, you can choose between two options: Nature and Personal. Apart from the color design, these styles also differ slightly in how the content is positioned. For example, in the Nature style, the header takes up the entire width. To adapt it to an RTL

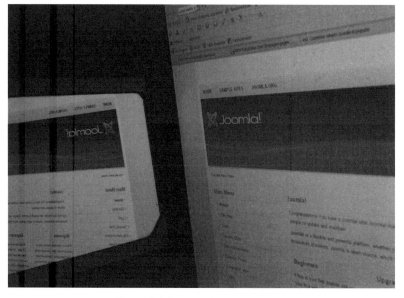

Figure 16.1   Joomla! in the mirror

orientation, you use the nature_rtl.css file. The Personal style has no separate RTL CSS because there is nothing else that needs to be switched that is specific to that style. The second, style-specific, file is added only if it actually exists.

The previous code uses rather complex PHP to determine whether an additional CSS file should be added for the selected style. It allows for a lot of flexibility because you could add another option to the color design without changing the code. However, if you don't need that flexibility, the following simpler code would accomplish the same thing as the previous code in a more straightforward manner:

```php
<?php if ($color=='nature') ?>
<link rel="stylesheet" href="<?php echo $this->baseurl ?>
/templates/your_name/css/nature_rtl.css" type="text/css" />
<?php endif; ?>
```

Testing RTL Mode

Even if you have not installed an RTL language, you can test whether your page is displayed properly in RTL mode. You just need to use a little trick. Each language installed in Joomla! has its own language folder where you can find a central control file for the language. For the English language, this file is called language/en-GB/en-GB.xml. It contains the `<metadata>` information on the reading direction (quite a long way down in the file).

```
<metadata>
<name>English (United Kingdom)</name>
<tag>en-GB</tag>
<rtl>0</rtl>
...
</metadata>
```

The `<rtl>` attribute in the English language is set to 0 by default. If you replace the 0 with a 1 and save the file, your template will automatically call the RTL CSS files and the page will be displayed accordingly.

```
<metadata>
<name>English (United Kingdom)</name>
<tag>en-GB</tag>
<rtl>1</rtl>
...
</metadata>
```

PHP Browser Switch

Chapter 15, "The System Template: Adapting and Modifying Output," pointed out the strange integration of the general.css file and asked you to ignore it for the time being. Now you will find out what it is all about.

Deep within Joomla! is a PHP function that can identify the browser used to view your site. Most browsers send this information automatically to the server, so that it just has to be read out there. You can now use this behavior when, for example, you want to output a special view for the iPhone. Joomla! can respond only to the most common browsers. If you add the following code to the template's index.php file, you can get Joomla! to tell you the browser and version being used. You can then adjust your design as necessary.

```php
<?php

// class located in libraries/joomla/application/Web/client.php
$browser= JApplicationWeb::getInstance('DetectClient') ;

var_dump($browser->client->mobile); // outputs mobile true or false
var_dump($browser->client->platform); //outputs platform;
var_dump($browser->client->browser); // outputs browser
?>
```

When you run this example, the var_dump() displays the information on your screen. When you actually use it in your template, you will likely use an if statement. For instance, to do something for only mobile devices, you could use the following code:

```php
<?php

// class located in libraries/joomla/application/Web/client.php
$browser= JApplicationWeb::getInstance('DetectClient') ;

if ($browser->client->mobile) :
  // Do something here like loading a special stylesheet
endif;

?>
```

For some designers, writing code to detect browsers is too uncomfortable or too theoretical. That is why Joomla! makes life easier for you. To clarify this, let's get back to integrating the general.css file.

With CSS3, you can now create elements with rounded corners without having to use complicated constructs with nested div containers and various background images. The browser implementation of this feature is sadly still lacking. Internet Explorer up to version 8 cannot cope with it at all, and even Firefox and Konqueror have trouble with it. To handle these cases, the PHP browser switch can help. It is questionable whether this solution is really the best to create rounded corners, but it is a good example to show how the browser switch works.

In the CSS folder of the Beez template, you will find general.css plus the files:

- general_mozilla.css
- general_konqueror_css
- general_opera.css

Tip

This construct is required so the browser recognition works properly.

Each of these files contains browser-specific CSS statements. Notice that the beginning of each file name is identical (general_), and the relevant browser follows the underscore.

Let's look at the integration of general.css in the index.php file of the template

```php
<?php
$files = JHtml::_('stylesheet','templates/your_name/css/general
.css',null,false,true);
if ($files):
if (!is_array($files)):
$files = array($files);
endif;
foreach($files as $file):
... // it continues on from here
?>
```

In the `JHtml` class of the Joomla! framework, there is a function that is responsible for integrating the stylesheets:

```php
function stylesheet($file, $attribs = array(), $relative = false,
[ca]$path_only = false, $detect_browser = true)
```

You can tell this function if you want it to detect the browser by setting the `$detect_browser` parameter to `true`. Joomla! then searches for all files having names that start with *general* followed by an underscore.

At the same time, it checks whether what comes after the underscore is identical to the identified browser type. If it is, this file is output together with the parent file, general.css. This is quite technical but also quite useful in some circumstances.

PHP Tricks

In this section I briefly mention a few PHP tricks for structuring the content in the index.php and introduce helpful functions from the Joomla! framework that can sometimes make your work much easier. I do not go into great detail, but I want to give you a taste of what Joomla! can really do.

Structuring the Homepage Differently—Access to the Views

Quite often you would like to structure the homepage differently than the rest of the site. The simplest solution would be to create a separate template for this view. But a separate template requires more effort and maintenance because then you have to manage two templates. You may find a second template to be the easier solution, because the template's index.php file stays much simpler, but adapting index.php isn't difficult.

With the following code:

```php
<?php
 $view =JRequest::getCmd('view');
?>
```

you can find out which view Joomla! is using to display the current content, and then you can adapt it accordingly:

```php
if ($view == 'featured')
{
// do something
}
else
{
// do something else
}
```

The values that have `$view` can have corresponding folders found in the the views folder of the component. In the case of com_content, the views are:

- `article` : article view
- `category`: category view
- `categories`: display of all categories
- `featured` : view of the homepage
- `form`: view that appears, for example, when editing the articles.

Outputting the Current Date with PHP

Sometimes you want to output the current date. You can do so easily using this little function:

```php
<?php $date = JFactory::getDate();
 echo $date;
?>
```

You can also format the date with custom settings, as shown in the following code.

```php
<?php $date = JFactory::getDate()->format("Y-m-d-H-i-s");
 echo $date;
?>
```

Table 16.1 shows the parameters that PHP offers:

Once again, Joomla! can make life easier for you because, depending on what language you are using, you may not want to use the date formats used in English. If your Web site is written in another language, you would want to display the date in the appropriate language format. The relevant language file is responsible for this. For example, to integrate the date in German format, you need the following statement:

```php
<?php $date = JFactory::getDate()->format(JText::_('DATE_FORMAT_
↪LC2'));
 echo $date;
?>
```

As you can see, the date format is integrated via a language string into the function. Here, it is DATE_FORMAT_LC2. You can find this string in the main language file of the

Table 16.1 **PHP Symbols Used to Format Dates**

Format Symbol	Description	Return Value
D	Day of the month, double digits with leading zero	01–31
D	Day of the week, abbreviated to three letters	Mon–Sun
l (lowercase "L")	Day of the week, written in full	Sunday–Saturday
F	Month as whole word, such as January or March	January–December
m	Month as number, with leading zero	01–12
M	Month as name with three letters	Jan–Dec
H	Hour in 24-hour format, with leading zero	00–23
i	Minutes, with leading zero	00–59
s	Seconds, with leading zero	00–59
Y	Four-digit year	2012
y	Two-digit year	12

corresponding language: language/en-GB/en-GB.ini or language/de-DE/de-DE.ini. You have the following formatting options:

- `DATE_FORMAT_LC="l, d F Y"`
- `DATE_FORMAT_LC1="l, d F Y"`
- `DATE_FORMAT_LC2="l, d F Y H:i"`
- `DATE_FORMAT_LC3="d F Y"`
- `DATE_FORMAT_LC4="Y-m-d"`
- `DATE_FORMAT_JS1="y-m-d"`

The data to the right of the equals sign corresponds to that in the PHP table. For example, if you have installed the German-language file and select `DATE_FORMAT_LC2`, the result will be Freitag, 18 März 2011 10:39.

17

The Default Templates and Their Features

As mentioned in Chapter 8, "Now for the Details: A First Look at The Templates," Joomla! has three default templates that differ not only in their design but also in their technical function range. This chapter introduces their particularities and illustrates their uses.

beez_20 and beez5 Templates

Joomla! has moved away from table-based layouts. The new HTML output is based on the template overrides from the old Beez 1.5 template. For greater clarity, the Cascading Style Sheet (CSS) class names were renamed and made more uniform. For template designers, this improvement offers a great advantage. The HTML output in the Joomla! default is clean and well formed. You no longer need to use template overrides to generate clean, standards-conforming code. The range of technical function of both Beez templates is almost identical (beez5 is also designed to be used with HTML5). They differ only in their graphical design. Here is a summary of the most important Beez features

- Accessibility
- Configurable position of navigation bar
- WAI-ARIA (Web Accessibility Initiative–Accessible Rich Internet Applications) landmark roles
- Automatic display of modules in accessible tabs
- Show-or-hide modules
- Show-or-hide columns
- beez_20, offering choice of Nature or Personal design
- beez5, offering HTML5 capabilities

Accessibility in General

As in Beez 1.5, the requirements for an accessible template design are implemented in beez_20. The most important ones are:

- Separation of content and layout
- Semantically logical structure
- Skip links
- Keyboard navigability
- Sufficient color contrasts

Chapter 12, "The Language Files," explained why we need skip links, and the necessity of thoughtful color choice should also be clear. Now we explore the structure in general.

Separation of Content and Layout

The goal of every design that can be displayed independently of the device it is viewed on, as well as adapted to different user requirements, is to achieve, to the largest possible degree, a separation of content and the various display forms because most browsers used today can cope fairly reliably with stylesheets. If you learned Web site design ten or even just five years ago (CSS1 was released in December 1996), you had to deal with unreliable rendering of the styles in different browsers and had practically no option other than using tables for your design. Today, this is no longer the case. Anyone who is still working with layout tables is using an obsolete and, in most cases, untenable technique and should adapt to the new processes.

Using stylesheets enables you to code the content of a Web site without concern for the rendering of the markup language. The design is specified in the stylesheets. This method has many advantages.

- People with disabilities can define custom user stylesheets for your Web sites in their browser if they need to. This means they can adapt and customize the display of your site as they wish.
- If you want to, you can offer several styles that the user can select from via a select box.
- Should you wish to implement a new design a few years later, you just need to change the stylesheets. The structure of the Web site remains untouched.

Semantically Logical Structure or the Concept of Linearization

Based on the separation of content and presentation, it becomes possible to structure the markup in such a way that its formal structure largely corresponds to that of the content. In other words:

- All elements of a document are structured in the source text in the correct and logical order regardless of whether they appear next to or below one another later on the screen.

- All elements are marked in accordance with their position and significance in the document (semantics): headings as headings, paragraphs as paragraphs, quotations as quotations, addresses as addresses, table data as table data, and so on. This makes it possible to further process the document automatically in various ways, such as for a comfortable output on a screen reader.

This concept appears not just in the templates but in the whole Joomla! default output. It was a central part of the development of Joomla! 1.6. In addition to better usability for assistive technologies, it offers search engine optimization and better operability with mobile devices. Not only can people with disabilities find their way around a Web site more easily, but search engines such as Google will also read your site better.

Think back to Chapter 2, "Accessibility: What Is It?" People with vision impairment navigate a Web site from top to bottom by jumping from heading to heading. If the heading hierarchies are not consistently nested, it can cause confusion.

Many people believe that the Web designer's sole responsibility is to create the appealing display they see on their monitor. The screen is not the only output medium for Web content, though, and most of the other output methods are not surface-oriented but use a linear approach. This means that the output devices process the content from top to bottom and as it actually appears in the source text. In linear form, not all aids, such as columns and color areas, are available. Numerous mobile devices also use output methods that display images but otherwise work in a linear fashion. This coincides nicely with the fact that "one word after the next" is ultimately the underlying principle of any kind of writing and also markup: if contents are implemented in the markup linearly, you automatically get a linear data stream, which can be used for further processing. The structure of the Beez templates is based on exactly this principle.

Let's have a closer look at this structure (see Figure 17.1). The implementation of a logical structure is not quite as simple anymore because of the increased complexity of Web sites.

Like many other templates, the Beez templates consist of

- A *frame document* that contains the various navigations and technical methods.

- An *inner document* that contains the actual content.

The headings are clearly structured and oriented because of the need for clear semantics. If you disable the stylesheets in your browser, the linear structure and the heading hierarchy of your template becomes visible. Even if you move through the page with the tab key, you can see its structure clearly: you are led through the page from top to bottom.

In the template are unseen intermediary headings that give details on the significance of individual page areas. *Unseen* in this case means that they are positioned beyond the visible area using CSS. They are not actually gone but simply have been taken out of the visual design.

```
<h3 class="unseen"><?php echo JText::_('TPL_BEEZ2_SEARCH'); ?></h3>
```

Figure 17.1   Content and frame document

These headings are meant to make navigation through the Web site easier for users of screen readers and to create a better overview of the overall site structure. In addition to the skip links described in Chapter 12, this is a good method of making the orientation in a long linear document easier.

beez_20: Selectable Design

Chapter 11, "The XML File and the Template Parameters," explained how you can equip templates with configurable stylesheets. Recall that in the beez_20 template you can choose between the designs Personal and Nature. The CSS integration of the nature.css and personal.css files via the template parameters, along with the general structure of the CSS files being used, are the basis for this method.

In addition to the CSS files responsible for the color design are two other files, position.css and layout.css, which take care of the general positioning and spacing. If you only want to change the color of the template, you can easily adjust personal.css or nature.css as you wish. The positioning of the content will remain untouched because is determined by the other files.

All style templates are modifiable, and template designers can add additional templates at any time. When designing the source code, I made sure that modifying the CSS files alone enables you to achieve a multitude of creative variations. The Beez templates also offer something like frameworks, so they can save you many editing steps.

Position of the Navigation Column

For design reasons or to make the Web site more search engine–friendly and accessible, it may be necessary, depending on your Web site concept, to position the navigation to the left or right of the content. Beez includes a parameter to switch between these positions. The navigation is positioned both visually and semantically on either side of the content and is formatted accordingly using CSS.

If you open the index.php file of the beez_20 template or the template you have already modified, you will find the following assignment around line 27:

```
$navposition = $this->params->get('navposition');
```

The value currently selected in the back end is assigned to the variable $navposition. The variable can have the value left or center. left is for positioning before the content, and center is for positioning after the content (see Figure 17.2).

The term right would seem more logical than center, but depending on how you design the CSS, you can place the navigation column in the center if you have a three-column design. In fact, it makes sense to output the column only if it actually contains content. Perhaps you will recall:

```
$showleft = ($this->countModules('position-4') or
➥$this->countModules('position-7') or $this->countModules('position-5'));
$showRightColumn = ($this->countModules('position-3') or
➥$this->countModules('position-6') or $this->countModules('position-8'));
```

Figure 17.2   Navigation after the content

The variables $showleft and $showRightColumn are true if they contain at least one of the specified modules.

A bit further down in the actual content of the document, an if query is used to respond to the value of this variable. The code for the navigation column appears twice in the file, once before and once after the content, But it is only wanted once in the output. On line 154 in the index.php file, directly following the breadcrumbs, you will find it for the first time:

```
<?php if ($navposition=='left' AND $showleft) : ?>
<div class="left1 <?php if ($showRightColumn==NULL){ echo
 'leftbigger';} ?>" id="nav">
<jdoc:include type="modules" name="position-7" style="beezDivision"
 headerLevel="3" />
<jdoc:include type="modules" name="position-4" style="beezHide"
 headerLevel="3" state="0 " />
<jdoc:include type="modules" name="position-5" style="beezTabs"
 headerLevel="2" id="3" /></div>
<?php endif; ?>
```

This is done by querying the value of the variable $navposition and outputting the code only if the value matches and there are actually modules in this column. Around line 208 you will find the same code again, but with two little changes:

```
<?php if ($navposition=='center' AND $showleft) : ?>
<div class="left <?php if ($showRightColumn==NULL){ echo
 'leftbigger';} ?>" id="nav">
<jdoc:include type="modules" name="position-7" style="beezDivision"
 headerLevel="3" />
<jdoc:include type="modules" name="position-4"
 style="beezHide" headerLevel="3" state="0 " />
<jdoc:include type="modules" name="position-5" style="beezTabs"
 headerLevel="2" id="3" /></div>
<?php endif; ?>
```

First, the code is output only if the position is set to center. Second, the navigation column contains a different CSS class (class="left ...") with which you can control its actual visual position. The CSS ID (id="nav") is the same for both positioning options, so that you can easily use it for a uniform design of the column contents via context selectors.

But the div container for the navigation contains more.

```
class="left <?php if ($showRightColumn==NULL){ echo 'leftbigger';} ?>"
```

The CSS class of the container is expanded by the CSS class `leftbigger` if there is no right column. This method enables you to make the navigation column a bit wider if you have only a two-column design. You can prevent overly wide, hard-to-read lines in the actual content area.

Let's now turn to a recently introduced structuring element.

JavaScript and WAI-ARIA

WAI-ARIA (Web Accessibility Initiative–Accessible Rich Internet Applications) is a technical specification of the Web Accessibility Initiative *(http://en.wikipedia.org/wiki/Web_Accessibility_Initiative)* intended to make it easier for people with disabilities to participate in today's increasingly complex and interactive Web offerings. It is particularly helpful where dynamic contents and user interfaces are concerned. It uses a combination of JavaScript, Ajax, HTML, and CSS.

At the beginning of the development of the Beez templates, this specification was still in its draft stage. WAI-ARIA, in the Candidate Recommendation version, was made available on January 18, 2011. Hopefully, it won't be long until the final version is ready.

Users of screen readers often ask the same question, especially when faced with large Web offerings and dynamically changing contents: "Where am I?" One reason for this popular question is the low semantic capacity of HTML, and another is that people using screen readers often lose track when something is suddenly hidden or shown. Sighted people can perceive this change with their eyes, but people who are blind can only follow it when the focus is set to the corresponding element. Focusing in this context simply means positioning the cursor on the corresponding place and therefore making the content placed there accessible.

Previously, we did not have the option of focusing all elements in HTML and XHTML. Only interactive elements such as links, buttons, and input fields were focusable. This changed with the arrival of WAI-ARIA and HTML5.

The scripts used within the Beez templates follow this technique so that the template design is accessible for people with disabilities.

WAI-ARIA—Landmark Roles: Initial Orientation Help

Landmark roles are intended to help people with disabilities find their way around a Web site more easily by describing individual page areas and their function within the page in more detail. The navigation has the role `navigation`, the search has the role `search`, the main content the role `main`. The implementation is very easy. The element to be marked is simply expanded by the corresponding role attribute. This tells users of modern screen readers what this role is:

```
<div id="main" role="main">
```

If you look at the source text of the Beez templates, you will not see these roles at first because the roles are only inserted into the document at runtime by the script hide.js in the JavaScript folder of the template.

If you were to write the roles directly into the source code, the page would not pass the validation test. This inconvenience will surely change in future when the WAI-ARIA elements are added to the HTML standard.

You can find a complete overview of the landmark roles at *www.w3.org/TR/wai-aria/roles#landmark_roles*.

If you plan to use a Beez template as the basis for your own template but change the structure of the individual page areas, you should ensure that you adapt the script accordingly.

Here is a quick example: if you change the id of the main content area, the script can no longer correctly assign the corresponding role to this area, because the landmark role is inserted, using this id, into the document object model (DOM).

```
if (document.id('main')) {
document.id('main').setProperties( {
role : 'main'
});
}
```

Showing and Hiding Modules and Page Areas

Showing and hiding certain page areas can be helpful to users and give them a better overview of the site, especially one with pages with a lot of content. Both Beez templates offer two different options for showing and hiding. One option allows you to completely show or hide the column with the additional information, and the other option allows you to show or collapse the modules as well, except for their headings.

Hiding Column

To test this functionality, you first need to place a module in the column for the additional information. Here you have the choice between the module positions: position-6, position-8, and position-3. It does not matter whether the navigation is located before or after the actual content. Whenever this column is displayed, a link called CLOSE INFO appears in the top right corner (see Figure 17.3).

By activating this link, the column is hidden, the link text is changed to OPEN INFO, and the column can then be enabled again by clicking on the link.

This function is controlled by JavaScript. All scripts mentioned here are based on the MooTools JavaScript framework, which does all the work for us in many places. To ensure that these scripts work as intended, you should check whether this framework has been loaded into the site. You may recall that the statement is JHtml::_('behavior. framework', true); in the index.php file.

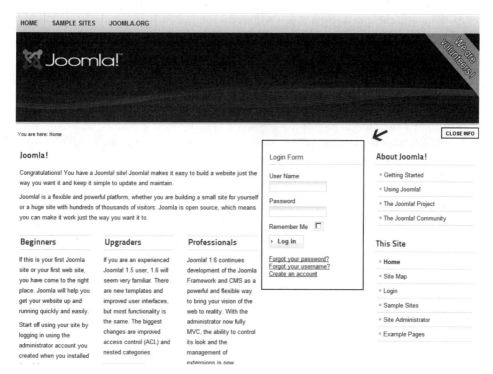

Figure 17.3   Link for showing and hiding the additional information

Showing and hiding the column is done by the file hide.js in the JavaScript folder of the template. In the index.php file of the template, you will find the required HTML code around line 194:

```
<div id="close">
<a href="#" onclick="auf('right')">
<span id="bild">
<?php echo JText::_('TPL_BEEZ2_TEXTRIGHTCLOSE'); ?></span></a>
</div>
```

The function auf ('right') in the file hide.js is called using the onclick event and controls the opening and closing of this area. (*Auf* means "open" in German, and *bild* means "image.")

So that this works in an accessible context as well, it is particularly important to have the focus in the right place and to correctly change the text within the link.

At the top of the index.php file, you will find a number of JavaScript variables that are required so that the integrated scripts can function. Among others, there are those that respond to the text link.

```
var rightopen='<?php echo JText::_('TPL_BEEZ2_TEXTRIGHTOPEN',true); ?>';
var rightclose='<?php echo JText::_('TPL_BEEZ2_TEXTRIGHTCLOSE'); ?>';
```

You control the text content of the JavaScript variables via the Joomla! language strings. If you want to customize them, you can do so using the language files. The variables var big and var small are also required so that this script can work.

Perhaps you remember that whenever the column with the additional information is hidden, the remaining column automatically gets wider. This also happens with showing and hiding. Because JavaScript is executed at runtime, you cannot use the Joomla! internal PHP function here to check if the corresponding column is present. You have to do it via JavaScript. Whenever the column is not present, the navigation column must use the class leftbigger. At the same time, the page area surrounding the actual content has to get narrower.

This is done using the percentage width specifications for the wrapper in the template parameters. The values entered there should correspond to the values that you specified in the position .css file for the areas wrapper and wrapper2. If you later make changes to these page areas in the CSS file, you should bear in mind that you also need to make these changes in the template parameters.

Hiding and Showing Modules

One of the biggest challenges when designing a Web site is creating a clear structure for the content. You often need to accommodate a lot of information, especially on the homepage, without overloading the page.

Both Beez templates have the option of representing modules in the form of sliders. The heading of the module is rendered first. By clicking on a plus symbol next to the heading, you can fold out the module to make its content visible. The plus symbol is then replaced by a minus symbol, and the module can be collapsed again (see Figure 17.4).

For this method, I have also used the accessible WAI-ARIA technique. The basis for the implementation is the, previously described modChrome concept of Joomla! and the hide.js file.

Note
Remember: the modChrome functions are in the HTML folder of the templates in the modules.php file. There, the output for all modules that have the style beezHide is determined.

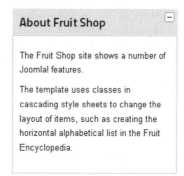

Figure 17.4   Module with foldout function

To use modules in collapsed format, you should integrate them into the template using the statement

```
<jdoc:include type="modules" name="position-8" style="beezHide"
 headerLevel="3" state="0" />
```

All modules located on position-8 are now displayed collapsed, with only their heading showing.

Perhaps you have noticed that this statement also has the attribute state. It controls whether the module is open or collapsed when first loaded.

If you select the value 0, it is collapsed when first loaded; with the value 1, it is folded out by default and the user can decide to close it. Do not forget to inform the visitors of your Web site that certain functions will work only if they allow cookies. To make the whole thing work across multiple pages, the current state of the module is recorded in a cookie.

The WAI-ARIA technique informs users of screen readers of the current state of the module. It is particularly important to inform them not only of the current focus but also to change the alternative text with the plus and minus symbols.

If you want to influence the alternative text or customize the graphics, you can do so using the JavaScript variables at the head of the index.php file:

```
var altopen='<?php echo JText::_('TPL_BEEZ2_ALTOPEN',true); ?>';
var altclose='<?php echo JText::_('TPL_BEEZ2_ALTCLOSE',true); ?>';
var bildauf='<?php echo $this->baseurl ?>/templates/<?php echo
➥$this->template; ?>/images/
plus.png';
var bildzu='<?php echo $this->baseurl ?>/templates/<?php echo
➥$this->template; ?>/images/
minus.png';
```

The alternative text is customizable in the language files, and the graphics can be replaced by adapting the specified path accordingly.

If you want to find out more about the WAI-ARIA technique used here, you can inspect the source code using the Firefox extension Firebug. You can then see that whenever the module is open, the corresponding element has the status `aria-expanded="true"`. If it is closed, it has the value `false`. The status informs users of screen readers of the state of the relevant module.

Accessible Tabs

Presenting content in *tabs* is becoming increasingly popular. There are already modules that add this function to Joomla!, though none of the modules offered come even close to fulfilling the requirements of accessibility. The solution used in Beez makes use of the WAI-ARIA techniques to increase accessibility. Again, the basis is a mixture of JavaScript and the `modChrome` concept.

To show the modules in tabs, you need to add them using the style beezTabs, as shown in the following code. The result is seen in Figure 17.5.

```
<jdoc:include type="modules" name="position-5" style="beezTabs"
 headerLevel="2" id="1" />
```

All modules placed on `position-5` are automatically arranged in tabs. Using the style beezTabs, you can control the HTML output. The attribute `id="3"` is essential because of the structure of the JavaScript. Imagine wanting to integrate modules into your template in this way in different places. The JavaScript function now needs clear information on where it should actually open or close the tabs. If this information is missing, the script is not going to work as you intended. You should use only numbers for the `id` you specify here.

The special features of the script are the WAI-ARIA attributes that are integrated into the source code using JavaScript.

The links for the tabs plus the associated content get a clear link from the ARIA attributes `aria-labelledby` and `aria-controls`. The module content has the

Figure 17.5　Modules in tab display

role `tabcontent`, and the link has the role `tab`. Current states can be made accessible for users of screen readers using the attributes `aria-selected`, `aria-hidden`, or `aria-expanded`.

Customizing Font Size

At the top of the layout, the user has the option of customizing the font size. The technical basis for this method can be found in the JavaScript file templates/your_name/ JavaScript/md_stylechanger.js. In the index.php file, you integrate a `div` container with the `id="fontsize"`. This area is initially empty and later is filled with content using JavaScript. If your visitors have disabled JavaScript, this function will not be available to them.

You may wonder why this function is necessary at all, given that every browser has a font enlargement function. Well, this technique is of special importance especially for seniors who may have some degree of vision impairment. Furthermore, people who know very little about their browser functionality and are happy to have a more obvious option.

beez5: Using HTML5

The beez5 template is hardly different from beez_20. The functions offered are almost identical. The only difference is that with beez5 you can use HTML5. If you look at the template parameters of beez5, you will see that you can choose between HTML5 and XHTML code for the output.

HTML5 offers a great number of new options and will surely entail a number of changes and improvements in the future, but it is still not a fully finalized standard (as of July 2012). Many of the options currently offered cannot be reliably applied in practice yet, but some others can be used without any problems.

We keep hearing rumors that this standard will not be fully completed until 2022. So the question is, why are we using it now? In fact it is the complete implementation of the HTML5 code into browsers that is not expected until 2022, but already, browser manufacturers are busy implementing HTML5.

The new structuring elements are an important feature of HTML5. These elements are a great improvement over HTML4 and XHTML, which suffered from low semantic significance. We now have really useful elements at our disposal for structuring the page and can beautifully structure a page with the elements. The following elements define the basic structure of the Web page:

- `header`
- `footer`
- `aside`
- `nav`

Elements such as the following will help you make the content more significant:

- `section`
- `article`
- `hgroup`

beez5—The index.php File

The HTML5 code used in beez5 uses only the elements that are already working fairly reliably. Only Internet Explorer up to version 8 causes problems. The solutions are described in Chapter 3, "CSS and HTML—Getting the Basic Structure into Shape."

In the page head, a script is inserted, integrating the unknown elements into the existing document structure:

```
<!--[if lt IE 9]>
<script type="text/JavaScript" src="<?php echo $this->baseurl ?>/
templates/beez5/JavaScript/html5.js"></script>
<![endif]-->
```

The integration of HTML5 in Joomla! is based on the template overrides and reacting to the selected markup language via the template parameters in the index.php file. Because the template allows for the use of two different markup languages, you need to address this option in index.php. In other words, the structure of the index.php file is quite complicated because a different HTML code must be output depending on the selected markup language. This begins when determining the document type. If you open index.php of the beez5 template, you will immediately see what I mean:

```
<?php if(!$templateparams->get('html5', 0)): ?>
<!DOCTYPE html PUBLIC "-//W3C//DTD XHTML 1.0 Transitional//EN"
 "http://www.w3.org/TR/xhtml1/DTD/xhtml1-transitional.dtd">
<?php else: ?>
<?php echo '<!DOCTYPE html>'; ?>
<?php endif; ?>
```

This concept continues throughout the entire page, and the HTML5 elements are only output if HTML5 is selected in the back end as well.

If you want to build your own HTML5 template later, it would be better if you remove all statements and XHTML elements and directly output the HTML5 code.

The HTML5 Overrides

The template overrides of the beez5 template output the content as HTML5. In other words, the content made available via the content component com_content is rendered as HTML5. You need to use a little trick to make these overrides function properly.

The reason for this has to do with the system. The template parameters are known to the system only if the template has already been loaded. But we would like to respond to the parameter beforehand, in this case, and load the HTML5 code. Unfortunately, this is not possible. So whenever XHTML code is selected as desired output, we need to get Joomla! to ignore the overrides and use the default output instead. This is done by adding the default XHTML layout using a PHP `require` statement. This statement copies the file that is required and inserts it in place of the `require` statement. Using the `if/else` statement, you either get the XHTML layout copied in or else you use the HTML5 code in this override.

In the file templates/beez5/html/com_content/article/default.php, you need the following code:

```
if ($templateparams->get('html5') != 1) :
require(JPATH_BASE.'/components/com_content/views/article/tmpl/
↪default.php');
/
else :
?>
<article class="item-page<?php echo $this->pageclass_sfx?>">
```

Again, the more elegant approach would be to just have the HTML5 override. Then you would not need to check the parameters, nor would you need the code to bring in the XHTML layout.

Atomic Template

The focus of the Atomic template is on using the CSS framework *Blueprint*. I provide a brief overview of its basic functions, but you can find a lot of further information at *www.blueprintcss.org*.

A CSS framework can be very useful if you can use it to its full extent. Ready CSS classes help you create complex layouts (see Figure 17.6).

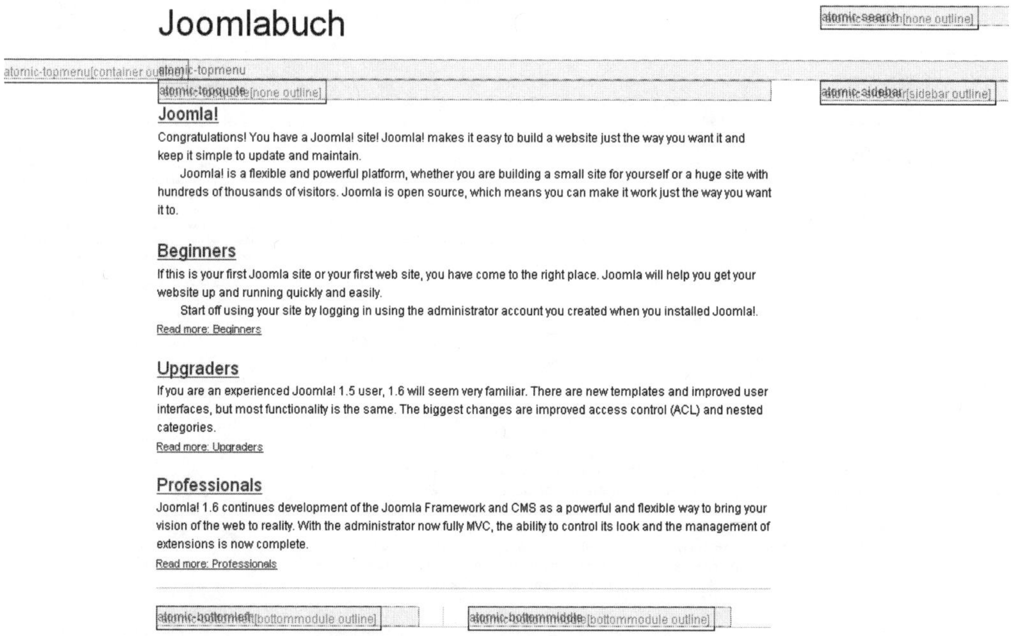

Figure 17.6   Module positions atomic

If you select this template in the back end and look at the page in the front end, you will not notice anything special at first. The template appears to be lacking all design, but it only looks this way because it has not been adapted to the present example content. In the template preview, you can see exactly where modules can be positioned and what these module positions are called.

Once you have placed the modules in the correct positions, the whole thing looks a lot prettier (see Figure 17.7).

The concept of the Blueprint CSS framework is based on a 24-column layout. The available workspace has a fixed width of 950 pixels in the default version and is divided into 24 columns of 30 pixels each. Each column has a right margin of 10 pixels, meaning the columns require 40 pixels of space. You can assign each columns a corresponding width by using the classes span-1 to span-24.

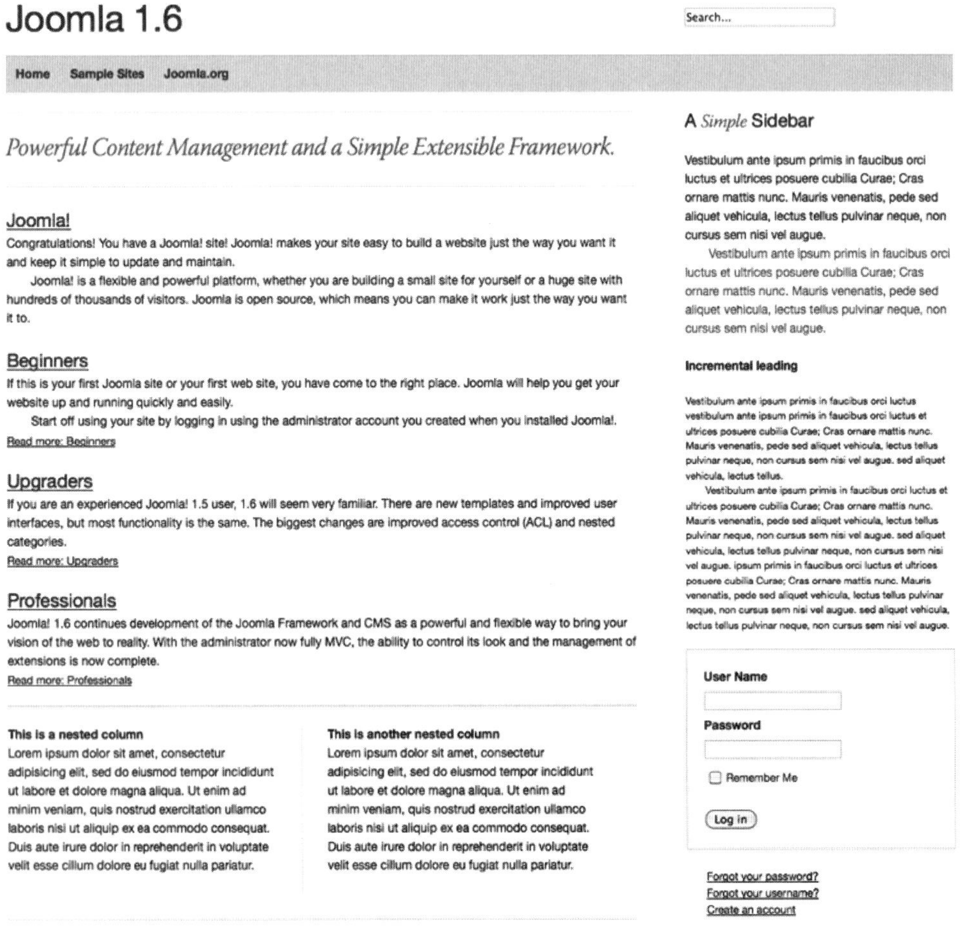

Figure 17.7   Atomic in action

Within this area, you can then place further columns or boxes as needed. Here is a quick example:

```
<div class="container">
<div id="header" class="span-24">
<p>Lorem Ipsum</p>
</div>
<div id="content" class="span-16">
<p>Lorem Ipsum</p>
</div>
<div id="sidebar" class="span-8">
<p>Lorem Ipsum</p>
</div>
<div id="footer" class="span-24 last">
<p>Lorem Ipsum</p>
</div>
</div>
```

In the screen.css file of the template, you can find CSS classes .span-1 to .span-24:

```
column, .span-1, .span-2, .span-3, .span-4, .span-5, .span-6, .span-7,
.span-8, .span-9, .span-10, .span-11, .span-12, .span-13, .span-14,
.span-15, .span-16, .span-17, .span-18, .span-19, .span-20, .span-21,
.span-22, .span-23, .span-24
{float:left;margin-right:10px;}
.last {margin-right:0;}
...
.span-8 {width:310px;}
...
.span-16 {width:630px;}
...
.span-24 {width:950px;margin-right:0;}
```

All elements with these classes are floated and have a specific width. The `div` with the class .span-24, for example, stretches over the full width, and the one with the class .span-8 stretches over eight columns, so it has an actual width of 310 pixels.

Many designers do not want a fixed page width but prefer fluid layouts with percentage specifications. This is also possible. In the folder css/blueprint/plugins/ you will find the liquid.css file, which takes care of exactly this task.

In addition to the already mentioned CSS files, you will also find, among others:

- print.css for printing
- ie.css specifically for Internet Explorer

The screen.css file described earlier is an aggregate of the original files typographie.css, reset.css, typography.css, grid.css, and forms.css, which were originally present in the framework. If you combine these files into one, the result is a clear performance increase, as only one file has to squeeze through the line.

18

Practical Implementation

The final four chapters of this book show you how you can put your previously acquired knowledge into practice and create your own individualized template. The example is based on the beez_20 template.

Let's develop a template for a music store using a layout I first created in Photoshop (see Figure 18.1).

The step-by-step instructions show you how you can quickly and effectively achieve your desired result. You do not necessarily have to follow the order of the steps, but this approach has proven successful in my everyday practical work, and it demonstrates how quickly you can customize the template to meet your requirements.

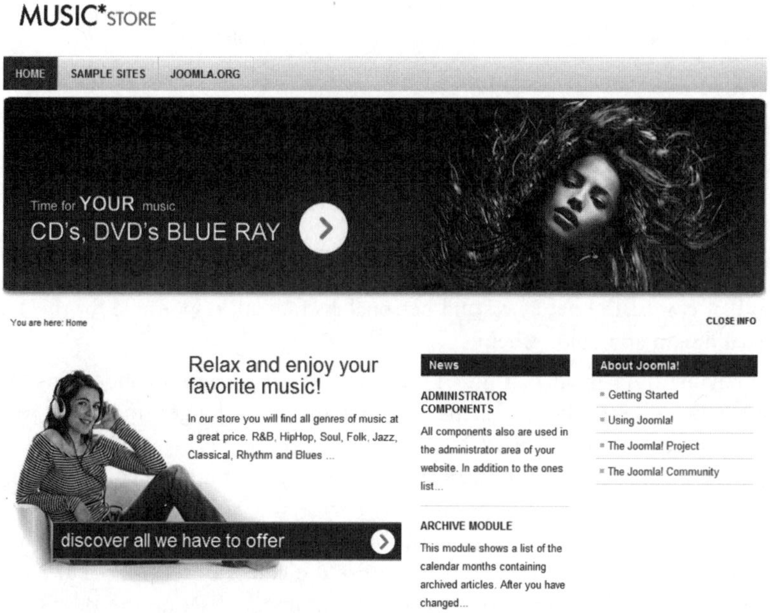

Figure 18.1   The design for the new template

The next three chapters show you how to:

- Restructure contents, adapt design, and then test it (Chapter 19, "Step by Step to a New Layout")

- Tidy up the template and integrate custom features (Chapter 20, "Integrating Custom Features")

- Install the template (Chapter 21, "Final Tasks: Fine-Tuning and Creating an Installable Zip Archive")

But before we get started, I want to add a few words on the structure of the underlying Beez template.

Concept of the Beez Templates

The Beez templates were built, among other reasons, to demonstrate the flexibility of Joomla! templates. Therefore, they contain a number of things that you do not really need in everyday use and that you can simply remove from your projects later. They are intended as a kind of instruction, or a pattern that shows you how you can solve certain problems in the quickest and most effective way. A good example is the structure of the Cascading Style Sheets (CSS) files, which enable you to implement practically any layout.

Note

In the final phase of this book I had a telephone conversation with someone from the Joomla! core team who complained about this complexity. He asked me why there are so many CSS statements that overwrite one another. This telephone conversation led me to explain the concept in a little more detail in this book.

The idea behind the Beez CSS concept was to create the highest possible degree of flexibility. These are the elementary CSS files and their responsibilities:

- The position.css file is responsible for the structure of the page.

- The layout.css file takes care of the margins, padding, sizes, and positioning within this frame layout.

- And, of course, the nature.css and personal.css files are responsible for the actual visual design and color scheme.

If you rename the personal.css file of the beez_20 template in a standard installation with the example files in such a way that the system can no longer find it, the result will be like the one shown in Figure 18.2.

As you can see, the positioning stays largely unchanged while the color, design, and therefore any kind of individuality is lost.

Whenever the discussion in the Joomla! forum revolves around CSS, I frequently notice that many people find it easy to customize the colors or font sizes but have problems with positioning individual page areas. For that reason. I set up the Beez templates

Figure 18.2   Designing the beez_20 template without personal.css

so you can use as many display variations as possible. I designed the structure in such a way that it can be used to implement almost any design easily by just changing a minimum of CSS. You can already achieve a great number of different positions by making choices in the Joomla! back end.

The pictures that follow give just a few examples. In Figure 18.3, the navigation is positioned, using the template parameter, to the left of the content. No modules are positioned in the column used for the additional information. The current menu item—here the homepage—is a two-column article design without leading articles.

In Figure 18.4, the navigation is again positioned, using the template parameters, to the left of the content. The newsflash module is set to `position-6` and enabled for the homepage. It is therefore now visible in the right column. The content is still output in two columns.

In the view shown in Figure 18.5, the client decided on a three-column presentation of the content with a leading article. This setting can be entered in the administrator back end using the parameters of the relevant menu item.

In Figure 18.6, the navigation is positioned to the right of the content. The corresponding settings can be entered in the administrator back end in the Template Manager. You may recall, both Beez templates offer the parameter Position of Navigation for this setting. If you select After Content there, the column that was previously positioned on

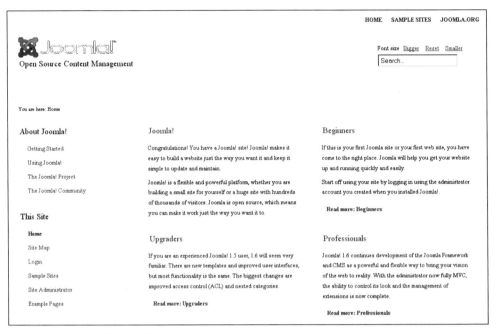

Figure 18.3   Two-column layout with two content columns

Figure 18.4   Three-column layout with two content columns

Figure 18.5   Three-column layout with three content columns and leading article

Figure 18.6   Three-column layout, content before navigation

the right will automatically move into the center. The articles themselves are presented in two columns.

In Figure 18.7, the articles are presented in one column, and the navigation is placed, using the template parameters, to the right.

These are just a few examples of the possible display variations that can be achieved using the back end alone and without altering any files. You probably know that Joomla! has a wide range of variations in terms of display of the contents.

You have the homepage, the blog view, the article view, the archive view, the category view, the editing view, and so on. You can create contacts pages, present links and news-feeds in structured form, or display search results, and this is by no means all you can do. All these views have to be formatted in the Joomla! default templates using CSS.

This explains why the CSS files of the two Beez templates are so large. If you are going to build your own template later, you will realize that you probably do not really need a lot of it. In most cases it makes sense to remove the CSS statements that are not required from the files, which can significantly improve the loading time of the page under certain circumstances.

Figure 18.7   Two columns, content before navigation, one content column

19

Step by Step
to a New Layout

Before we start implementing the design into the template structure, we should first think about the content structure and the structure of the site as a whole and compare the desired result with the current design to determine the necessary steps. The simplest way to do this is to move step by step, from top to bottom, through the site. The desired layout is shown in Figure 19.1.

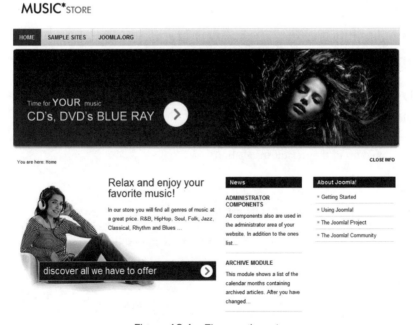

Figure 19.1 The new layout

The basis for the design is the beez_20 template you renamed and installed Joomla! together with the example data. If you have not read the previous chapters, please go back to Chapter 11, "The XML File and the Template Parameters," to learn about the template XML file. There you will learn the steps required to rename your template with a custom name. If possible, work with the Firefox browser—you will need its plug-in, Firebug, a lot.

If you now look at the default installation of Joomla! and compare it to our desired layout, you will see a few differences. Let's discuss them one by one.

Step 1: Positioning the Navigation

Let's start by changing the menu navigation so that it is positioned the way you want it.

Problem

The navigation is in the left column. For the new design, you want to position it on the right.

Action

Navigate in the back end to Extensions and select the Template Manager. Click on the default style of your template and change the parameter for positioning the navigation to After Content. When you save your changes, the navigation should be in the right column.

Step 2: Filling the Center Column with Content

Next, we look at getting the content into the center column.

Problem

You want to display two articles from lower-level areas in the center column, but there is no center column in the default installation.

Action

To output content from lower-level areas, the module *Articles Category* is useful. It is particularly flexible in its display and offers many selection options. To position the module in the center column, you can choose from the following module positions, in this order:

1. position-6
2. position-8
3. position-3

If you forget this position later, the template preview in the back end will quickly tell you how the modules are positioned in the template.

Tip

In the Template Manager, go to the Templates tab and click on the word Preview directly below the template name. If the preview is not enabled there, you need to enable it by clicking on the Options button above the template overview and then enabling the preview.

Go to the Module Manager in the back end and create a new module of the type *Articles Category*.

1. Enter the word *News* as title.

2. Position it on `position-6`.

3. On the right, select the Filtering Options and enter 2 in the Count field: two articles are then output. In the Category field, select All Categories for now as these are only example contents.

4. Select Display Options. As you can see, you can determine the heading hierarchy of the output articles here. For now you can leave it set to `h4`. Set Linked Titles to yes and Introtext to show. Then you still have the option of specifying the displayed number of characters of the introductory text. In my example, I chose 100.

5. You need to assign the module to the menu item Home, as it should be displayed only on the homepage. You can do this via the settings in the category Menu Assignment. Change the Module Assignment to Only on the Pages Selected, then click on Clear Selection to remove all the checkmarks. Click on the tab for the Main Menu, then click the box next to Home to select the menu item Home.

Do not forget to publish the module if its status is unpublished. After you save, the page should look as shown in Figure 19.2.

Optimizing Step 2: More Meaningful Names for Module Positions

You know that module positions

- `position-6`
- `position-8`
- `position-3`

are used in what is now the center column. But these abstract names have little meaning for the site editors who will be responsible for maintaining the site later. You should think about renaming the module positions with more meaningful, and therefore more

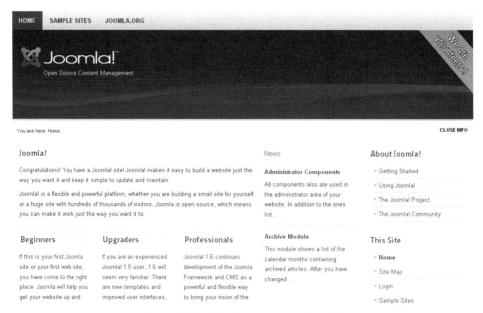

Figure 19.2   Result after steps 1 and 2

memorable, names. Theoretically, and depending on the concept, there are two different approaches. You can choose names that describe the module position in the design, such as

- `middle-top`
- `middle-middle`
- `middle-bottom`

Or, you can choose names that tell something about the content of the modules, such as

- `news`
- `login`
- `search`

This is, of course, dangerous if one day you want to place modules in this position that have nothing to do with that content.

On the other hand, you could also mix both types of names:

- `middle-news`
- `middle-login`
- `middle-search`

The concept you choose depends greatly on your own preferences for the site structure and the amount of content. I decided to use this version:

- `middle-top`
- `middle-middle`
- `middle-bottom`

Actions

To rename the module positions and make sure the page still works properly, you need
to replace the names used in the index.php file in all places where they are used with the
new names. You also need to save the module positions in the XML file so they are still
available in a new installation. If you want, you can also add a description for these positions in the template's language file.

Adapting the index.php File

Open the index.php file of the template and navigate down until you find these lines
(about line 190):

```
<div id="right">
<a id="additional"></a>
<jdoc:include type="modules" name="position-6"
 style="beezDivision" headerLevel="3"/>
<jdoc:include type="modules" name="position-8"
style="beezDivision" headerLevel="3" />
<jdoc:include type="modules" name="position-3"
 style="beezDivision" headerLevel="3" />
</div>
```

As you can see, this is where the module positions position-6, position-8,
and position-3 are integrated.

Replace the name attribute of the jdoc:include statement with your new
position names:

```
<div id="right">
<a id="additional"></a>
<jdoc:include type="modules" name="middle-top"
 style="beezDivision" headerLevel="3"/>
<jdoc:include type="modules" name="middle-middle"
 style="beezDivision" headerLevel="3" />
<jdoc:include type="modules" name="middle-bottom"
 style="beezDivision" headerLevel="3" />
</div>
```

The right column is displayed only if it also has content. This is achieved, as you know, using the function countModules() (see Chapter 13, "Modules—Dynamics within the Presentation").

Our example uses the auxiliary variable $showRightColumn for this, which is defined at the very top of the document:

```
$showRightColumn =($this->countModules('position-3') or
➥$this-> countModules('position-6') or
➥$this->countModules('position-8'));
```

But because the module position names have now changed, you also need to change them here accordingly:

```
$showRightColumn = ($this->countModules('middle-top') or
➥$this-> countModules('middle-middle') or
➥$this->countModules('middle-bottom'));
```

Otherwise the following request cannot work as intended:

```
<?php if ($showRightColumn) : ?>
//show right column
<?php endif; ?>
```

Adapting the XML File

The newly renamed module positions now have to be entered in the XML file of the template as well so that they are automatically available for selection in the back end later.

Insert them in the appropriate place in the XML file templateDetails.xml:

```
<position>middle-top</position>
<position>middle-middle</position>
<position>middle-bottom</position>
```

Once you have carried out these steps and all files are saved, have a look at the page in the front end. You will see the consequences of your actions.

The center column is gone. Why?

The News module positioned there is still on position-6, but this position no longer exists in your template. You must position this module on the position middle-top. Once you have done that, it will all look as it should again.

Adapting Language Files

Chapter 13 explained how you can integrate an explanation of the relevant module positions into the template-specific language file. The responsible file is the template-internal language file with the extension: sys.ini, templates/your_name/language/en-GB/en-GB. your_name.sys.ini.

Insert the explanations there for the three new positions following the pattern TPL_ YOUR_NAME_POSITION_MIDDLE-TOP="Middle Position Top".

Step 3: Adjusting the Number of Articles

The next thing you need to do is change the number of articles that are displayed on this page.

Problem

In the main content of your new layout, you want only one article to be presented on the homepage, but there are four in the default setup—a leading article at the top and below it three columns with one article each.

Action

In the back end, go to the menu item of the homepage (Home) in the main menu and select the following settings under Layout Options:

- Leading Articles: 1
- Intro Articles: 0
- Links: 0
- Pagination: Hide
- Pagination Results: Hide

Now you should see only one article.

Once you have carried out these steps, the page structure should correspond to your draft without having touched the structure in index.php, but just by using the setting options in the back end. You can now move on to designing the Web site itself.

Step 4: Visually Designing the Header

Now it's time to work on getting the header to match the new design.

Problem

You can see that in the new draft the logo is located above the navigation bar, and the search field has an image button in the form of a double arrow. In the actual Beez templates, the navigation bar is visually arranged above the logo.

Actions

To make creative design changes to the Cascading Style Sheets (CSS) of the Web site, Firebug is an indispensable aid, because it saves you from painstakingly searching for the responsible CSS statements in the various CSS files.

Adapting the Main Menu

To position the logo above the navigation bar, first use Firebug to look at the properties of the main menu (see Figure 19.3).

You can see that the main menu here has an absolute position, `<ul class="menu">`. This lets you locate it in the semantically correct position after the logo in the document

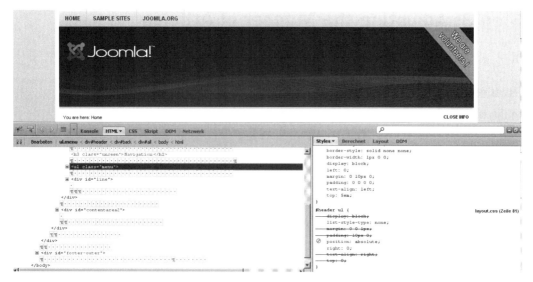

Figure 19.3   Properties of the main menu

but visually before the logo. Keeping a logical semantic document flow is important, as described in Chapter 2, "Accessibility: What Is It?"

But now you want to place the navigation bar after the logo as well (as shown in Figure 19.4), which you can easily achieve by removing the absolute positioning.

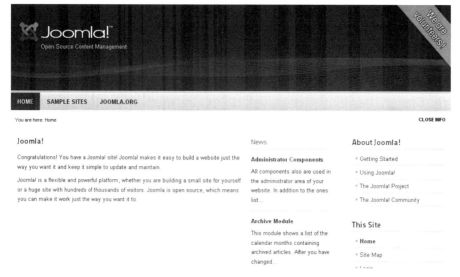

Figure 19.4   Menu below the logo

The CSS statements for this can be found in the layout.css file in line 81, so you change this:

```
#header ul
{
display:block;
margin:0px 0px 1px 0px;
text-align:right;
list-style-type:none;
padding:10px 0px 10px 0px;
position:absolute;
top:0;
right:0px;
}
```

to this:

```
#header ul
{
display:block;
margin:0px 0px 1px 0px;
text-align:right;
list-style-type:none;
padding:10px 0px 10px 0px;
}
```

And now the menu is below the logo.

Formatting the Logo Area

The area surrounding the logo with the blue background is very tall (see Figure 19.5). Let's have a closer look at its formatting.

You can see that the logo is enclosed by a div container with the class .logo-header. This container is assigned a minimum height of 200 pixels and a background image in the personal.css file (line 94). Now remove both those lines.

The background image disappears, as expected, but sadly the height stays the same (see Figure 19.6).

The reason is that there is a fallback in the position.css file. Both styles of the Beez template require a minimum height for this area. In the Personal style, this height is a little bit taller than in the Nature style. That's why the height that was actually determined in position.css was then overwritten in personal.css. To now remove the height altogether, go to the position.css file at line 225 and remove the min-height of 159 pixels.

But this action is not enough to get the logo area to the correct height. For one thing, the enclosing h1 with the id="logo" has a padding, and for another, the header padding is 8 em (see Figure 19.7).

This is because the region that contains the search box and the font enlargement button has been positioned absolutely, so it is located after the navigation bar in the page

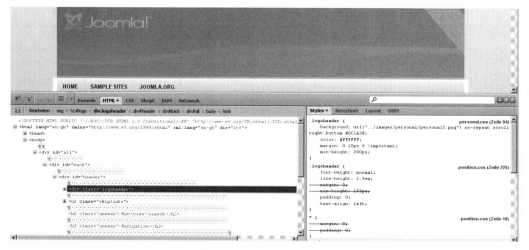

Figure 19.5   Logo header

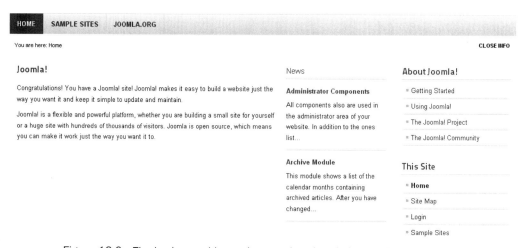

Figure 19.6   The background image is gone, but the whole area is still too high.

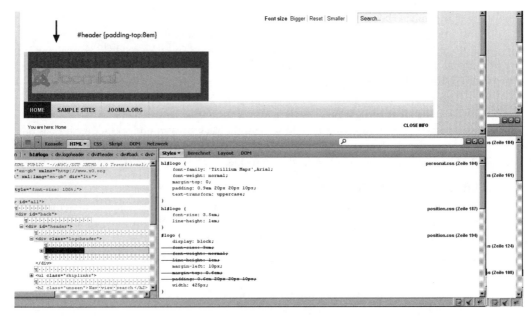

Figure 19.7   Padding header and H1

structure but is positioned visually at the top left. To make things clearer, try looking at the page without stylesheets. In Firefox, you can find this function under View → Page Style → No Style.

If you were now to enlarge the page font, the page areas would overlap without this padding. You can adapt the padding of the h1 in line 104 of the personal.css file to 0.5 em from top and bottom. The specification in ems is useful in this case because it ensures that the proportions are kept even if the font is enlarged.

```
h1#logo
{
font-family: 'Titillium Maps', Arial;
padding: 0.5em 0px;
text-transform:uppercase;
font-weight:normal;
margin-top:0;
}
```

And now the logo moves up a bit.

The padding of the header can be adapted in line 91. I used an initial padding-top of 2 em.

```
#all #header
{padding-top:2.0em ;
}
```

The result is shown in Figure 19.8.

In the next step, you just need to replace the logo using the template parameters.

I created a logo in the appropriate size in Photoshop and then loaded the image using the Media Manager into the system's Images folder. It is then directly integrated into the template via the template parameters.

If you want to design an accessible site, you should make sure your logo does not have a transparent background. People with vision impairments sometimes use their own stylesheets. If, for example, a yellow font against a black background was set in this custom stylesheet and the text or signet in your logo is also black, the logo would remain invisible.

The result with the new logo is shown in Figure 19.9.

Integrating Image Button for the Search

A form without buttons is difficult for most people to use. Our layout will therefore have an image with two arrows as a Send button. I created this image in Photoshop; to integrate it into the layout, you need to take the following steps.

1. Go to the Module Manager in the back end and open the Search module that is displayed on all pages. It will be in `position-0`.

2. Choose the following in the Basic options:

   Search Button: yes
   Button Position: right
   Search Button Image: yes

3. Save the module.

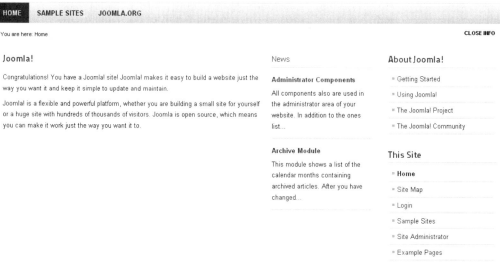

Figure 19.8   The header and logo now look just as intended.

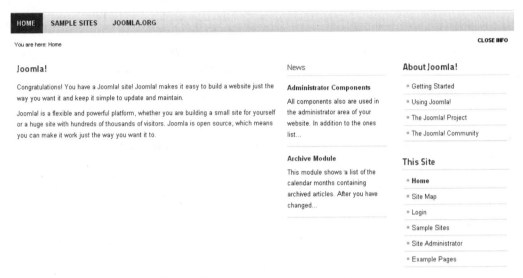

Figure 19.9   The new logo is now visible.

In the front end you will now see something that looks like a button but in fact isn't one. If you inspect the output code, you can see that the image is output as a button, but the path used leads nowhere. The formatting of this pseudo-button is determined by its class, .button.

```
<input type="image" value="Search" class="button"
→src="/joomlabook_ installation/"
→onclick="this.form.searchword.focus();"/>
```

To integrate your own graphic, you need to store it under the name *searchButton.gif* in the images folder of your template. Make sure you input the correct spelling and get the file extension right; otherwise the graphic will not be displayed.

The result (shown in Figure 19.10) is still not quite right.

Figure 19.10   Custom button displayed still needs
a few CSS changes to fit seamlessly.

The class .button interferes with the display of the graphic. You can make changes around line 289 of the personal.css file. Here you will see this statement:

```
#header form .button
{
border:solid 0px #ddd;
background:#ccc url(../images/personal/button.png);
color:#333;
padding:4px !important
}
```

Now change the background color to #fff and set the padding to 0:

```
#header form .button
{
border:solid 0px #ddd;
background:#fff;
color:#333;
padding:0 !important
}
```

Now your button should look as you intended.

Checking Semantics

We discussed the importance of having a semantically logical structure in Chapter 2. You now need to check whether the visual structure corresponds to the content structure. You have two options for doing this:

1. See how the template reacts when you move through the page using the keyboard.
2. Look at the page without stylesheets.

Problems with Keyboard Navigation

If you move through the page using the keyboard, you will notice that the sequence of the elements in focus no longer corresponds to the visual presentation. The tabbing starts with the skip links, then goes to the navigation, and only then to the font size options and the search. But the visual presentation demands that the font size and search options appear before the navigation (see Figure 19.11).

To keep the tabbing order in the same order as the visual display, the font size and the search areas must be moved to before the navigation in the index.php file.

You will also notice on your own display that the site description *Open Source Content Management* is not visible, though it is taking up space. This is because it has been assigned a white font color using CSS, which doesn't show against a white background. Let's fix

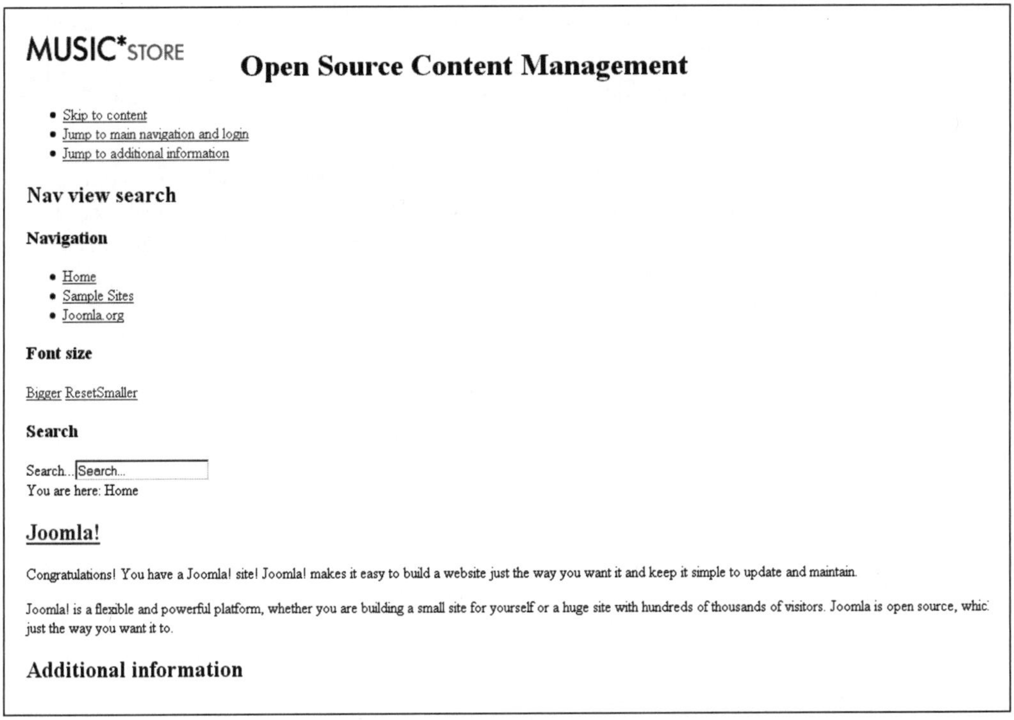

MUSIC*STORE   **Open Source Content Management**

- Skip to content
- Jump to main navigation and login
- Jump to additional information

Nav view search

Navigation

- Home
- Sample Sites
- Joomla.org

Font size

Bigger ResetSmaller

Search

Search... [Search...]
You are here: Home

Joomla!

Congratulations! You have a Joomla! site! Joomla! makes it easy to build a website just the way you want it and keep it simple to update and maintain.

Joomla! is a flexible and powerful platform, whether you are building a small site for yourself or a huge site with hundreds of thousands of visitors. Joomla is open source, whic just the way you want it to.

Additional information

Figure 19.11   Page without stylesheets

this so you can see the text. Around line 83 of the personal.css file, the font color for this site description is specified. Replace the color white with a very dark gray:

```
#logo span
{
color:#333;
padding-left:50px;
font-size:0.3em !important;
text-transform:none;
font-family:arial, sans-serif
}
```

Now that we can see the site description, we can decide what we want to do with it. According to our layout, it should not be visible. Yet such a description can contain useful information on the Web site's content, which is especially important for people with impaired vision and for search engines. You can edit the text of this site description in the template parameters and customize it as you wish. Because my example is about a music store, I added the following text:

> Find your music: R&B, HipHop, Soul, Folk, Jazz, Classical, Rhythm and Blues and more

This text gives information about the purpose and content of the Web site and feeds relevant keywords to search engines. You now need to hide this text from visual users. To do this, open the template's index.php file. As you can see, the logo is added around line 116:

```
<h1 id="logo">
<?php if ($logo): ?>
<img src="<?php echo $this->baseurl ?>/<?php echo
htmlspecialchars($logo); ?>" alt="<?php echo
htmlspecialchars($templateparams->get('sitetitle'));?>" />
<?php endif;?>
<?php if (!$logo ): ?>
<?php echo htmlspecialchars($templateparams->get('sitetitle'));?>
<?php endif; ?>
<span class="header1">
<?php echo htmlspecialchars($templateparams->
get('sitedescription'));?>
</span>
</h1>
```

Before we deal with the site description, notice that the logo has an alternative text assigned. This text is defined by the Site Title set in the template parameters. We have not yet changed this alternative text, and should do so now. I used the logo title *Music Store*. Now change your site title in the template style parameters to Music Store. If you look at the source text, you can see that the logo now has that alternative text.

The page description is in the h1 in a span with the class .header1. To make this area invisible in the visual presentation, you need to position the span outside of the visual area of the Web site using CSS:

```
position:absolute;
left:-3000px;
top:-3000px
```

Do not use display:none, because then the text is invisible even for users of screen readers. As a solution to this problem, the Beez template offers the predefined class .unseen, which you can also find in the invisible subheadings.

Now replace the class header1 with unseen:

```
<span class="unseen">
<?php echo htmlspecialchars($templateparams->
 get('sitedescription'));?>
</span>
```

In the visual presentation, you will no longer see this subheading. It will become visible only if you disable the stylesheets.

Now let's move on to the order of the content. Around line 138 of the index.php file you will see the `div` container with the `id="line"`. This container holds the font enlargement and the text field for the search. You need to move this whole container to just above the navigation in the document structure, which is the `jdoc` statement on line 136:

```
<h2 class="unseen"><?php echo JText::_('TPL_BEEZ2_NAV_VIEW_SEARCH');
<div id="line">
<div id="fontsize"></div>
<h3 class="unseen"><?php echo JText::_('TPL_BEEZ2_SEARCH'); ?></h3>
<jdoc:include type="modules" name="position-0" />
</div> <!-- end line -->
<h3 class="unseen"><?php echo JText::_('TPL_BEEZ2_NAVIGATION'); ?></h3>
<jdoc:include type="modules" name="position-1" />
```

If you look at the page and navigate using the keyboard, you will see that the order is now correct.

But if you look at the page with the stylesheets disabled, there is a little error, as shown in Figure 19.12.

The text order of the content in this heading no longer corresponds to the actual content order. You should change the order in the language file. It should no longer say `Nav View Search`, but instead, `View Search and Navigation`.

```
<h2 class="unseen"><?php echo JText::_('TPL_BEEZ2_NAV_VIEW_SEARCH');
 ?></h2>
```

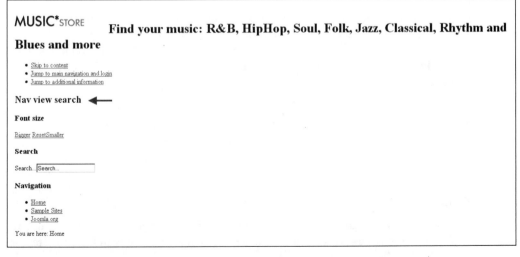

Figure 19.12   The invisible subheading is not quite right anymore.

The language string `TPL_BEEZ2_NAV_VIEW_SEARCH` should therefore be changed in the language file of your template:

```
TPL_BEEZ2_NAV_VIEW_SEARCH="View Search and Navigation"
```

Remember that the language file can be found under templates/your_name/language/en-GB/en-GB.your_name.ini.

Adapting Language Strings and Language File

You can also remove all the Beez names from the language strings in the index.php file and adapt them in accordance with your template name. Change all the `TPL_BEEZ2` language keys to start with `TPL_YOUR_NAME`, as in this example. Replace

```
<h2 class="unseen"><?php echo JText::_('TPL_BEEZ2_NAV_VIEW_SEARCH');
 ?></h2>
```

with:

```
<h2 class="unseen"><?php echo
 JText::_('TPL_YOUR_NAME_NAV_VIEW_SEARCH'); ?></h2>
```

Now you need to make the same changes in the language file as well.

```
TPL_BEEZ2_NAV_VIEW_SEARCH="View Search and Navigation"
```

becomes:

```
TPL_YOUR_NAME_NAV_VIEW_SEARCH="View Search and Navigation"
```

Your editor's search-and-replace function can make this work much easier for you. Don't forget: the language file also contains the language strings for the template parameters used in the back end. These are defined in the template's XML file around line 60. Please also make the necessary changes there.

Here is a brief example:

```
<field name="wrapperSmall" class="validate-numeric" type="text"
➥default="53" label="TPL_YOUR_NAME_FIELD_WRAPPERSMALL_LABEL"
➥description="TPL_YOUR_NAME_FIELD_WRAPPERSMALL_DESC"
➥filter="integer" />
```

Result

The header now corresponds to our draft in terms of both design and semantics. You have even begun to tidy up and adapted the language files in accordance with the template.

Step 5: Integrating the Module Position for the Header Picture

In this step you want to add your header picture in such a way that you can display different pictures on different pages.

Problem

Below the navigation, you want to display a header picture that may need to be replaced on the subpages with a different picture, depending on circumstances.

Action

You need to provide a module position in the index.php file directly below the navigation, from which the image can later be loaded onto the page. I created the image in Photoshop and uploaded it to the system's images folder using the Media Manager. It has a width of 960 pixels and a height of 240 pixels.

Open the template's index.php file and insert a module position there directly after the `header` and before the content. For this position, you should use a meaningful name, such as `headerimage`.

```
...
</div>
<!-- end header -->
<jdoc:include type="modules" name="headerimage" />
<div id="<?php echo $showRightColumn ? 'contentarea2' : 'contentarea';
?>">
...
```

The `jdoc:include` statement was not assigned a style attribute, so the module output will be displayed without surrounding elements in the HTML code.

Now you need to remember to add the position `headerimage` to the positions that already exist in the XML file.

```
<position>headerimage</position>
```

Once these preparations are complete, you can create a module of the type *Custom-HTML*. Select a meaningful module title, assign the module the position `headerimage`, place the desired image in the textbox provided, and make sure the image is displayed on all pages.

In my example, the result looks like the one shown in Figure 19.13.

The image is too narrow for the whole layout: it is aligned to the left, and on the right the result is an unattractive space. To solve this problem, several steps are necessary.

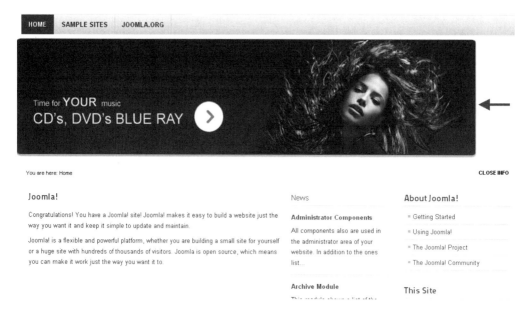

Figure 19.13   The inserted graphic is too narrow.

Adding a Class to Surrounding div

To make CSS formatting possible in this area, you first need a uniquely identifiable `div` container that surrounds the image.

You have two options. The first is to simply place this `div` in the index.php file around the `jdoc:include` statement, but then you need to make sure this code is output only if there actually is a module loaded in that position. This is done using the function `countModules()`.

```
<?php if ($this->countModules('headerimage') :?>
<div id="headerimage">
<jdoc:include type="modules" name="headerimage" />
</div>
<?php endif ; ?>
```

The second option is to use the already existing code more effectively.

The Module Class Suffix

If you output a module of the type *Custom*, the content of the textbox is automatically surrounded by a `div` container with the class `.custom`. Joomla! offers the option of adding a suffix to this class, which allows individual formatting using CCS. You can find this setting (shown in Figure 19.14) in all modules under Advanced Options.

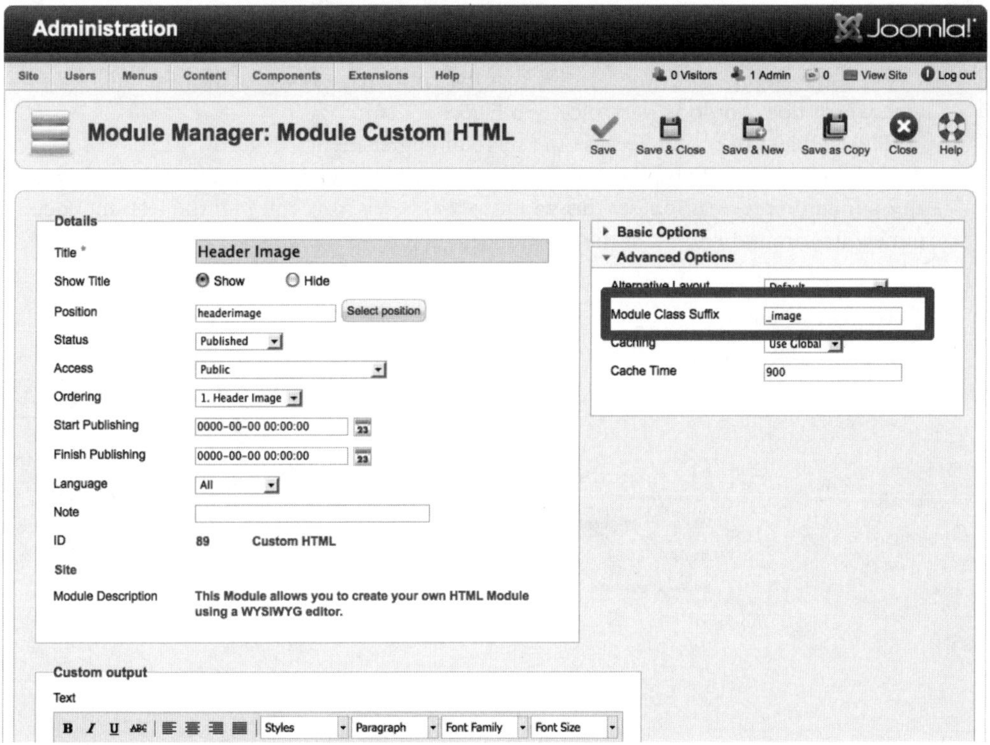

Figure 19.14   Module Class Suffix

If you enter _image here and save the module, you get the following result:

```
<div class="custom_image">
<p><img src=/images/template/headerimage.jpg"
border="0" /></p>
</div>
```

You can now individually format this div using CSS. You should make the formatting changes in the personal.css file of the template.

To center the image, you need the following code:

```
.custom_image
{text-align:center }
```

Chapter 3, "CSS and HTML: Getting the Basic Structure into Shape," mentioned that it is possible to assign two different classes to one element: <div class="custom image">. If you want this as an additional class instead of a suffix on the existing class, you need to insert a space before the actual text in the module in the field for the suffix (see Figure 19.15). This example uses a suffix instead.

Once this step is done, you can see that the entire page is wider than the inserted picture, which does not look very nice (see Figure 19.16).

This problem occurred because the surrounding element <div id="all"> has a maximum width of 1050 pixels. You now need to adapt it to your image width. To get an optimum representation, set this width to 980 pixels. You will find the relevant code somewhere around line 32 of the position.css file:

```
#all
{ margin: 0 auto;
max-width:980 ;
padding: 0px;
text-align: left;
}
```

Figure 19.15   Space before actual text

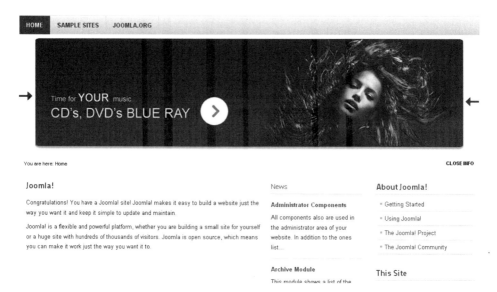

Figure 19.16   Unattractive spacing on left and right

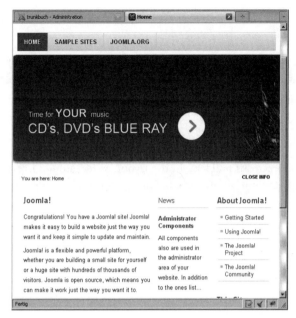

Figure 19.17   Display of page after shrinking in browser

You may wonder why the page has a maximum width and not a fixed width. It is so the user can shrink it, even at small resolutions, without unattractive horizontal scrollbars appearing. If you try this now, however, you will notice that it does not shrink. The size of the image automatically stretches the page out. You can use CSS to prevent the page from stretching. If you assign the container surrounding the image the property overflow:hidden, the image will be automatically cut off when you shrink the page. This is no big deal in most cases, because such images usually just serve as decoration. Make this change, shown below, in the personal.css file. In Figure 19.17, you can see the result if the page is reduced.

```
.custom_image
{
text-align:center;
overflow:hidden
}
```

Step 6: Adapting the Footer

Next you check the footer section for any changes that are necessary.

Problem

If you scroll all the way down, you will see that the change of the maximum page width has resulted in the footer being too wide (see Figure 19.18).

Figure 19.18   The footer is wider than the actual content.

Action

You can quickly correct this problem. In the layout.css file, around line 1402, the footer is assigned a maximum width of 1020 pixels. Change this value to 950 pixels:

```
#footer
{
padding:15px 10px 15px 20px;
text-align:right;
margin:0 auto;
display:block;
max-width:950px;
overflow:hidden
}
```

Step 7: Adapting the Minimum Height of Content

In this step, you get rid of some unneeded modules and tweak some CSS to make the display look better.

Problem

Your layout calls for only one menu in the right column, but there are still two there: About Joomla! and This Site. Disable This Site via the Module Manager.

There are a few other modules the layout does not use. Please also disable Login Form, Shop, Book Store, and Contribute.

You can now see a relatively large, white empty space above the footer (see Figure 19.19).

The culprit is the predefined minimum height of the div container that surrounds the content:

```
<div id="main">
```

You can find the CSS specifications for it in the position.css file somewhere near line 84. Adapt the minimum height to 320 pixels.

```
#main
{
padding: 10px 0px 20px 0px;
```

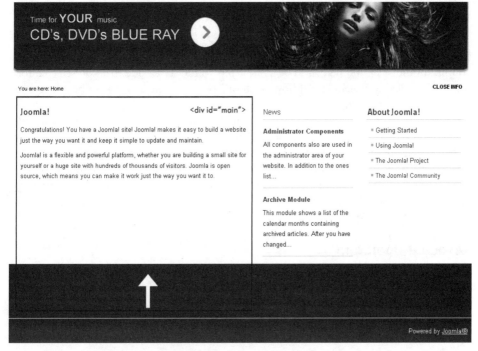

Figure 19.19   Space above footer

```
position: relative;
min-height:320px;
}
```

Step 8: The First Tests

You have finished positioning the content on the homepage. Now it's time for the first tests! Here is where the first important questions arise.

- How does the design behave when the font is enlarged?
- Can the page be operated using the keyboard?
- Will your design be represented correctly in all browsers?

Font Enlargement

As you probably already know, you can influence the representation of the page in the browser in different ways. Most browsers offer the option of enlarging the entire page with all content, which unfortunately can result in certain page areas being pushed outside of the viewport and only being reachable by scrolling horizontally. The other option is to just display the enlarged font.

In Firefox you will find this setting in View → Zoom. Make sure the option Zoom Text Only is enabled. The WCAG 2 (see Chapter 2) demands a possible font size adaptation in this mode of 200 percent. The value refers to the start value that you selected for your default display. Regardless of how small or large your font is, it has to be possible to enlarge it by 200 percent.

In the test, your layout is as meek as a lamb. Even at a zoom level of 300 percent and a resolution of 800 × 600 pixels, the layout still looks as it should (see Figure 19.20).

But watch out: in the example texts, we only use the English language with words that are much shorter than in other languages, such as German and Dutch. If you write a site in another language and a very long word appears in the navigation, it will stretch the page area in which it is located. Consequently, the page cannot be shrunk quite as far when the font is enlarged.

Keyboard Operation

If you use the keyboard to move through the page, the tabbing happens in the right order. The visual presentation corresponds to that of the content. So in this respect, your page passes the test.

Figure 19.20   Text zoom of 300 percent at a resolution of 800 × 600 pixels

Browser Check

The different implementation of CSS still causes display errors in the individual browsers from time to time. We have been working with Firefox up to now, so we already know that all is well here. Opera and Safari also represent everything as intended. Even Internet Explorer in versions 7, 8, and 9 behaves itself.

Responsibility for the correct display in Internet Explorer 7 falls to a special CSS file specifically designed to fix problems with that browser. You will find it in the CSS file of the template.

You should include it in the head of the index.php file via the conditional comments:

```
<!--[if IE 7]>
<link href="<?php echo $this->baseurl ?>/templates/<?php echo
➥$this->template; ?>/css/ie7only.css"
rel="stylesheet" type="text/css" />
<![endif]--
```

The file does not contain many statements because the main goal when designing the concept of the template was to avoid as many bugs as possible.

Internet Explorer 6 is old but is still used in large companies or developing countries. From a developer's point of view, you should probably not support it anymore, but many clients would like to have a clean display here as well. If you know your way around it a little bit, it only takes a few tweaks to sort out the display errors. I cover Internet Explorer 6 only superficially because it really is a thing of the past.

The design in Internet Explorer does not look all that bad. The head is too deep, and the whole page too wide (see Figure 19.21), but it can be quickly fixed. The CSS file responsible for fixing it is ieonly.css file, which is also integrated into the template's index.php file via the conditional comments and used by all Internet Explorer versions through version 6.

Additionally, CSS statements added directly to the head of the file make it possible to integrate special CSS statements only for the Personal style in the standard Beez. Because you are working with the personal.css file in this case, you need to take care of the statements used there.

```
<!--[if lte IE 6]>
<link href="<?php echo $this->baseurl ?>/templates/<?php echo
➥$this->template; ?>/css/ieonly.css"
rel="stylesheet" type="text/css" />
<?php if ($color=="personal") : ?>
<style type="text/css">
#line
{ width:98% ;
}
.logoheader
{
height:200px;
```

Figure 19.21   Display in IE6

```
}
#header ul.menu
{
display:block !important;
width:98.2% ;
}
</style>
<?php endif; ?>
<![endif]-->
```

As you can see, this code contains a height specification for the `div` container `.logoheader`. The statement is no longer required in this case, so you can simply remove it. As a result, the head moves up a bit. You can make this change directly in the ieonly.css file. In line 30 is another height specification for this area, which must also be deleted. Once you have done so, the header will have the desired height.

Now you need to adapt the width of the layout. Because Internet Explorer 6 does not know the statement `max-width`, you must work with *expressions*, which produce a similar result. Changing line 17 to:

```
#all { width: expression(document . body . clientWidth > 980? "980" :
  "auto"); }
```

ensures that the page now has the width you want it to have. You proceed in the same way for the display of the footer:

```
#footer-inner
{ width: expression(document . body . clientWidth > 980 ? "940" :
 "auto"); }
#footer { width: expression(document . body . clientWidth > 980 ?
 "955" : "auto"); }
```

Finally, you need to adapt the height of the content area. As you will recall, #main had a minimum width. In Internet Explorer 6, you give this area an explicit width, because it does not know the statement min-height. Here you can make use of one of its bugs. If you use the statement height in a standards-conforming browser, the area you assign this property to will only get as high as specified in the height property regardless of the size of its content. The rest is simply cut off. But Internet Explorer stretches the area according to its content regardless of what is specified in the CSS. It makes it at least as high as the specified height prescribes, though.

If you now assign a height of 300 pixels to #main in the ieonly.css file, your layout corresponds more or less to your expectations. Change line 56 to:

```
#main
{
height:300px;
}
```

The largest part of the work is done. In the next steps, we deal with formatting the content.

Step 9: Customizing Typography

In this step you customize the typography so that it matches your design.

Problem 1

The Beez template uses Arial in the body text and the Web font Titillium Maps for the main headings. The layout is only uses Arial, so you need to remove the Web font Titillium Maps.

Action 1

The font formatting can be found in the personal.css file. Right at the top, the Web font Titillium Maps is embedded into the CSS using the @fontface statement. As you can see, several fonts are loaded, which is necessary for wider browser compatibility. These fonts are located in the template's fonts folder.

In this case, you can simply delete all these statements because they are not necessary.

Now you need to check whether the file has references to this font in other places, and if yes, replace them with Arial. The easiest approach is to use the search function of your editor. Once you have done that, all headings should also be presented in Arial.

To get rid of unnecessary ballast, you can now delete the entire fonts folder and remove the reference in the template's XML file to this folder.

Problem 2

All links are represented in blue. When the user hovers over them with the mouse, the background turns blue and the text color white. But your layout dictates a very dark red (#990000) for the link color. When the mouse hovers over it, the background is supposed to turn dark gray (#333), and the font color should stay the same. The links in the center column should be black and represented in uppercase (`text-transform:uppercase`). The main navigation keeps the same design, but on hovering, the blue background color is replaced by red. In the menu in the right column, the links should have a red text color on hovering. And a few headings are to have a blue color.

Action 2

All required formatting can be found in the personal.css file, which is responsible for the color design. Go ahead and look for all statements that have anything to do with links, and then change the foreground and background colors accordingly. Once again, Firebug can help. You can also try customizing the color with the search-and-replace function, but then you need to know that the blue represented on hovering over the links is a different blue than the link color itself. The link color is slightly darker, so the links are clearly distinct from the text.

Your result should initially look like the one shown in Figure 19.22.

The links are adapted, so now work your way once more through the file from top to bottom and edit all headings that have a blue color.

Step 10: Formatting Module Headings

In this step, you attack the module headings to make them look the way you want.

Problem

The module headings in the right and center columns are to have a dark brown background and white text color. The font size should have a uniform height.

Action

Once again, you can gradually approach your goal with the help of Firebug. Start with the center column. If you look at the source text in the h3, you will see that it contains three nested `span` elements that are automatically integrated into the code via `style="beezDivision"` of the `jdoc.include` statement. Originally, this code is

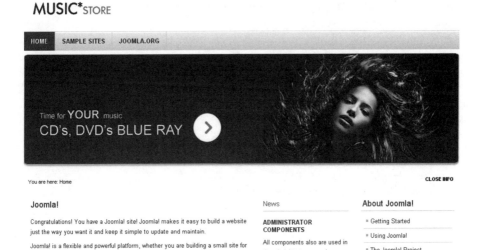

Figure 19.22   Result after customizing color

intended to give the heading background images for rounded corners. In our case, these elements inflate the code unnecessarily and should be removed from the layout:

```
<h3>
<span class="backh">
<span class="backh2">
<span class="backh3">
News
</span>
</span>
</span>
</h3>
```

Open the file templates/your_name/HTML/modules.php. In the function mod-Chrome_beezDivision($module, &$params, &$attribs), you find these spans and can remove them there:

```
...
<?php if ($module->showtitle) { ?> <h<?php echo $headerLevel;
➥?>><?php echo $module->title; ?> </h<?php echo $headerLevel; ?>>
...
```

Make sure you proceed with care. If you remove a little bit too much or not enough, it can quickly result in display errors.

Once you have removed these spans, it is much easier to format the headings via the context selectors #right h3 (that is, the center column, despite the id="right") and #nav h3 in the personal.css file.

Start with the heading in the navigation column; you will find the corresponding CSS in line 324 of personal.css. Change the font size, padding, line height plus text, and background color.

```
#nav h3
{
border-bottom:solid 1px #ddd;
font-family: Arial, sans-serif ;
color:#fff;
background:#302c29;
font-size:1.1em;
padding:3px 10px;
font-weight:bold;
line-height:1.4em
}
```

The same statements are also needed in the center area with the id="right". So you do not need to write the same thing again, you can simply add the second selector to the first one, separated by a comma.

```
#nav h3, #right h3
{
border-bottom:solid 1px #ddd;
font-family: Arial, sans-serif ;
color:#fff;
background:#302c29;
font-size:1.1em;
padding:3px 10px;
font-weight:bold
line-height:1.4em
}
```

You should then see the result shown in Figure 19.23.

Now there is just a bit of tidying up left to do. You just removed the spans from the module headings. Now you should check whether you also need to remove them from the CSS. After all, the CSS files should not be any bigger than absolutely necessary.

The search function of your editor can be very helpful here. Make sure you leave all h3 with the class .js-heading untouched, because these headings are required for the foldout modules.

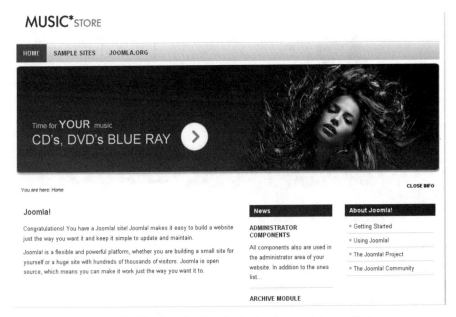

Figure 19.23   Result after designing the module headings

Step 11: Assigning a Background Image to the Homepage Article

In your layout is a background image behind the homepage article, showing a woman resting on a sofa (see Figure 19.24).

To achieve this result, you can integrate a module and add a background image to it using the Module Class Suffixes, or you can assign a background image to the article itself. Both approaches require direct access to the CSS files and are appropriate only if these articles are not constantly being changed.

Before you start with the actual formatting, you first change the content of the homepage article, because after all it's about music. Locate the article, currently called Joomla!, and change the title to:

> Relax and enjoy your favorite music!

Change the text to the following and put a Read More break at the end:

> In our store you will find all genres of music at a great price. R&B, HipHop, Soul, Folk, Jazz, Classical, Rhythm and Blues . . .

Change Read More Text in the Article Options on the right to:

> discover all we have to offer

Figure 19.24   This is what the homepage article should look like.

Now disable the linked titles. If both the Read More text and the title are output as links, that is because of settings entered in the menu. Go to the Menu Manager and in the menu item Home in the Article Options, you will find the parameter Show Title with Read More. Choose Hide to avoid this duplication (see Figure 19.25).

If you inspect the code with Firebug, you will see that the article itself is located in a div container with the class leading-0. This container is enclosed by another container

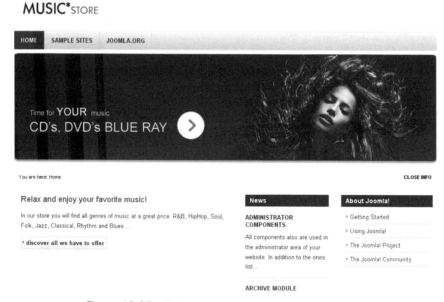

Figure 19.25   This is the result after the text changes.

with the class `items-leading`, which is in turn enclosed in a container with the class `blog-featured`. Awareness of this structure helps you with the special formatting for this area.

With the context selector `.blog-featured .leading-0`, you can now influence the display of this article specifically, without the formatting having an effect in other places. The following steps are necessary to achieve this:

1. The background image has to be created in Photoshop and saved in the images folder of the template. In my case, it is 400 pixels wide and 280 pixels high.

2. The CSS formatting has to specified in the personal.css file.

First, you need to assign the previously created background image to the `div` container with the class `leading-0` and align the image on the left. It should not be repeated automatically. The text itself is shorter than the background image, so the whole container needs to have a minimum height corresponding to the image height. To make sure the text is not over the image, the container gets a padding on the left of 220 pixels. Figure 19.26 shows how the article is positioned in the document structure.

Figure 19.26   Positioning the article in the document structure

The following code is used to position the article:

```
.blog-featured .leading-0
{
background:#fff url(../images/earphones.jpg) bottom left no-repeat;
min-height:290px;
padding-left:220px
}
```

The next chapter discusses the integration of background images in more detail. The following brief explanation will suffice for now.

The heading of this homepage article should be noticeably larger than that of all other articles:

```
#main .blog-featured .leading-0 h2
{font-size:2em; line-height:1.0em}
```

The reason I inserted the parent element #main is to make use of the principle of inheritance. The layout.css file contains this statement:

```
#main .items-leading h2
```

It is initially higher ranking than .blog-featured .leading-0 h2. To make things clearer, I made the path toward h2 in the document structure more precise and thus created a higher-ranking statement.

Finally, you still need to deal with formatting the Read More link. Again, you need to be precise and specific to achieve the desired effect. The link gets a brown background color and a background image with an arrow. The required graphic was created in Photoshop and saved in the template's images folder. The background image is positioned at the far right. The surrounding container has a padding on the left, but you now want the link to move further to the left. To achieve this, specify a negative margin of −170 pixels:

```
#main .blog-featured .leading-0 p.readmore a:link,
#main .blog-featured .leading-0 p.readmore a:visited
{
background: #302c29 url(../images/arrow_leading.png)
no-repeat top right;
color: #fff;
border: 0;
margin-left: -170px;
margin-top: 50px;
display: block;
font-weight: normal;
font-size: 1.8em;
padding: 10px 10px;
```

```
border-top: 2px solid #999;
border-bottom: 2px solid #999
}
```

All other formatting should be self-explanatory. In the end, you just need to make sure that the link behaves as it should when hovered over, when active, or when in focus. How about a red background color? To make it all look really good, the background of the arrow graphic needs to be red too:

```
#main .blog-featured .leading-0 p.readmore a:hover,
#main .blog-featured .leading-0 p.readmore a:active,
#main .blog-featured .leading-0 p.readmore a:focus
{
background: #990000 url(../images/arrow_leading_hover.png) no-repeat top
right !important;
color: #fff
}
```

That's it for now. But before you lean back and relax, you need to do a few final tests.

Step 12: Final Tests

Visually, the layout now corresponds to your expectations, at least in Firefox. But some errors may still have crept in. You are not yet sure if the layout works in all browsers, or perhaps you made a mistake while editing the CSS files or rearranging the index.php file. The basis for a browser-compatible, uniform display is always valid, well-formed code.

Validating CSS

Start by checking your CSS for validity. If you are working locally and using the Web developer tools for validating, and you select Validate local HTML, you need to know that the pages are checked automatically for conformance with the standards of CSS 2.1. But the Beez templates use properties from the CSS 3 standard in some places, which invariably results in errors.

If your page is on the Internet, you can validate your styles directly via the W3C Validation Service. There, you have the option of setting defaults for the CSS version (see Figure 19.27).

The validator is available in many languages. You can find it at *http://jigsaw.w3.org/css-validator/*.

Validating HTML

The HTML validator can help you track down structural errors in your template. If you later decide to generate your output via HTML5, you should ensure that you specify this option in the validator (see Figure 19.28).

You can find the W3C Markup Validation Service at *http://validator.w3.org*.

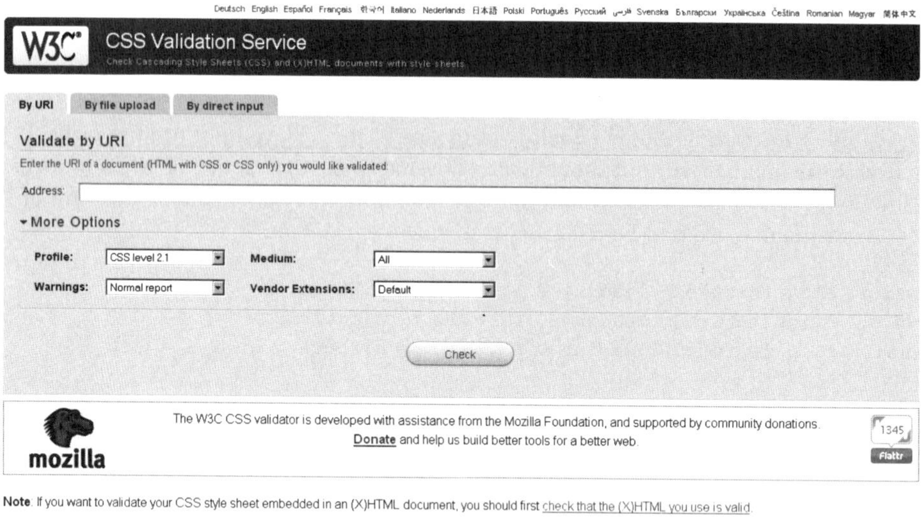

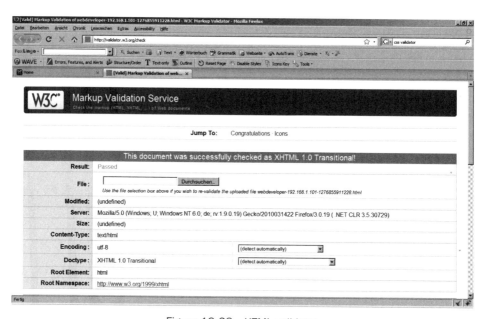

Figure 19.27   CSS validator

Figure 19.28   HTML validator

Browser Check

Browser checks are best carried out by actually looking at your site in different browsers. But Adobe offers BrowserLab, a useful tool for checking the display of a page in various browsers. With BrowserLab, you can choose in which browsers the page, specified by its URL, should be tested (see Figure 19.29).

The tool then presents the display in the form of a screenshot. The only drawback is that you need an Adobe ID to be able to use this tool. You can find Adobe BrowserLab at *https://browserlab.adobe.com.*

If you now check your page for its display, you get the following result:

Firefox: OK

Opera: OK

Safari: OK

IE 9: OK

IE8: OK

IE7: OK

IE6: Not quite right!

All is well except for Internet Explorer 6, which is being awkward (see Figure 19.30).

Figure 19.29   Display of the Joomla! page in Adobe BrowserLab

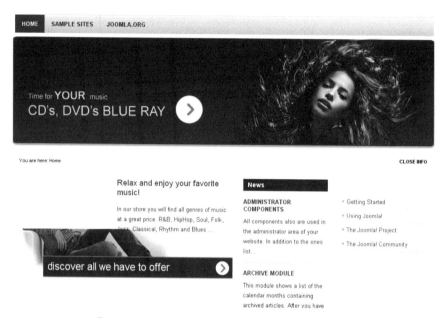

Figure 19.30   Display errors in Internet Explorer 6

The background image is cut off, and the background color of the heading in the navigation column has disappeared. Fortunately, the solution for these display errors is not very complicated.

As you might expect, the `div` container `.blog-featured .leading-0` needs a height because Internet Explorer 6 does not know the property `min-height`. You can quickly fix the problem. In the ieonly.css file, just insert the following lines:

```
.blog-featured .leading-0
{height:300px}
```

The missing background color of the heading can be traced back to the `hasLayout` property of Internet Explorer. The quick and painless solution is the property `zoom:1`:

```
#nav h3
{zoom:1}
```

If you want to know more about this, please go back and review Chapter 3.

Accessibility Checks

Chapter 7, "Tools," introduced a number of useful tools for checking accessibility. If accessibility is important to you, please go back and work through the different checks.

Chapter 7 also discussed the Juicy Studio Accessibility extension for Firefox, and it's worth mentioning again. With this extension, you can check the color contrast and color differences of a site. The color choice is a central design element and should support all users, even those who have limited visual perception, in taking in the information from your site.

Juicy Studio shows you, quickly and in a structured way, where problems with your color design might arise. Figure 19.31 shows a typical example of using this program.

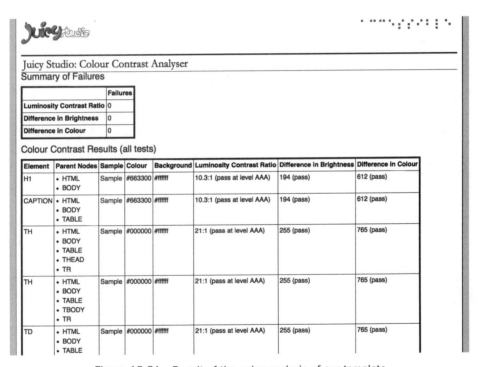

Figure 19.31   Result of the color analysis of our template

20

Integrating Custom Features

The page layout now looks as we wanted it to, but technically it is not yet up to our expectations. We are currently using text in our header image, and that is bad both for search engine optimization and for accessibility reasons. We also want to use HTML5 rather than the core layouts, which use XHTML. We fix both of these issues in this chapter.

The Header Image—A Background Image?

When you look at the header image, you can see that it is a text graphic. This means that the important text information is inaccessible by Google and by visual devices. Of course, you could enter this information in the alternative text of the graphic or add a meaningful title to the enclosing link, but that is not an optimal solution. It would be much better if the graphic could be integrated as a background image and the text was really text.

You can integrate background images into the page using Cascading Style Sheets (CSS). In Chapter 19, "Step by Step to a New Layout," you already used abbreviated notation to integrate them:

```
#mydiv
{
background:#000 url(../images/mypicture.jpg) bottom left no-repeat
}
```

You can also specify the formatting using the properties `background-image`, `background-position`, `background-color`, and `background-repeat`.

```
#mydiv
{
background-image:url(../images/mypicture.jpg);
background-position: bottom left;
background-repeat: repeat-x;
background-color:#000
}
```

Both methods require specifying a path to the image you want to use.

Tip

You should use the long notation if you want to use CSS to overwrite individual properties in later statements.

You do not have to specify background-color, background-repeat, and background-position, but they can be helpful. If you do not specify anything for background-repeat, the background image will be automatically tiled over the whole width and height of your element. If you select repeat-x, it will be repeated horizontally. repeat-y results in vertical repeating.

If you omit the specification of the background position, it will automatically be aligned in the top left corner of your element. bottom left results in alignment at the bottom left. The other options are bottom right and top right.

Whenever you assign a background image to an area, you should watch what happens when the user enlarges the font. If your element contains text, its height will automatically adapt to the selected font size. To avoid unattractive effects, you should make the background image slightly larger from the start.

A very cool and popular treatment is to add color gradients to elements. If you are using such a gradient, you should additionally assign a background color corresponding to one of the color values from the gradient to the entire element.

For example, say you created a gradient from black to white in Photoshop that corresponds exactly to the height of your element in an unscaled display. You assigned the property bottom left repeat-x to this background image.

The image is aligned at the bottom right and tiled horizontally. If someone now changes the font size, the element automatically becomes higher, but the background image does not. The selected background color is showing at the top. You can avoid this effect by specifying the same color for the background color as the one that your gradient graphic ends with. In this example, it would be black.

When using background images, you might wonder what to do about their information content in terms of accessibility. Background images are not accessible for visual devices. If you are using background gradients, this question does not generally arise because they are completely without meaning. In fact, it would be incorrect to make them "audible."

If you go back to our layout and look at the header image, you have to ask yourself whether the pretty lady contributes anything to the information content of the page.

Not really, but she does convey emotions and creates a certain atmosphere. To me, she seems passionate, full of energy, yet still somehow calm. She is completely "in" the music. The image might have an entirely different effect on you, which isn't surprising, because you are a different person with your own experiences and feelings. When you use such emotionally charged photos, you are generally not able to describe their effect on people who cannot see these pictures. You could offer a neutral description, such as "dancing woman," but that does not contribute anything to the information content of the page. For that reason, you can safely and with good conscience send the photo into the background.

Editing Module Content

To prepare the Header Image module, you first need to change its content. Go to the Module Manager and select the Header Image custom module that you created in Chapter 19. Now remove the image from the module and type in the text that is written on the image. Then link the entire text to an existing article.

In our design, individual words are formatted smaller than others. Insert a span element around the small words in the a element (see Figures 20.1 and 20.2). This element will later enable you to select separate formatting for these words.

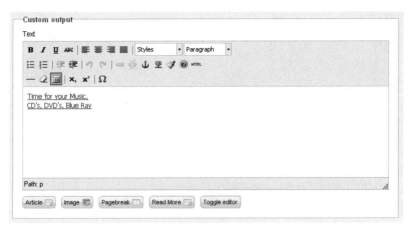

Figure 20.1   Edited text

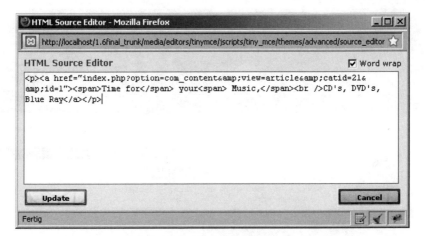

Figure 20.2   Editing the text in the editor's HTML mode

Adapting CSS

Once you have changed the content, you need to edit the CSS that controls the appearance. Remember, you already created a selector for this area in the personal.css file. Now specify the following formatting there (you can see the result in Figure 20.3):

```
.custom_image {
overflow: hidden;
min-height:125px;
background:#554d46 url(../../../images/template/headerimage.jpg)
top left no-repeat;
color:#fff;
font-size:2.2em;
padding:90px 500px 20px 30px;
margin:10px ;
}
```

Your image is still in the images/template folder, which you can access via the Media Manager. Because you want to access this image in your CSS, you need to go three levels up in the document tree. The whole area has been assigned a background color and a minimum height. The minimum height corresponds to the image height if you add the top and bottom padding. Please do not assign a fixed height; otherwise the container maintains this height even when the user changes the font size. The font size is set to 2.2 em for now, and the font color to white.

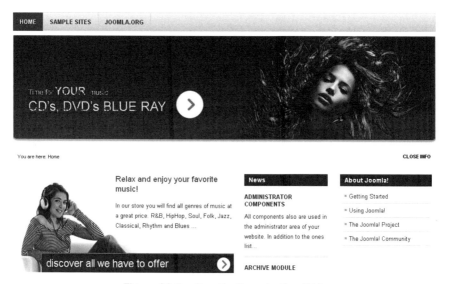

Figure 20.3   Result after adapting CSS

Now you just need to format the link corresponding to the layout. You assign a white font color, a special arrow image as a background image, the correct padding, and a smaller font for the words designated to be smaller (see Figure 20.4).

You can make these changes with the following code:

```
.custom_image p
{
line-height: 1.2em;
}
.custom_image p a:link,
.custom_image p a:visited
{
background: url(../images/arrow_headerimage.png) center
right no-repeat;
padding: 10px 70px 10px 0;
display: block;
text-transform: uppercase;
color: #fff;
text-decoration: none
}
.custom_image p a:hover,
.custom_image p a:active,
.custom_image p a:focus
{
```

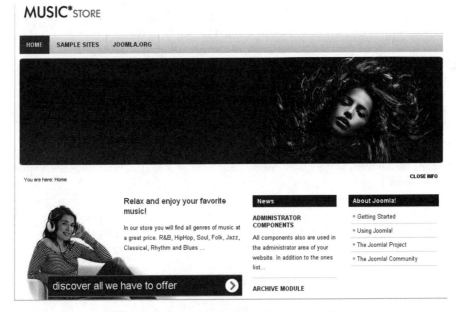

Figure 20.4   Result with changed background image

```
text-decoration: underline
}
.custom_image p a span
{
text-transform: none;
font-size: 0.7em
}
```

Now that you have replaced the text graphic, change the image in the images/template folder to one without the text graphic.

Background Images in the Module's Own HTML

Custom HTML modules now allow you to add a background image using a module parameter. Editors can insert or change background images autonomously without having to alter the CSS itself.

Via the option Background Image, you have direct access to the media manager and therefore to all available graphics. The graphics are inserted as inline styles into the surrounding HTML element of the module. Here is an example:

```
<div class="custom_image" style="background-image: url('/joomlabook/
➥images/joomla_black.gif')">
<p>Module content</p>
</div>
```

You should set up your template for this use to achieve the desired result. Only the background image itself is integrated. There are no specifications about where the image is positioned or whether it should be repeated. The height of the `div` container is also not automatically adapted to the height of the image. All of these settings are left in the hands of the template designer and can be modified with the help of the Module Class Suffix.

To ease the use of the inline style background image, the long notation was used so that you can still change all other properties.

Browser Check

All standards-conforming browsers display your page as intended. Only Internet Explorer 6 and Internet Explorer 7 have problems (see Figure 20.5).

The reason this problem occurs is that Internet Explorer relies on its `hasLayout` property for this value. The paragraph in question does not have this property and therefore does not have the intended right margin of 50 percent of the parent element.

For Internet Explorer 7, a simple snippet in the ie7only.css file quickly fixes the problem:

```
.custom_image p
{zoom:1}
```

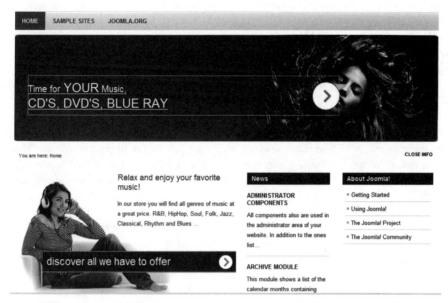

Figure 20.5   Internet Explorer 7: The paragraph with the text is too wide.

In Internet Explorer 6, the display problems are also easy to fix. Because it lacks the property `min-height`, you need to assign a fixed height to the surrounding `<div>` element using the class `.custom_image`. Also, it requires the property `zoom:1` in order to force the element to have layout. Remember that the fixes to Internet Explorer 6 are made in the index.php file.

For Internet Explorer 7, you do not need to do this because the property `overflow:hidden` automatically gives the element layout.

```
.custom_image
{height:125px}

.custom_image,
.custom_image p
{zoom:1}
```

Using HTML5 Effectively

In principle, HTML5 is nothing more than an advanced version of HTML 4.01. HTML5 does not define the language itself but rather what the browser does with the code and how it builds its document object model (DOM) from it. The DOM describes in a tree structure all of the elements that are present. It forms the basis for our work because it provides the basic structure we have to work with.

But what does that mean for us in practice? Semantics are not the strong point of HTML 4.01/XHTML. HTML5 introduces a multitude of new elements that can remedy this weakness (`<header>`, `<footer>`, `<section>`, `<nav>`, `<aside>`, `<article>`, `<hgroup>`).

Especially in terms of accessibility, these elements can contribute a lot toward making a Web site easier to use. HTML5 also offers a multitude of other new features (`<video>`, `<canvas>`, etc.) that are quite technical and not always fully usable yet due to insufficient browser support in some cases. I have therefore limited the HTML5 used in beez5 to the semantic expressions. These extensions are used not only in the index.php file but also for the default output of the content. For this reason, I have created HTML5 overrides, as you already know. Based on the overrides, we'll now prepare our new template for output with HTML5.

But HTML5 and XHTML Are Not the Same

I recently read that you can simply turn an XHTML page into an HTML5 page by changing the doctype. The question is, what is this supposed to achieve? Well, it achieves nothing, because the new features of HTML5 are not used, and changing the doctype alone does not automatically make it a better Web site. If you want to get your page to HTML5, you should do so consistently and use its capabilities to the extent that they are usable today.

The following section contains a brief overview of HTML5. I cannot write a complete description of HTML5—there are whole books available on this topic and many resources can be found online—but maybe you will still get an impression of what it is all about.

Chapter 17, "The Default Templates and Their Features," pointed out that the implementation of HTML5 in beez5 is not as clean as we would like. Because you have the choice in the template between the presentation of HTML5 and XHTML, the code of the index.php file and the overrides becomes unnecessarily inflated. You can avoid this problem by opting for only the HTML5 version and omitting the XHTML variation. Here are the steps involved.

1. The HTML5 code from the Beez template from the template overrides has to be copied over into your template.
2. The index.php file needs to be adapted accordingly.
3. The JavaScript for Internet Explorer has to be added to index.php.
4. The CSS needs to be adapted.
5. The XML file needs to be adapted to include the added files. You will do this final step in Chapter 21, "Final Tasks: Finc-Tuning and Creating an Installable Zip Archive."

Adding the HTML5 Overrides

Because the beez5 is your model template, you simply need to go into the HTML folder in the first step and copy the com_content folder into your own HTML folder. That is, copy templates/beez5/html/com_content to templates/your_name/html/.

At first glance, this step does not result in any change because of the code itself. Because you have the choice between XHTML and HTML5 in the beez5 template, this selection causes a reaction in the overrides, and the HTML5 code is output only if it was selected in the template parameters. There is no such parameter in your template, so you want to remove the if statement and the XHTML code.

Let's first look at a simple example. Please open the file templates/your_name/html/com_content/article/default.php. Starting around line 20, you will find the following code:

```
. . . .
if ($templateparams->get('html5') != 1) :
require(JPATH_BASE.'/components/com_content/views/article/tmpl/
↪default.php');
//possibly replace with JPATH_COMPONENT.'/views/...'

else :
JHtml::addIncludePath(JPATH_COMPONENT.DS.'helpers');
?>
The HTML5 code is here


<?php endif; ?>
```

This code checks the html5 parameter, and if it is not selected, it uses the core layout, which is in XHTML. It uses the require() statement to bring in a copy of the core layout, and then jumps to the endif statement at the end of the file. However, if HTML5 was selected in the parameters, the code that follows the else statement, which is an HTML5 version of the layout, is used.

If you delete the code snippets in italics from the code (starting with the if statement, through and including the else statement, plus the final endif statement), the HTML5 output will always be used. The overrides will then work as expected. This is the code you would have left:

```
JHtml::addIncludePath(JPATH_COMPONENT.DS.'helpers');
?>
The HTML5 code is here
```

If you do this and then look at the output, you will see HTML5. Please remember that we just adapted the output of the article view, so you need to go to such a view in your site (see Figure 20.6).

Following this pattern, you now need to edit all views and remove the HTML5 query. Remember to delete the final <?php endif; ?> as well. Otherwise you will get a PHP

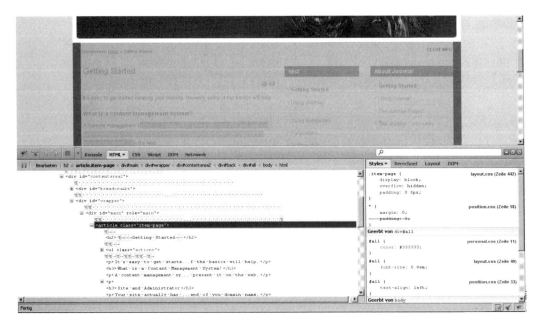

Figure 20.6   Article view in HTML5

error message. In some views, you will find only a closing curly bracket } instead of `<?php endif; ?>`, like this: `<?php } ?>`. This is just another notation that leads to the same result. The default_articles.php and default_children.php files under the category view are a little different. In those files, delete this code:

```
if ($templateparams->get('html5') != 1) :
    require JPATH_BASE.'/components/com_content/views/category/tmpl/
➥default_articles.php';
    //evtl. ersetzen durch JPATH_COMPONENT.'/views/...'
    return;
endif;
```

Warning

For these two files, do not delete the `<?php endif; ?>` at the end because it is the end of a different `if` statement.

Once you have deleted that code, you will see in your browser that some of the formatting has been lost, even in Firefox. This is no big deal for now; it happens because previously present `div` containers that are innately block-level elements have now been replaced by HTML5 elements, which are not block-level by default.

For example,

```
<div class="item-page">
```

becomes

```
<article class="item-page">
```

You will change the CSS later on to make the elements block level. But first, you need to prepare the index.php file for use with HTML5.

Adapting index.php

Open the index.php file. You can also open index.php of the beez5 template in parallel and use it to copy the required elements from there directly into your template. This method saves you some typing.

First you change the doctype from

```
<!DOCTYPE html PUBLIC "-//W3C//DTD XHTML 1.0 Transitional//EN"
 "http://www.w3.org/TR/xhtml1/DTD/xhtml1-transitional.dtd">
```

to

```
<!DOCTYPE html>
```

The simple doctype is a real bonus: finally, an expression that is easy to remember!

\<header>

The `<header>` is intended for introductory content, such as the first heading or the navigation. It does not have to be used only for the header area of a page; it can also be used as the head of subordinate areas. Now replace the header `<div>` with the HTML5 element `<header>`.

So,

```
<div id="header">
```

becomes

```
<header id="header">
```

Please remember that these elements also have to be closed again. So where your `<div>` element was closed previously, you now need to close your `<header>` element.

```
</header>
```

<nav>

Every site has navigation, and this is what the <nav> element is for—to enclose the link lists to internal and external pages.

Because you used the template parameters to position the navigation column before and after the content, it appears twice in the index.php file: once directly following the head area and once following the column for the additional information. Replace the <div> elements with the HTML5 element <nav> in both places that have the id="nav". This is one of them:

```
<nav class="left1 <?php if ($showRightColumn==NULL){ echo
 'leftbigger';} ?>" id="nav">
</nav>
```

Now mark the horizontal navigation in the head with the <nav> element. This navigation is currently output without surrounding elements.

```
<nav>
<jdoc:include type="modules" name="position-1" />
</nav>
```

<aside>

Many sites present additional information or additions to the main content in a sidebar. To mark these sidebars, you use the element <aside>. Change the <div> element containing the id="right" to the HTML5 element aside:

```
<aside id="right">
<a id="additional"></a>
<jdoc:include type="modules" name="middle-top" style="beezDivision"
 headerLevel="3"/>
<jdoc:include type="modules" name="middle-middle" style="beezDivision"
 headerLevel="3" />
<jdoc:include type="modules" name="middle-bottom" style="beezDivision"
 headerLevel="3" />
</aside><!-- end right -->
```

<footer>

The footer informs the user of copyright and relevant links to other documents. Replace the <div> element containing the id="footer" with the HTML5 element <footer>.

```
<footer id="footer">
<jdoc:include type="modules" name="position-14" />
<p>
<?php echo JText::_('TPL_YOUR_NAME_POWERED_BY');?> <a href="http://
↪www.joomla.org/">Joomla!&#174;</a>
</p>
</footer>
```

Adding the JavaScript File to Deal with Internet Explorer

We could content ourselves with a job well done if it weren't for Internet Explorer up to version 9, which once again breaks rank. It does not recognize the new HTML5 elements, so you need to insert them at runtime into the DOM of the browser via JavaScript.

A corresponding script can be found in the beez5 template: templates/beez5/javascript/html5.js. Please copy this file into the JavaScript folder of your template and integrate it into the document head via the conditional comments for all versions of Internet Explorer below version 9:

```
<!--[if lt IE 9]>
<script type="text/javascript" src="<?php echo $this->baseurl ?>
↪/templates/<?php echo $this->template; ?>/javascript/html5.js"></script>
<![endif]-->
```

Now even Internet Explorer can understand the elements introduced in HTML5 and can interpret and implement the assigned styles.

Adapting CSS

As mentioned previously, our design has become a bit messy because of the HTML5 elements and insufficient browser implementation of its elements. If the browser does not know the elements, it usually treats them like <span> elements, which invariably are inline elements.

In Firefox 4 and Internet Explorer 9, most elements are now correctly interpreted. But to convert these elements in all other browsers to block-level elements, you need to explicitly specify so in your CSS. Please add the following statement to your personal.css file:

```
article, aside, footer, header, hgroup, nav, section
{display:block;}
```

Now it should all work as intended, and your template should work with HTML5 as well. But you will probably still need to tweak and fine-tune the CSS in a few places.

21

Final Tasks:
Fine-Tuning and Creating an
Installable Zip Archive

We are nearing the completion of our template. Before you can create an installable zip archive, you should fine-tune the template and add the finishing touches.

Fine-Tuning

The overall appearance of a site is dependent not just on its basic structure but also on the content it displays. If you design a site and then fill it with content, in most cases, you will have to readjust the stylesheets after adding the content. The spacing has to be adapted to the specific content. One such place is with the print stylesheet.

Creating a Print Stylesheet

Joomla! offers you the option of a print preview. Its formatting is controlled via the CSS file integrated in the component.php file. If the user wants to print your page directly from the browser, you can directly affect this design using a print stylesheet.

The stylesheet is integrated into the print preview via `media="print"` in your CSS statement.

```
<link rel="stylesheet" href=" <?php echo $this->baseurl ?>/templates/
↪<?php echo $this->template; ?>/css/print.css" type="text/css"
↪media="print" />
```

Here you can target the content to be presented. Using the CSS property `display:none`, you can hide specified page areas to achieve an optimized display. Always consider the user's ink cartridge when deciding which page areas to hide. I always make sure to hide large graphics, such as the header image in our example, because their significance is rather low. The navigation is also usually not of interest when printing the page.

Adjusting error.php and offline.php

You can also create your own error page (error.php) and a custom page for the offline message (offline.php). Remember to adjust the paths to the CSS files and the language strings if necessary.

Right-to-Left View

If you want to make your template available for right-to-left (RTL) languages, you should check the relevant CSS file and optimize it if necessary. If you do not care to do this, you can simply remove the appropriate code from the index.php file.

Removing Superfluous Files

Check whether all the files stored in the template are in fact required. During the development process, especially, it is easy to leave behind files, such as unused graphics and CSS files, that are no longer needed in the finished design.

Creating Previews

You will probably recall that in the Template Manager in the Joomla! back end, you need a small and a large thumbnail. You should now add these graphics, which you should put in the top-level directory of your template.

The template_thumbnail.png file is responsible for the small display and template_preview.png is responsible for the enlarged display. Neither graphic has a fixed size specified, but for uniform display, you should adhere to the size of the models. For the thumbnails, the default templates use an approximate size of 206 × 150 pixels.

Figures 21.1 and 21.2 show examples of previews that are too small or too large.

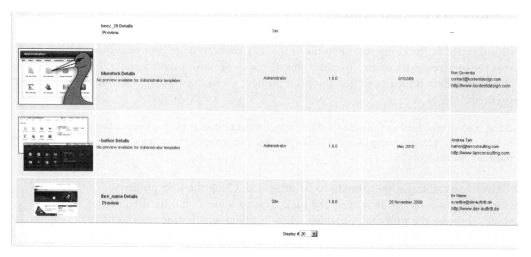

Figure 21.1   Thumbnail too small

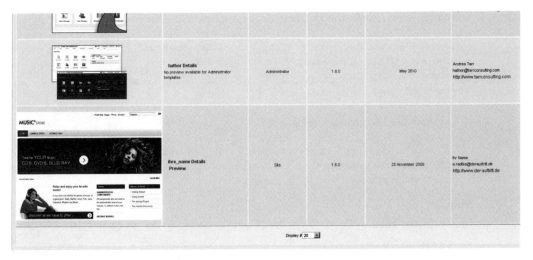

Figure 21.2   Thumbnail too large

The larger preview is also not fixed in its size. In my opinion, it should not be wider than 640 pixels, so it does not overlap the window below at a lower resolution.

Changing Favicon

Remember to replace your favicon; otherwise, the Joomla! favicon is used by default.

Optimizing index.php

The index.php file also frequently contains relics from the different development stages. In our case, this primarily concerns the template parameters. The source template allows you to choose between two styles: *Nature* and *Personal*. The new template does not have this option, so you need to change index.php accordingly, as follows.

Step 1

In the index.php file, remove the assigned color variable at about line 25.

```
$color = $this->params->get('templatecolor');
```

Step 2

Around line 55, the CSS of the style specified in the back end is loaded depending on the setting.

- personal.css
- nature.css

You only need the personal.css file.

You can now remove the variable $color and insert the file name:

```
<link rel="stylesheet" href="<?php echo $this->baseurl ?>/templates/
➥<?php echo $this->template; ?>/css/<?php echo
➥htmlspecialchars($color); ?>.css"
➥type="text/css" />
```

You now need to change the code to:

```
<link rel="stylesheet" href="<?php echo $this->baseurl ?>/templates/
➥<?php echo $this->template; ?>/css/personal.css"
➥type="text/css" />
```

Step 3

In line 58, the RTL styles are integrated. There are separate files for each style.

- personal_rtl.css
- nature_rtl.css

Both files can be removed. It is sufficient to use the single template_rtl.css file. Remove the following code that adds those two files:

```
<?php
if (file_exists(JPATH_SITE. DS . '/templates/beez_20/css/' .
$color . '_rtl.css')) :?>
<link rel="stylesheet" href="<?php echo $this->baseurl ?>/templates/
➥<?php echo $this->template; ?>/css/<?php echo $color ?>_rtl.css"
➥type="text/css" />
<?php endif; ?>
```

The statements from the personal_rtl.css file are not required in the new layout. If you do not want to offer your Web site in an RTL language, you can remove all stylesheets that relate to RTL.

Step 4

For Internet Explorer 6, there are statements that should only come into effect if you have selected the style Personal. You will find this code around line 60:

```
<!--[if lte IE 6]>
<link href="<?php echo $this->baseurl ?>/templates/<?php echo
➥$this->template; ?>/css/ieonly.css" rel="stylesheet"
➥type="text/css" />
<?php if ($color=="personal") : ?>
<style type="text/css">
#line
{ width:98% ;
}
```

```
#header ul.menu
{
display:block !important;
width:98.2% ;
}
</style>
<?php endif; ?>
<![endif]-->
```

You can simply copy the statements inserted within the PHP `if` query over into the ieonly.css file and then delete them together with the PHP query.

Only the reference to Internet Explorer 6 CSS should remain:

```
<!--[if lte IE 6]>
<link href="<?php echo $this->baseurl ?>/templates/<?php echo
➥$this->template; ?>/css/ieonly.css" rel="stylesheet"
➥type="text/css" />
<![endif]-->
```

Step 5
Now that you aren't using the other color files, nature.css and nature_rtl.css, you can delete them.

You have now cleaned up your index.php file and removed the extraneous code.

Adapting the XML File
Templates can be installed within Joomla! via the Extension Manager. Here, the system requires a neat package where nothing can be missing.

In the course of building your template, you have made changes to the templateDetails.xml file as needed, so you just have a couple of things to do. You need to remove the <field> element for the template parameter by simply deleting it.

```
<field name="templatecolor" type="list" default="nature"
label="TPL_YOUR_NAME_FIELD_TEMPLATECOLOR_LABEL"
description="TPL_YOUR_NAME_FIELD_TEMPLATECOLOR_DESC" filter="word">

<option value="nature">TPL_YOUR_NAME_OPTION_NATURE</option>
<option value="personal">TPL_YOUR_NAME_OPTION_PERSONAL</option>
</field>
```

As you already know, you can assign default values to the form fields so that they are already present, even for the first installation. If you now look at the XML file, neither the site title nor the site description show such a default value. You can add them now if you wish. To ensure that this default value can be translated, you should use language strings here.

Finally, if you added any files or folders to the root, make sure you add them to this XML file. Similarly, if you deleted any root files or folders, remove them here. While you worked through the example, you added and removed files for this custom template, but you didn't add or remove any at the root level, so you don't need to make any changes now.

Once these steps are complete, you can finally prepare the template for installation.

Creating a Zip Archive

Joomla! templates are installed as zip archives, as all extensions are. This is not rocket science—it's quick and easy. Go to your cleaned-up and optimized template folder and zip everything it contains (see Figure 21.3).

Once your files are zipped, you should check your archive by installing *your* template in a new Joomla! installation.

I hope all went well and you now have as much fun creating templates as I do!

Figure 21.3   The files to include in your zip archive

Appendix

Useful Links

Joomla!

- *www.joomla.org*
- *http://api.joomla.org*
- *http://developer.joomla.org*
- *http://forum.joomla.org*
- *Joomla! 2.5: Beginner's Guide: http://cocoate.com/j25*
- *The Official Joomla! Book: http://officialjoomlabook.com*

Assistive Technologies

- JAWS: *www.freedomscientific.com/fs_downloads/jaws.asp*
- Windows eyes: *www.gwmicro.com*
- Virgo: *www.baum.de/cms/en/*
- Accessibility Overview: *http://msdn.microsoft.com/en-en/windows/bb735024.aspx*

CSS

- *www.alistapart.com/topics/code/css/*
- *www.meyerweb.com*
- *www.meyerweb.com/eric/css/edge/*
- *http://css-tricks.com*
- *http://lea.verou.me/css3-secrets/*
- *www.colorzilla.com/gradient-editor/*
- *www.webdirections.org/blog/let-the-web-move-you-css3-animations-and-transitions/*
- *http://tympanus.net/Tutorials/OriginalHoverEffects/index7.html*
- *http://flipc.blogspot.com/2009/02/damn-ie7-and-inline-block.html*

- *www.smashingmagazine.com/2010/07/19/how-to-use-css3-media-queries-to-create-a-mobile-version-of-your-website/?goback=.gde_2071438_member_44034332*
- *http://nimbupani.com/drop-shadows-with-css3.html*
- *www.dzinepress.com/2009/11/50-useful-css-professional-techniques/*
- *http://cssglobe.com/post/3714/css-sprites-rounded-corners/*
- *http://tympanus.net/codrops/2010/05/03/pimp-your-tables-with-css3/*
- *http://net.tutsplus.com/tutorials/html-css-techniques/10-css3-properties-you-need-to-be-familiar-with/*
- *http://designbeep.com/2010/12/28/42-powerful-css3-techniquestutorials-and-experiments-with-demos/*
- *http://css3pie.com*
- *http://trentwalton.com/2010/07/05/non-hover/*

HTML5

- *http://dev.w3.org/html5/spec/*
- *www.whatwg.org/specs/web-apps/current-work/multipage/*
- *www.html5rocks.com*
- *http://html5demos.com*
- *http://thinkvitamin.com/code/getting-started-with-html5-video/*
- *http://thinkvitamin.com/code/html5-audio-unplugged/*
- *http://thinkvitamin.com/code/fun-with-html5-forms/*
- *www.unmatchedstyle.com/podcast/html5-is-the-future.php*
- *http://dev.opera.com/articles/view/new-structural-elements-in-html5/*
- *www.net-kit.com/20-html5-video-players/*
- *www.impressivewebs.com/bold-italic-html5/*
- *www.smashingmagazine.com/2010/11/10/learning-to-love-html5/*
- *www.html5accessibility.com*

Design

- *http://grid.mindplay.dk*

Typography

- *www.smashingmagazine.com/2011/03/14/technical-web-typography-guidelines-and-techniques/*
- *http://sixrevisions.com/css/css-typography-01/*
- *www.google.com/webfonts*
- *http://webfonts.info/wiki/index.php?title=Main_Page*

- *www.fontsquirrel.com*
- *www.dafont.com*
- *http://cufon.shoqolate.com/generate/*

Colors

- *www.colourlovers.com*
- *http://kuler.adobe.com*
- *http://juicystudio.com/services/luminositycontrastratio.php*
- *http://blogs.sitepoint.com/21-stimulating-color-palette-tools-for-designers/*

Icons

- *www.iconfinder.com*

JavaScript

- *http://mootools.net*
- *http://jsfiddle.net/Wzekb/*

WAI ARIA

- *www.w3.org/WAI/intro/aria.php*
- *www.w3.org/TR/wai-aria-practices/*
- *http://dev.opera.com/articles/view/introduction-to-wai-aria/*

Checker Tools

- Colour Contrast Analyser: *www.juicystudio.com/services/colourcontrast.php*
- *www.visionaustralia.org.au/info.aspx?page=628*
- Vischeck: *http://vischeck.com*
- Cynthia Says: *www.contentquality.com*
- Validator: *www.htmlhelp.com*
- Wave: *www.wave.webaim.org*
- Accessibility Toolbar Mozilla/Firefox: *http://cita.disability.uiuc.edu/software/mozilla/*
- Webdeveloper Toolbar: *https://addons.mozilla.org/en-US/firefox/addon/web-developer/*
- Firebug: *https://addons.mozilla.org/en-US/firefox/addon/firebug/*
- Developer Toolbar for Internet Explorer: *www.microsoft.com/downloads/en/details.aspx?FamilyID=95e06cbe-4940-4218-b75d-b8856fced535*
- *https://addons.mozilla.org/en-US/firefox/addon/juicy-studio-accessibility-too/*
- Wcag2-Checker: *http://achecker.ca/checker/index.php*

Helpful Functions

jdoc:include	Type	Style	Additional Attributes
	head		
	component		
	message		
	modules	none	name
		xhtml	name
		rounded	name
		table	name
Beez Templates			
		beezDivision	name, headerLevel
		beezHide	name, headerLevel, state
		beezTabs	name, id

Function	Description
`$this->params->get('YOUR_PARAMETER')`	Access to the template parameters
`JFactory::getApplication()`	Load framework
`$app=JFactory::getApplication()` `$app->getCfg('sitename')`	Site name from configuration
`JFactory::getDocument();`	Load document properties
`$doc=JFactory::getDocument();` `$doc->get('title')`	Document title
`countModules('YOUR_MODULPOSITION')`	Count modules
`JHTML::_('behavior.framework', true)`	Integrate MooTools
`$this->language;`	Current language
`$this->baseurl`	Base URL
`$this->direction`	Reading direction
`$this->template`	Current template
`JText::_('TPL_YOUR_NAME_YOUR_STRING')`	Insert language string
`JRequest::getCmd('view')`	Current view
`JFactory::getDate()`	Accessing current date
`defined('_JEXEC') or die;`	Security check

CSS Classes Used and Their Elements

Templates

Template beez_20

File Name	ID/Class Name	HTML Elements	Line (approx.)	Description
index.php	#all	div	108	Encloses all elements except footer
	#back	div	109	Is within the div#all Use: rounded corners, drop shadows
	#header	div	110	Header area
	.logoheader	div	111	Logo, page title, and site description
	#logo	h1	112	Logo, page title, and site description
	.header1	span	120	Site description
	.skiplinks	ul	124	Skip links
	.u2	a	125, 126, 128	Position skip links outside of viewport
	.unseen	h2 h3 span	131, 186 132, 136 109, 111	Position elements outside of viewport Example: invisible intermediary headings
	#line	div	134	Font size and module position position-0 Example: Search
	#fontsize	div	135	Font size
	.fontsize	p		Font size
	.larger	a		Enlarge font
	.reset	a		Reset font size
	.smaller	a		Reduce font size
	#contentarea, #contentarea2	div	142	Encloses the actual content If right column is present, contentarea; otherwise, contentarea2
	#breadcrumbs	div	143	Breadcrumb trail
	.left1 .left	div div	152 206	Navigation column before the page content: left1 Navigation column after the page content: left
	#nav	div	152, 206	Navigation column

(continues)

Template beez_20 (*continued*)

File Name	ID/Class Name	HTML Elements	Line (approx.)	Description
	`.leftbigger`	div	152, 206	Right column is collapsed or not present
	`#wrapper`	div	161	Encloses the `div#main`
	`#wrapper2`	div	161	
	`.shownocolumns`	div	161	Neither right nor left column are shown
	`#main`	div	163	Content
	`#top`	div	166	Module position `position-12`
	`.error`	div	171	Error messages, system notices
	`#close`	div	189	Link for showing and hiding right column
	`#Image`	span	191	Link text
	`#right`	div	196	Right or middle column
	`#additional`	a	197	Anchor for skip link
	`.wrap`	div	216	Cancels `floats`
	`#footer-outer`	div	224	Footer area
	`#footer-inner`	div	226	Module position debug
	`#bottom`	div	228	Contains the following four `div`s:
	`.box`	div	229, 230, 231	Boxes for modules
	`.box1`	div	229	Module position `position-9`
	`.box2`	div	230	Module position `position-10`
	`.box3`	div	231	Module position `position-11`
	`#footer-sub`	div	240	Footer
	`#footer`	div	243	Contains module position `positon-14` and `Powered by Joomla!`

Template beez5

File Name	ID/Class Name	HTML Elements	Line (approx.)	Description
`index.php`	`#all`	div	96	Encloses all elements except footer
	`#back`	div	97	Is within the `div#all`
	`#header`	div	99	Header area
		header	101	

(*continues*)

Template beez5 (*continued*)

File Name	ID/Class Name	HTML Elements	Line (approx.)	Description
	.logoheader	div	103	Logo, page title, and site description
	#logo	h1	104	Logo, page title, and site description
	.header1	span	111	Site description
	.skiplinks	ul	116	Skip links
	.u2	a	117, 118, 120	Position elements outside of viewport
	.unseen	h2 h3	123, 194 124	Position elements outside of viewport
	#line	div	126	Font size and module position position-0
	#fontsize	div	127	Font size
	.fontsize	p		Font size
	.larger	a		Enlarge font
	.reset	a		Reset font size
	.smaller	a		Reduce font
	#header-image	div	131	Contains module position position-15 or header image
	#contentarea, #contentarea2	div	142	Encloses the actual content If right column present, contentarea; otherwise, contentarea2
	#breadcrumbs	div	143	Breadcrumb trail
	.left1 .left1 .left .left	div nav div nav	152 152 224 226	Navigation column before the page content left1 Navigation column after the page content: left
	#nav #nav	div nav	152, 206 152, 206	Navigation column
	.leftbigger .leftbigger	div nav	152, 206 152, 206	Right column is collapsed or not present
	#wrapper #wrapper2	div div	169 169	Encloses the div#main

(*continues*)

Template beez5 (*continued*)

File Name	ID/Class Name	HTML Elements	Line (approx.)	Description
	`.shownocolumns`	`div`	169	Neither right nor left column are shown
	`#main`	`div`	171	content
	`#top`	`div`	174	Module position `position-12`
	`.error`	`div`	179	Error messages, system notices
	`#close`	`div`	197	Link for showing or hiding right column
	`#Image`	`span`	199	Link text
	`#right` `#right`	`div` `aside`	204 206	Right column
	`#additional`	`a`	209	Anchor for skip link
	`.wrap`	`div`	240	Cancels `floats`
	`#footer-outer`	`div`	248	Footer area
	`#footer-inner`	`div`	251	Module position debug
	`#bottom`	`div`	253	Contains the following `div`s
	`.box`	`div`	255, 258, 261	Boxes for modules
	`.box1`	`div`	255	Module position `position-9`
	`.box2`	`div`	258	Module position `position-10`
	`.box3`	`div`	261	Module position `position-11`
	`#footer-sub`	`div`	267	Footer
	`#footer` `#footer`	`div` `footer`	270 272	Contains module position `position-14` and `Powered by Joomla!`

Template Atomic

File Name	ID/Class Name	HTML Elements	Line (approx.)	Description
`index.php`	`.container`	`div`	45, 60	Should really be the all-enclosing `div`
	`.space`	`hr`	46	
	`.joomla-header`	`div`	47	Page name

(continues)

Template Atomic (*continued*)

File Name	ID/Class Name	HTML Elements	Line (approx.)	Description
	.span-16	div	47, 61, 86	Width from *Blueprint*
	.append-1	div	47, 61, 86	Padding from *Blueprint*
	.joomla-search	div	51	Module position atomic-search
	.span-7	div	51, 69, 75, 81	Width from *Blueprint*
	.last	div	51, 75, 81	Borders from *Blueprint*
	.joomla-footer	div	86	Copyright notes
	.colborder	div	69	Borders and frames from *Blueprint*

Components

Component com_content

View	File Name	ID/Class Name	HTML Elements	Line (approx.)	Description
featured	default.php	#blog-featured	div	19	Contents of homepage
		.items-leading	div	28	Leading items
		.leading-0 .leading-1 etc.	div	30	Individual leading item
		.system-unpublished	div	30, 58	Formats the display of unpublished content if you are logged into the front end
		.items-row	div	56	Row contains columns
		.cols-1 .cols-2 etc.	div	56	Row with columns, number of columns
		.row-0 .row-1 etc.	div	56	Row with columns, number of columns
		.item	div	58	An article
		.column-1 .column-2 etc.	div	58	Columns, number of columns
		.row-separator	span	66	Separator
		.items-more	div	74	List with further articles

(continues)

Component com_content (*continued*)

View	File Name	ID/Class Name	HTML Elements	Line (approx.)	Description
		.pagination	div	80	Page numbers
		.counter	p	83	Page number of pages in total: Page 1 of 2
	default_ item.php	.system- unpublished	div	19	Formats the display of unpublished content if you are logged into the front end
		.actions	ul	33	Icon list
		.print-icon	li	35	Print icon
		.email-icon	li	40	E-mail icon
		.edit-icon	li	46	Edit icon
		.article-info	dl	62	Details on an article
		.article-info- term	dt	63	Definition term
		.parent- category-name	dd	66	Parent category
		.category-name	dd	77	Category name
		.create	dd	88	Date of creation
		.modified	dd	93	Date it was last modified
		.published	dd	98	Date of publication
		.createdby	dd	103	Author
		.hits	dd	117	Number of hits
		.readmore	p	140	Read More link
		.item-separator	div	160	Separator
	default_ links.php				
article	default.php	.item-page	div	19	Article
		.actions	ul	38	Icon list
		.print-icon	li	41	Print icon
		.email-icon	li	47	E-mail icon
		.edit-icon	li	52	Edit icon
		.article-info	dl	75	Details on an article

(*continues*)

Component `com_content` (*continued*)

View	File Name	ID/Class Name	HTML Elements	Line (approx.)	Description
		`.article-info-term`	`dt`	76	Definition term
		`.parent-category-name`	`dd`	79	Parent category
		`.category-name`	`dd`	90	Category name
		`.create`	`dd`	101	Date of creation
		`.modified`	`dd`	106	Date last modified
		`.published`	`dd`	111	Date of publication
		`.createdby`	`dd`	116	Author
		`.hits`	`dd`	130	Number of hits
`categories`	`default.php`	`.categories-list`	`div`	16	Elements of category view
		`.category-desc`	`div`	29	Category description
	`default_items.php`	`.first`	`li`	13	First list element
		`.last`	`li`	22	Last list element
		`.item-title`	`span`	27	Category name
		`.category-desc`	`div`	32	Category description
		`.article-count`	`dl`	38	Number of subcategories
`category` (`list bzw. default view`)	`default.php`	`.category-list`	`div`	16	Elements of category view
		`.subheading-category`	`span`	28	Subheading
		`.category-desc`	`div`	34	Category description
		`.clr`	`div`	41	Cancels `floats`
		`.cat-items`	`div`	45	Filter and table with articles
		`.cat-children`	`div`	50	Child categories
	`default_articles.php`	`#adminForm`	`form`	32	Form
		`.filters`	`fieldset`	34	Filter

(*continues*)

Component `com_content` (*continued*)

View	File Name	ID/Class Name	HTML Elements	Line (approx.)	Description
		`.hidelabeltxt`	`legend`	35	Legend
		`.filter-search`	`div`	39	Filter
		`.filter-search-lbl`	`label`	40	Filter: article title, author, or number of hits
		`#filter-search`	`input`	41	Input field for filter term
		`.inputbox`	`input`	41	Input field for filter term
		`.display-limit`	`div`	46	Number of items
		`.category`	`table`	56	Table with articles
		`.list-title`	`th`	60	Table header article title
		`#tableOrdering`	`th`	60	Article title
		`.list-date`	`th`	65	Table header article date
		`#tableOrdering2`	`th`	65	Article date
		`.list-author`	`th`	71	Table header author of article
		`#tableOrdering3`	`th`	71	Author of article
		`.list-hits`	`th`	77	Table header number of hits
		`#tableOrdering4`	`th`	77	Number of hits
		`.system-unpublished`	`tr`	89	Formats display of unpublished content if you are logged into the front end
		`.cat-list-row0` `.cat-list-row1` etc.	`tr`	89, 91	Table row with article
		`.list-title`	`td`	95	Article title
		`.actions`	`ul`	100	Icon list
		`.edit-icon`	`li`	101	Edit icon
		`.list-date`	`td`	109	Date of article
		`.createdby`	`td`	116	Author of article
		`.list-hits`	`td`	134	Number of hits

(*continues*)

Component `com_content` (*continued*)

View	File Name	ID/Class Name	HTML Elements	Line (approx.)	Description
		`.register`	`a`	151	Link for registering to lead whole article
		`.pagination`	`div`	168	Page numbers
		`.counter`	`p`	171	Page number of pages in total: Page 1 of 2
	`default_children.php`	`.first`	`li`	12	First list element
		`.last`	`li`	21	Last list element
		`.item-title`	`span`	27	Category name
		`.category-desc`	`div`	32	Category description
category (blog view)	`blog.php`	`.blog`	`div`	16	Encloses the following elements
		`.subheading-category`	`span`	27	Subheading
		`.category-desc`	`div`	36	Category description
		`.clr`	`div`	43	Cancels `floats`
		`.items-leading`	`div`	51	Encloses leading articles
		`.leading-0` `.leading-1` etc.	`div`	53	Encloses each leading article
		`.system-unpublished`	`div`	53, 80	Formats display of unpublished content if you are logged into the front end
		`.items-row`	`div`	78	Row with columns
		`.cols-1` `.cols-2` etc.	`div`	78	Row with columns, number of columns
		`.row-0` `.row-1` etc.	`div`	78	Row with columns, number of rows
		`.item`	`div`	80	Article
		`.column-1` `.column-2` etc.	`div`	80	Column, number of columns

(continues)

Component com_content (*continued*)

View	File Name	ID/Class Name	HTML Elements	Line (approx.)	Description
		.row-separator	span	88	Separator
		.cat-children	div	105	Child categories
		.pagination	div	114	Page numbers
		.counter	p	116	Page number of pages in total: Page 1 of 2
	blog_children.php	.first	li	12	First list element
		.last	li	21	Last list element
		.item-title	span	26	Category name
		.category-desc	div	32	Category description
	blog_item.php	.system-unpublished	div	23	Formats display of unpublished content if you are logged into the front end
		.actions	ul	37	Icon list
		.print-icon	li	39	Print icon
		.email-icon	li	44	E-mail icon
		.edit-icon	li	49	Edit icon
		.article-info	dl	65	Details on article
		.article-info-term	dt	66	Definition term
		.parent-category-name	dd	69	Parent category
		.category-name	dd	80	Category name
		.create	dd	91	Date of creation
		.modified	dd	96	Date last modified
		.published	dd	101	Date of publication
		.createdby	dd	106	Author
		.hits	dd	120	Number of hits
		.readmore	p	143	Read More link
		.item-separator	div	163	Separator
	blog_links.php	.items-more	div	15	List with further articles

(continues)

Component `com_content` (*continued*)

View	File Name	ID/Class Name	HTML Elements	Line (approx.)	Description
archive	default.php	.archive	div	15	Elements of archive view
		#adminForm	form	21	Form
		.filters	fieldset	22	Filter
		.hidelabeltxt	legend	23	Legend
		.filter-search	div	24	Filter
		.filter-search-lbl	label	26	Filter: article title, author, or number of hits
		#filter-search	input	27	Input field for filter term
		.inputbox	input	27	Input field for filter term
		.button	button	33	Button
	default_items.php	#archive-items	ul	17	Archived articles
		.row	li	19	List element with an article
		.article-info	dl	31	Details on article
		.article-info-term	dt	32	Definition term
		.parent-category-name	dd	35	Parent category
		.category-name	dd	47	Category name
		.create	dd	58	Date of creation
		.modified	dd	63	Date last modified
		.published	dd	68	Date of publication
		.createdby	dt	73	Author
		.hits	dt	87	Number of hits
		.intro	div	96	Introduction of article
		.pagination	div	104	Page numbers
		.counter	p	105	Page number of pages in total: Page 1 of 2
form	edit.php	.edit	div	32	Editing view
		.item-page	div	32	Article

(continues)

Component `com_content` (*continued*)

View	File Name	ID/Class Name	HTML Elements	Line (approx.)	Description
		`#adminForm`	`form`	39	Form
		`.form-validate`	`form`	39	Form
		`.formelm`	`div`	43, 49, 70, 74, 80, 85, 90, 94, 100	`div`-enclosed individual form elements
		`.formelm_buttons`	`div`	55	Button
		`.form-note`	`div`	105	Note in editing view
		`.formelm_area`	`div`	113, 121, 125	Surrounding element

Component `com_contact`

View	File Name	ID/Class Name	HTML Elements	Line (approx.)	Description
featured	`default.php`	`#blog-featured`	`div`	18	Contents of contact component
		`.pagination`	`div`	27	Page numbers
		`.counter`	`p`	30	Page number of pages in total: Page 1 of 2
	`default_items.php`	`#adminForm`	`form`	24	Form
		`.filters`	`fieldset`	25	Filter
		`.hidelabeltxt`	`legend`	26	Legend
		`.display-limit`	`div`	28	Number of articles
		`.category`	`table`	35	Table with contacts
		`.item-num`	`th`	38	Table header: number
		`.item-title`	`th`	41	Table header: name of contact
		`.item-position`	`th`	45	Table header: position of contact
		`.item-email`	`th`	50	Table header: e-mail
		`.item-phone`	`th`	55, 61, 67	Table header: phone and fax number

(continues)

Component `com_contact` **(***continued***)**

View	File Name	ID/Class Name	HTML Elements	Line (approx.)	Description
		`.item-suburb`	`th`	73	Table header: suburb
		`.item-state`	`th`	79, 85	Table header: state
		`.odd` `.even`	`tr`	96	Alternate table rows get one of these classes
		`.item-num`	`td`	97	Number
		`.item-title`	`td`	101	Name of contact
		`.item-position`	`td`	107	Position of contact
		`.item-email`	`td`	113	E-mail
		`.item-phone`	`td`	119, 125, 131	Phone, fax, and cell-phone number
		`.item-suburb`	`td`	137	Suburb
		`.item-state`	`td`	143, 149	State
		`.pagination`	`div`	160	Page numbers
		`.counter`	`p`	162	Page number of pages in total: Page 1 of 2
		`.item-separator`	`div`	176	Separator
categories	default.php	`.categories-list`	`div`	16	Contents of contact component
		`.category-desc`	`div`	25, 31	Category description
		`.base-desc`	`div`	25, 31	Category description of selected category
	default_ items.php	`.first`	`li`	12	First list element
		`.last`	`li`	21	Last list element
		`.item-title`	`span`	26	Category name
		`.category-desc`	`div`	32	Category description
		`.contact-count`	`dl`	39	Number of contacts in category
category	default.php	`.contact-category`	`div`	14	Contents of contact component in category view
		`.category-desc`	`div`	26	Category description
		`.clr`	`div`	33	Cancels `floats`

(continues)

Component com_contact (*continued*)

View	File Name	ID/Class Name	HTML Elements	Line (approx.)	Description
		.cat-children	div	40	Child categories
	default_children.php	.first	li	12	First list element
		.last	li	21	Last list element
		.item-title	span	26	Category name
		.category-desc	div	32	Category description
	default_items.php	#adminForm	form	22	Form
		.filters	fieldset	24	Filter
		.hidelabeltxt	legend	25	Legend
		.display-limit	div	27	Number of articles
		.category	table	33	Table with contacts
		.item-title	th	37	Table header: name of contact
		.item-position	th	41	Table header: position of contact
		.item-email	th	46	Table header: e-mail
		.item-phone	th	51, 57, 63	Table header: phone, fax, and cellphone number
		.item-suburb	th	69	Table header: suburb
		.item-state	th	75, 81 83	Table header: state
		.system-unpublished	tr	93	Formats unpublished content if you are logged into the front end
		.cat-list-row0 .cat-list-row1 etc.	tr	93, 95	Table row with contact data
		.item-title	td	98	Title of contact
		.item-position	td	104	Position of contact
		.item-email	td	110	E-mail
		.item-phone	td	116, 122, 128	Phone, fax, and cellphone number

(*continues*)

Component com_contact (*continued*)

View	File Name	ID/Class Name	HTML Elements	Line (approx.)	Description
		.item-suburb	td	134	Suburb
		.item-state	td	140, 146	State
		.pagination	div	158	Page numbers
		.counter	p	160	Page number of pages in total: Page 1 of 2
contact	default.php	.contact	div	14	Individual contact
		.contact-name	span	22	Name of contact
		.contact-category	span	27, 33	Category name
		#selectForm	form	39	Form
		.inputbox		41	Input field
		.contact-image	span	51	Image of contact
		.contact-position	p	57	Position of contact
		.contact-miscinfo	div	105	Further information
		Class from php: .jicons-icons .jicons-text .jicons-none	span	106	Classes used depending on parameter selected
		.contact-misc	div	109	Additional content
	default_address.php	.contact-address	div	17	Address of contact
		Class from PHP: .jicons-icons .jicons-text .jicons-none	span	19, 61, 72, 82, 92, 102	Classes used depending on parameter selected
		.contact-street	span	25	Street
		.contact-suburb	span	30	Suburb
		.contact-state	span	35	State
		.contact-postcode	span	40	Postal code
		.contact-country	span	45	Country

(continues)

Component `com_contact` (*continued*)

View	File Name	ID/Class Name	HTML Elements	Line (approx.)	Description
		`.contact-contactinfo`	`div`	57	E-mail, phone, fax, and cellphone number, Web site
		`.contact-emailto`	`span`	64	E-mail
		`.contact-telephone`	`span`	75	Phone number
		`.contact-fax`	`span`	85	Fax number
		`.contact-mobile`	`span`	95	Cellphone number
		`.contact-webpage`	`span`	104	Web site
	`default_articles.php`	`.contact-articles`	`div`	13	Articles by contact
	`default_form.php`	`.contact-error`	`div`	31	Error messages
		`.contact-form`	`div`	36	Contact form
		`#emailForm`	`form`	37	Form
		`.form-validate`	`form`	37	Form
		`.form-required`	`p`	38	Required information
		`.contact-email`	`div`	41	Input fields
		`#contact-formname`	`input`	46	Input field name
		`.inputbox`	`input`	46, 52, 58, 64	Input field
		`#contact-emailmsg`	`label`	49	E-mail
		`#contact-email`	`input`	52	Input field e-mail
		`.required`	`input`	52, 64	Required information
		`.validate-email`	`input`	52	Input field e-mail
		`#contact-subject`	`input`	58	Input field subject
		`#contact-textmsg`	`label`	61	Message
		`#contact-text`	`textarea`	64	Input area subject

(*continues*)

Component `com_contact` (*continued*)

View	File Name	ID/Class Name	HTML Elements	Line (approx.)	Description
		#contact-email-copy	input	69	Send copy of message to own address
		.button	button	76	Button
		.validate	button	76	Button
	default_links.php	.contact-links	div	17	Additional information
	default_profile.php	.contact-profile	div	14	Surrounding element
		#users-profile-custom	div	14	Surrounding element

Component `com_newsfeeds`

View	File Name	ID/Class Name	HTML Elements	Line (approx.)	Description
categories	default.php	.categories-list	div	16	Newsfeeds category view
		.category-desc	div	26, 32	Category description
		.base-desc	div	26, 32	Category description of selected category
	default_items.php	.first	li	12	First list element
		.last	li	21	Last list element
		.item-title	span	26	Category name
		.category-desc	div	31	Category description
		.newsfeed-count	dl	37	Number of newsfeeds
category	default.php	.newsfeed-category	div	15	Newsfeeds category view
		.category-desc	div	27	Category description
		.clr	div	34	Cancels `floats`
		.cat-children	div	41	Child categories
	default_children.php	.first	li	12	First list element
		.last	li	21	Last list element

(*continues*)

Component `com_newsfeeds` (*continued*)

View	File Name	ID/Class Name	HTML Elements	Line (approx.)	Description
		`.item-title`	`span`	26	Category name
		`.category-desc`	`div`	32	Category description
		`.newsfeed-count`	`dl`	39	Number of newsfeeds
	`default_ items.php`	`#adminForm`	`form`	24	Form
		`.filters`	`fieldset`	25	Filter
		`.hidelabeltxt`	`legend`	26	Legend
		`.display-limit`	`div`	28	Number of articles
		`.category`	`table`	34	Table with newsfeeds
		`.item-title`	`th`	38	Table header: Feed name
		`#tableOrdering`	`th`	38	Feed name
		`.item-num-art`	`th`	44	Column number of articles
		`#tableOrdering2`	`th`	44	Number of articles
		`.item-link`	`th`	50	Table header: Feed link
		`#tableOrdering3`	`th`	50	Feed link
		`.system-unpublished`	`tr`	62	Formats display of unpublished content if you are logged into the front end
		`.cat-list-row0` `.cat-list-row1` etc.	`tr`	62, 64	Table row with newsfeeds
		`.item-title`	`td`	67	Feed name
		`.item-link`	`td`	79	Feed link
		`.pagination`	`div`	92	Page numbers
		`.counter`	`p`	94	Page number of pages in total: Page 1 of 2
newsfeed	`default.php`	`.newsfeed`	`div`	39	Outputs a newsfeed
		Class from php: `.redirect-ltr` `.redirect-rtl`	`h1`	41	Main heading

(*continues*)

Component `com_newsfeeds` (*continued*)

View	File Name	ID/Class Name	HTML Elements	Line (approx.)	Description
		Class from php: `.redirect-ltr` `.redirect-rtl`	h2	45	Subheading
		`.feed-description`	div	52	Feed description
		`.feed-item-description`	div	73	Feed content

Component `com_weblinks`

View	File Name	ID/Class Name	HTML Elements	Line (approx.)	Description
categories	default.php	`.categories-list`	div	16	Web links category view
		`.category-desc`	div	26, 32	Category description
		`.base-desc`	div	26, 32	Category description of selected category
	default_items.php	`.first`	li	13	First list element
		`.last`	li	22	Last list element
		`.item-title`	span	27	Category name
		`.category-desc`	div	32	Category description
		`.weblink-count`	dl	38	Number of Web links
category	default.php	`.weblink-category`	div	14	Web links category view
		`.category-desc`	div	26	Category description
		`.clr`	div	33	Cancels `floats`
		`.cat-children`	div	38	List with child categories
	default_children.php	`.first`	li	12	First list element
		`.last`	li	21	Last list element
		`.item-title`	span	26	Category name
		`.category-desc`	div	32	Category description
		`.weblink-count`	dl	39	Number of Web links

(*continues*)

Component `com_weblinks` (*continued*)

View	File Name	ID/Class Name	HTML Elements	Line (approx.)	Description
	`default_ items.php`	`#adminForm`	`form`	34	Form
		`.filters`	`fieldset`	36	Filter
		`.hidelabeltxt`	`legend`	37	Legend
		`.display-limit`	`div`	38	Number of articles
		`.category`	`table`	45	Table with Web links
		`.title`	`th`	50	Table header: Web link name
		`.hits`	`th`	54	Table header: number of hits
		`.system-unpublished`	`tr`	64	Formats the display of unpublished content if you are logged into the front end
		`.cat-list-row0` `.cat-list-row1` etc.	`tr`	64, 66	Table row with Web links
		`.title`	`td`	69	Web link name
		`.actions`	`ul`	116	Icon list
		`.edit-icon`	`li`	117	Edit icon
		`.hits`	`td`	131	Number of hits
		`.pagination`	`div`	145	Page numbers
		`.counter`	`p`	147	Page number of pages in total: Page 1 of 2
form	`edit.php`	`.edit`	`div`	32	Editing view
		`#adminForm`	`form`	38	Form
		`.form-validate`	`form`	38	Form
		`.formelm`	`div`	42, 47, 51, 56, 61	Form elements
		`.formelm-buttons`	`div`	65	Button

Component `com_search`

View	File Name	ID/Class Name	HTML Elements	Line (approx.)	Description
search	default.php	.search	div	14	Search form
	default_error.php	.error	div	15	Error messages
	default_form.php	#searchForm	form	14	Search form
		.word	fieldset	16	Input field for search term
		#search-searchword	input	20	Input field for search term
		.inputbox	input	20	Input field for search term
		.button	button	21	Button
		.searchintro	div	24	Number of search results
		.phrases	fieldset	30	Search options
		.phrases-box	div	33	Radio buttons for selecting search options
		.ordering-box	.div	36	Select order
		.ordering	label	37	Order
		.only	fieldset	45	Limit search
		#area-	input	50	Limit search
		.form-limit	div	60	Number of search results per page
		.counter	p	66	Page number of pages in total: Page 1 of 2
	default_results.php	.search-results	dl	14	Search results
		.result-title	dt	16	Title
		.result-category	dd	27	Category
		.small	span	28	Category
		.result-text	dd	33	Content
		.result-created	dd	37	Date created
		.pagination	div	44	Page numbers

Component com_users

View	File Name	ID/Class Name	HTML Elements	Line (approx.)	Description
login	default.php				
	default_login.php	.login	div	14	Encloses login area
		.login-description	div	22	Login description
		.login-image	img	30	Login image
		.login-fields	div	42	Input fields
		.button	button	46	Login button
	default_logout.php	.logout	div	13	Logout area
		.logout-description	div	21	Logout description
		.logout-image	img	29	Logout image
		.button	button	38	Logout button
profile	default.php	.profile	div	14	Profile
	default_core.php	#users-profile-core	fieldset	16	User profile core data
	default_custom.php	#users-profile-custom	fieldset	23	User profile additional data
		.users-profile-custom	fieldset	23	User profile additional data
	default_params.php	#users-profile-custom	fieldset	23	Surrounding element
	edit.php	.profile-edit	div	20	Edit profile
		#member-profile	form	25	Form
		.form-validate	form	25	Validatable form
		.optional	span	41	Optional input
		.validate	button	53	Validatable button
registration	complete.php	.registration-complete	div	13	Heading after completed registration
	default.php	.registration	div	17	Registration
		#member-registration	form	22	Form
		.form-validate	form	22	Validatable form

(continues)

Component `com_users` (*continued*)

View	File Name	ID/Class Name	HTML Elements	Line (approx.)	Description
		`.optional`	span	38	Optional input
		`.validate`	button	49	Validatable button
`remind`	`default.php`	`.remind`	div	17	Password forgotten
		`#user-registration`	form	24	Form
		`.form-validate`	form	24	Validatable form
`reset`	`complete.php`	`.reset-complete`	div	16	Reset password
		`.form-validate`	form	23	Form
	`confirm.php`	`.reset-confirm`	div	16	Surrounding element
		`.form-validate`	form	23	Form
	`default.php`	`.reset`	div	17	Reset password
		`#user-registration`	form	24	Form
		`.form-validate`	form	24	Form

Component `com_wrapper`

View	File Name	ID/Class Name	HTML Elements	Line (approx.)	Description
`wrapper`	`default.php`	`.contentpane`	div	25	Content of wrapper component
		`#blockrandom`	iframe	36	Iframe
		`.wrapper`	iframe	42	Iframe

Modules

Modules Chrome Template beez_20

Style	File Name	ID/Class Name	HTML Elements	Line (approx.)	Description
`beezDivision`	`modules.php`	`.moduletable`	div	22	Contents of modules
		`.backh`	span	24	For example, for rounded corners

(*continues*)

Modules Chrome Template beez_20 (*continued*)

Style	File Name	ID/Class Name	HTML Elements	Line (approx.)	Description
		.backh2	span	24	For example, for rounded corners
		.backh3	span	24	For example, for rounded corners
beezHide	modules.php	.moduletable_js	div	42	Modules
		.js_heading	h	43	Heading
		.backh	span	43	For example, for rounded corners
		.backh1	span	44	For example, for rounded corners
		.opencloselink	a	47	Link to open and close
		#link_ with module ID	a	47	Link to open and close
		.no	span	48	Image
		.module_content	div	51	Collapsible content
		#module_ with module ID	div	52	Collapsible content
beezTabs	modules.php	#area-mit	div	84	Tab
		.tabouter	div	84	Tab
		.tabs	ul	84	List with tab
		.tab	li	87	Individual tab
		#link_ with module ID	a	87	Tab
		.linkopen	a	87	Tab
		.linkclosed	a	87	Tab, link generated via JS
		.tabcontent	div	95	Tab content
		.tabopen	div	95	Open tab
		.tabclosed	div	95	Closed tab
		#module_ with module ID	div	95	Content
		.unseen	a	99	Elements outside of viewport
		#next_ with module ID	a	99	Link to next tab content

Modules Chrome Template beez5

Style	File Name	ID/Class Name	HTML Elements	Line (approx.)	Description
`beezDivision`	`modules.php`	`.moduletable`	`div`	22	Contents of modules
		`.backh`	`span`	24	For example, for rounded corners
		`.backh2`	`span`	24	For example, for rounded corners
		`.backh3`	`span`	24	For example, for rounded corners
`beezHide`	`modules.php`	`.moduletable_js`	`div`	42	Modules
		`.js_heading`	`h`	43	Heading
		`.backh`	`span`	43	For example, for rounded corners
		`.backh1`	`span`	44	For example, for rounded corners
		`.opencloselink`	`a`	47	Link to open and close
		`#link_` with module ID	`a`	47	Link to open and close
		`.no`	`span`	48	Image
		`.module_content`	`div`	51	Collapsible content
		`#module_` with module ID	`div`	52	Collapsible content
`beezTabs`	`modules.php`	`#area-mit`	`div`	84	Tab
		`.tabouter`	`div`	84	Tab
		`.tabs`	`ul`	84	List with tabs
		`.tab`	`li`	87	Individual tab
		`#link_` with module ID	`a`	87	Tab
		`.linkopen`	`a`	87	Tab
		`.linkclosed`	`a`	87	Tab, link generated via JavaScript
		`.tabcontent`	`div`	95	Tab content
		`.tabopen`	`div`	95	Open tab
		`.tabclosed`	`div`	95	Closed tab

(continues)

Modules Chrome Template beez5 (*continued*)

Style	File Name	ID/Class Name	HTML Elements	Line (approx.)	Description
		#module_ with module ID	div	95	Content
		.unseen	a	99	Elements outside of viewport
		#next_ with module ID	A	99	Link to next tab content

Module mod_articles_archive

File Name	ID/Class Name	HTML Elements	Line (approx.)	Description
default.php	.archive-module	ul	13	Archived articles

Module mod_articles_categories

File Name	ID/Class Name	HTML Elements	Line (approx.)	Description
default.php	.categories-module	ul	13	List of categories

Module mod_articles_category

File Name	ID/Class Name	HTML Elements	Line (approx.)	Description
default.php	.category-module	ul	13	List of categories
	.mod-articles-category-title	a	23, 61, 87, 123	Category name
	.mod-articles-category-hits	span	26, 32, 90, 96	Number of hits
	.mod-articles-category-writtenby	span	40, 103	Author
	.mod-articles-category-category	span	46, 108	Parent category
	.mod-articles-category-date	span	51, 113	Date of creation, publication, or last modification
	.mod-articles-category-introtext	p	54, 116	Intro text of articles
	.mod-articles-category-readmore	p	60, 122	Read More link of articles

Module `mod_articles_latest`

File Name	ID/Class Name	HTML Elements	Line (approx.)	Description
default.php	.latestnews	ul	13	List of latest contributions

Module `mod_articles_news`

File Name	ID/Class Name	HTML Elements	Line (approx.)	Description
default.php	.newsflash	div	13	Contents of module
_item.php	.newsflash-title	h	15	Article heading
	.readmore	a	35	Read More link
horizontal.php	.newsflash-horiz	ul	14	List of articles
	.article-separator	span	22	Separator
vertical.php	.newsflash-vert	ul	13	List or articles
	.newsflash-item	li	16	List element with an article
	.article-separator	span	19	Separator

Module `mod_articles_popular`

File Name	ID/Class Name	HTML Elements	Line (approx.)	Description
default.php	.mostread	ul	13	List of most popular articles

Module `mod_banners`

File Name	ID/Class Name	HTML Elements	Line (approx.)	Description
default.php	.bannergroup	div	16	Encloses all banners
	.banneritem	div	22	Encloses a banner each
	.clr	div	106	Cancels floats
	.bannerfooter	div	111	Footer area

Module `mod_breadcrumbs`

File Name	ID/Class Name	HTML Elements	Line (approx.)	Description
default.php	.breadcrumbs	div	14	Breadcrumbs
	.pathway	a	25	Breadcrumbs link

Module `mod_custom`

File Name	ID/Class Name	HTML Elements	Line (approx.)	Description
default.php	.custom	div	13	Content of module

Module `mod_feed`

File Name	ID/Class Name	HTML Elements	Line (approx.)	Description
default.php	.feed	div	21	Content of module
	.newsfeed	ul	61	List with newsfeeds
	.newsfeed-item	li	69	List element with a newsfeed
	.feed-link	h4	77	Feed heading
		h5	74	

Module `mod_footer`

File Name	ID/Class Name	HTML Elements	Line (approx.)	Description
default.php	.footer1	div	13	Copyright
	.footer2	div	14	License information

Module `mod_languages`

File Name	ID/Class Name	HTML Elements	Line (approx.)	Description
default.php	.mod_languages	div	14	Languages
	.pretext	div	16	Text appears before language selection
	.posttext	div	32	Text appears after language selection

Module mod_login

File Name	ID/Class Name	HTML Elements	Line (approx.)	Description
default.php	#login-form	form	15, 33	Login form
	.login-greeting	div	17	Greeting after login
	.logout-button	div	25	Logout button
	.button	input	26, 52	Button
	.input	fieldset	47	Input fields
	.pretext	div	34	Text before input fields
	.userdata	fieldset	37	Input fields for user name and password
	#form-login-username	p	38	User name
	#modlgn_username	input	40	Input field user name
	.inputbox	input	40, 44, 49	Input fields
	#form-login-password	p	42	Password
	#modlgn-passwd	input	44	Input field password
	#form-login-remember	p	47	Save login data
	#modlgn-remember	input	49	Input field save login data
	.posttext	div	76	Text after input fields

Module mod_menu

File Name	ID/Class Name	HTML Elements	Line (approx.)	Description
default.php	.menu	ul	16	List with menu items
	ID from PHP:	ul		Configurable ID via parameter: Menu Tag ID
	.current	li	27	Active menu item in lowest level
	.active	li	31	Active menu items
	.parent	li	39	Parent element
	#item- plus ItemId	li	42	List element

(continued)

Module mod_menu (*continued*)

File Name	ID/Class Name	HTML Elements	Line (approx.)	Description
default_ component.php	Class from PHP		14, 27, 31, 35	Configurable class via parameter: Link CSS style
	.image-title	span	18	Link text
default_ separator.php	.image-title	span	17	Link text
	.separator	span	23	Separator
default_url. php	Class from PHP		14, 27, 31, 36	Configurable class via parameter: Link CSS style
	.image-title	span	18	Link text

Module mod_random_image

File Name	ID/Class Name	HTML Elements	Line (approx.)	Description
default.php	.random-image	div	13	Images

Module mod_related_items

File Name	ID/Class Name	HTML Elements	Line (approx.)	Description
default.php	.relateditems	ul	13	Article list

Module mod_search

File Name	ID/Class Name	HTML Elements	Line (approx.)	Description
default.php	.search	div	14	Search
	#mod_search_ searchword	input	16	Input field for search term
	.inputbox	input	16	Input field for search term
	.button	input	20, 22	Button

Module mod_stats

File Name	ID/Class Name	HTML Elements	Line (approx.)	Description
default.php	.stats-module	dl	13	Statistical data

Module mod_syndicate

File Name	ID/Class Name	HTML Elements	Line (approx.)	Description
default.php	.syndicate-module	a	13	Feed link

Module mod_users_latest

File Name	ID/Class Name	HTML Elements	Line (approx.)	Description
default.php	.latestusers	ul	12	List of latest users

Module mod_weblinks

File Name	ID/Class Name	HTML Elements	Line (approx.)	Description
default.php	.weblinks	ul	12	List of Web links

Module mod_whosonline

File Name	ID/Class Name	HTML Elements	Line (approx.)	Description
default.php	.whosonline	ul	22	List of users who are online

Module mod_wrapper

File Name	ID/Class Name	HTML Elements	Line (approx.)	Description
default.php	#blockrandom	iframe	27	Iframe
	.wrapper	iframe	33	Iframe

Index

inform IT.com THE TRUSTED TECHNOLOGY LEARNING SOURCE

InformIT is a brand of Pearson and the online presence for the world's leading technology publishers. It's your source for reliable and qualified content and knowledge, providing access to the top brands, authors, and contributors from the tech community.

✦Addison-Wesley **Cisco Press** EXAM/**CRAM** **IBM** Press. **QUE** ‡‡ PRENTICE HALL **SAMS** | Safari'

LearnIT at InformIT

Looking for a book, eBook, or training video on a new technology? Seeking timely and relevant information and tutorials? Looking for expert opinions, advice, and tips? **InformIT has the solution.**

- Learn about new releases and special promotions by subscribing to a wide variety of newsletters. Visit **informit.com/newsletters**.

- Access FREE podcasts from experts at **informit.com/podcasts**.

- Read the latest author articles and sample chapters at **informit.com/articles**.

- Access thousands of books and videos in the Safari Books Online digital library at **safari.informit.com**.

- Get tips from expert blogs at **informit.com/blogs**.

Visit **informit.com/learn** to discover all the ways you can access the hottest technology content.

Are You Part of the **IT** Crowd?

Connect with Pearson authors and editors via RSS feeds, Facebook, Twitter, YouTube, and more! Visit **informit.com/socialconnect**.

inform IT.com THE TRUSTED TECHNOLOGY LEARNING SOURCE

✦Addison-Wesley **Cisco Press** EXAM/**CRAM** **IBM** Press. **QUE** ‡‡ PRENTICE HALL **SAMS** | Safari'

FREE
Online Edition

Your purchase of *Joomla!*® ***Templates*** includes access to a free online edition for 45 days through the Safari Books Online subscription service. Nearly every Addison-Wesley Professional book is available online through Safari Books Online, along with thousands of books and videos from publishers such as Cisco Press, Exam Cram, IBM Press, O'Reilly Media, Prentice Hall, Que, Sams, and VMware Press.

Safari Books Online is a digital library providing searchable, on-demand access to thousands of technology, digital media, and professional development books and videos from leading publishers. With one monthly or yearly subscription price, you get unlimited access to learning tools and information on topics including mobile app and software development, tips and tricks on using your favorite gadgets, networking, project management, graphic design, and much more.

Activate your FREE Online Edition at
informit.com/safarifree

STEP 1:   Enter the coupon code: KYYHEBI.

STEP 2:   New Safari users, complete the brief registration form.
Safari subscribers, just log in.

If you have difficulty registering on Safari or accessing the online edition,
please e-mail customer-service@safaribooksonline.com